TRIPPING THE BARDO WITH TIMOTHY LEARY

My Psychedelic Love Story

JOANNA HARCOURT-SMITH

Copyright © 2013 Joanna Harcourt-Smith
All rights reserved.
ISBN-10: 1484826493
ISBN-13: 9781484826492
Library of Congress Control Number: 2013912748
CreateSpace Independent Publishing Platform
North Charleston, South Carolina

A Future Primitive Book

Book cover designed by Marion Wasserman

Any resemblance to any character living or dead is purely intentional. All protagonists and antagonists are described as I remember them, warts and beauty and all. I apologize in advance for not painting them as they saw themselves, but as Oscar Wilde said,

"Memory is the diary that we all carry about with us."

Dedicated to whistleblowers past, present, and future, and to all the government agents who made the wrong career choice

TABLE OF CONTENTS

Acknowledgements	ix
Foreword	xiii
Taking Psychedelics Literally: Spiritual Evolution Beyond the Narrative Mind By Richard Doyle	xiii
Preface	xxi
Part I	
The Wheel of Fortune	1
1 Tommy the Tumbling Dice	3
Fall 1972	
2 Lara	7
Lausanne, 1967	
3 The Domain of the Witch	11
Spring 1972	
4 George Sand Meets Jeanne d'Arc	15
September, 1972	
5 Huxley and Heineken	19
Summer 1968	
6 America with a K	23
November 15, 1969	
7 Alexis	27
Washington, DC, 1970	
8 Michel	31
September 1972	
9 Hope Fiends Abound	47
New York City, Fall 1972	
10 Un Jeu de Piste, For Real	51
November 1972	

11 The Universal Solvent	55
12 Everything	61
13 Acid Queen	65
14 Wheel of Fortune, Turn Round, Round	67
15 The Bill	73
16 Suits	77
17 Escape	81
18 The Soup Thickens	87
19 Lightning Strikes Twice	91
Gstaad, 1957	
20 The White Scarf	95
November 1972	
21 The Play's the Thing	99
22 Love Circuits	103
23 A Telephone Conversation	107
24 Alone Together	111
December 1972	
25 Two Wings Are Better Than One	117
26 Moonfields	119
27 No Room at the Inn	121
Christmas 1972	
28 Christmas Eve with Warhol	125
St. Moritz, December 1972	
29 The Sacred Waters of the Ganges	127
Vienna, New Year's 1973	
30 The Yellow Peril	131
New Year's 1973	
31 The Shadow of Death	135
January 11, 1973	

Bardo Express
Part II
The Turnkey	139
32 Prestomico	141
Beirut, January 16, 1973	
33 The Afghani Connection	147
Kabul, January 19, 1973	

34 Aegean Dreams	155
35 We Walk the Plank	161
January 19, 1973	
36 The Prodigal Son Returns	163
Cairo, January 19, 1973	
37 The Queen of Diamonds	171

Bardo Express

Part III

Mind at Large 175

38 The Iron Door	177
January 20, 1973	
39 Angel of Mercy	181
40 The Sorcerer's Apprentice	183
41 Case Closed	187
February 19, 1973	
42 Tripping in Prison	189
March 1973	
43 Are You Going to San Francisco?	193
44 The Folsom Prison Blues	197
45 Ginsberg Redefines Prison in Sanskrit	199
46 The Three Fates of Watergate	205
Summer 1974	
47 Starseed	209
48 The Hundred Dollar Man	211
49 Cops and Robbers	215
50 Mummy at Folsom	217
Christmas 1974	
51 Tripping with Franklin's Clear Light	221
52 A Mean Scene	225
53 Up Against the Wall	229
54 Walking the Line	233
55 Room 660	235
56 Making Love with Mr. D	241
57 In the Mouth of the Beast	245
58 The Right Side of the Law	249

Bardo Express
Part IV
- The Flash Point ... 253
  - 59 Charlie Thrush ... 255
  - 60 The Country Club Prison ... 259
  - 61 Presidents Come and Go ... 265
    August 8, 1974
  - 62 Is There Anybody Out There? ... 267
    Minneapolis, 1974
  - 63 The Watergate Hotel ... 271
  - 64 Four and Twenty Blackbirds ... 275
  - 65 Queen Mary, Save Us ... 277
  - 66 Virginia Church and Charlie Thrush Begin to Sing ... 281
  - 67 The Gun ... 287
  - 68 Dennis Dies ... 291
  - 69 The Flophouse of Mirrors ... 297
  - 70 James and Nora Joyce ... 301
  - 71 This Is the End, Beautiful Friend ... 305

Epilogue ... 311
- Postscript: Up and Out of the Ashes ... 321

Appendix 1
- Alcoholics Anonymous Step 8 ... 325
  Santa Fe, Spring 1990

Appendix 2
- Prison Timetable ... 329
  January 20, 1973 to April 21, 1976

ACKNOWLEDGEMENTS

Every book has its Godmothers and Godfathers, protective beings prodding and protecting until the last word is written.

I began writing this book when I was 30 years old and pregnant on a beach in Rosarito, Baja California. It was early December. My mother had died in September, and Timothy Leary was somewhere being Timothy Leary.

Laurie Becklund, a reporter from the *San Diego Tribune*, offered to help me put what we then called "Chain of Change" on paper. We worked together for a few months, then were swept separate ways by life's turbulence. Thank you, Laurie; you are this book's first Godmother.

Time passed and I came to live in Santa Fe. I was recently sober and working as a cook, wanting nothing more than to be a writer. I took classes with Miriam Sagan, and for years we wrote and read to each other. Thank you, Miriam Sagan, you are one of the Fairy Godmothers of this book—you and everyone I came to trust and love in the classes.

I met with Natalie Goldberg during the first Iraq war. We went to demonstrations at the Quaker House on Canyon Road, protested the war on the Plaza, wrote and read to each other. Thank you, Natalie Goldberg. You have supported my writing for many years, telling me that writing is what makes a writer. I name you Honorary Godmother.

And then there was John Lash. We lived together and I watched him write books, mimicking and learning from him. I thank you and name you Honorable Godfather. You rewrote what I wrote, birthing English prose out of my French-English writing. You pulled this story out of me when I was afraid to tell it.

In 1994, I met Elana Freeland, a skilled writer and brilliant analyst of the Sixties Revolution. Together, we carried this memoir a long way. In a finished form at last, I showed it to agents and it was rejected over and over again. Discouraged and afraid, I disappeared from Elana's life.

Ali McGraw read the story and gently coaxed me to just get back on the horse and go on. I believed her and held my faith. Thank you, Ali.

At a gallery opening, I met Dina McQueen whose Master's degree was in memoir writing. She sat with me and my memoir for a year as I handwrote and she typed and made suggestions. Out of our adventure together, I wrote a whole new book about the same events, got an agent—and was again rejected by the straight publishing world. Dina, you are a shining Fairy Godmother of this memoir.

I kept writing in a village in Spain, in the rain in Brussels, and in the fracas of London.

Deep friendships with women have kept me going while keeping me whole: Jennie Dietrich, Tina LeMarque, the mending people in AA. Many people have shown up to help me gather the fragments of my lost soul.

Sir Peter Anderson, Secretary General of the Conch Republic in Key West, has had my back for 35 years. Peter, you are my Chief of Love Security.

After 14 years, Elana and I ran into each other (appropriately enough) at the Santa Fe post office. We had both recently lived in Europe and were back in Santa Fe. Feverishly, we took up the book again, this time determined to finish, reading aloud and discussing, me writing and she cutting, pasting, slashing and burning. An editor who understands your story and rhythm is a blessed gift! I could not have done this without you, Elana, then or now. Your skill and compassion for my story have carried me through. You are the Doula Midwife of this adventure.

To my team of amazing friends and sisters who have helped me surf crazy waves and wait out the doldrums, thank you! Mela, my steady breeze. Linda, Cynthia, Hugh, Big Al, and Lenya, I love you and thank you.

Close to my heart and at my side are the fantastic Baldwin Brothers: Ian Baldwin, true friend of many lives; Philip Baldwin, with his real and down-to-earth support; and Michael Baldwin, founder of the Marion Institute, philanthropist extraordinaire, and my kindness guru.

I dedicate this book to my children Lara, Alexis, and Marlon, and to my grandchildren Harper, Sasha, and Nicolas. You are the life that lives on, the reason to live, the bridges to many other stories.

And finally there is Jose Luis G. Soler who came to share my life some years ago. Thank you for whispering, shouting, and forever insisting, "Finish your book."

Thank you to all for walking and having walked with me.

FOREWORD

TAKING PSYCHEDELICS LITERALLY: SPIRITUAL EVOLUTION BEYOND THE NARRATIVE MIND

BY RICHARD DOYLE

The fire of God is fallen from heaven, and hath burned up the sheep, and the servants, and consumed them; and I only am escaped alone to tell thee.
   - Job 1:16

After eating five grams of psilocybe cubensis . . . I realized that we are one with God, and he loves us. Now if that isn't a hazard to this country, I don't know what is.
   - Bill Hicks

A familiar and now tired dictum emerged from comedian Robin Williams' manic psychedelic improv: "If you remember the 1960s, you weren't there."

While contemporary neuroscientific models of memory—some of it emerging out of research into psychedelics in the 1950s and

1960s—reminds us that our recall is no more to be trusted than our politicians, this bit of unintentional Drug War agit prop about our cultural amnesia encourages us not to remember this period of revolution *at all*. And, of course, according to George Santayana's dictum, if we don't remember the past, we'll be condemned to repeat it.

It is a profound grace, then, that we have Johanna Harcourt-Smith, who "escaped alone to tell thee," to recount her gripping, well-told, and unsparing account of this period of cultural, political and spiritual transformation essential to our present. Harcourt-Smith tells us her truth, and in so doing reminds us that it is not only crucial to recall what the 1960's were about, what happened in them, and to whom, but in fact what the 1960s *were*.

Consider the effect, for example—if we can cut through the fog of the now nearly 50-year Drug War—of beginning our story about the psychedelic Sixties by focusing on the locale of one of its most significant experiments: The Marsh Chapel at Boston University.

In the so-called "Good Friday Experiment" of 1962, Harvard Divinity grad student Walter Pahnke, acting under the supervision of Dr. Timothy Leary and the Harvard Psilocybin Project, conducted a controlled study into the nature of what William James called "religious experience." Walter Pahnke and Leary administered psilocybin and niacin respectively—yes, on Good Friday—to two groups of volunteers in a double blind experiment designed to test the hypothesis that religious experiences could be enabled by drugs.

The study had precursors: James himself had sampled peyote, and Gordon Wasson announced the very existence of psilocybin to the world in *Life* magazine in 1957 after a thorough-going mystical experience at the hands of Mazatec *curandera* Maria Sabina, and he did so with the help of a CIA-financed airplane.

And the study had sequels: In 2006, a group at Johns Hopkins University repeated the study with 21st century research protocols, including permission from the Drug Enforcement Administration (DEA) to even handle the now felonious Schedule 1 compound, and came to very similar conclusions in an article whose title speaks volumes about both studies as well as the nature of the Drug War: *Psilocybin Can Occasion Mystical-Type Experiences of Meaningful and Long Lasting Significance*.

In other words, psychedelic research, from its inception to its prohibition and its recent renascence, has always been inexorably bound up with spiritual quest. This should hardly shock the careful observer, who would note the early prohibition and eventual legalization of peyote as a sacrament for the Native American Church; the DEA seizure of the psychedelic sacrament *ayahuasca* from a branch of a Brazilian church in Taos, New Mexico, as well as the subsequent 2009 U.S. Supreme Court decision upholding the right of that church to its sacrament under the Religious Freedom Restoration Act of 1994; and the continuing efforts of Rastafarian devotees to have legal access to now quasi-legal medical marijuana for spiritual purposes. If these hypothetically careful observers looked further to less legally sanctioned quests, they would find that online databases of information related to psilocybin contain so many references to God that Google yielded 428,000 results as of October 2012 for a query pairing the two terms.

Writing of her initial interest in LSD and Leary, Harcourt-Smith writes of Laura Huxley that "God in her language sounded like an adventure that could happen between a man and a woman who loved each other very much." Harcourt-Smith, a young aristocrat with a diamond clear mind that saw through the crumbling paradigms of Cold War mainstream culture but not yet beyond them, sought out Leary as the "one person best qualified to answer all of my questions about LSD and God . . ."

Leary himself began The League of Spiritual Discovery to facilitate the spiritual quest that he and others had found themselves on after taking psilocybin and then LSD. Even before LSD was accidentally discovered by Swiss chemist Albert Hofmann in 1943, a 1932 Austrian novel by Leo Perutz, *St. Peter's Snow*, presciently focused on the effects that an ergot-based compound would have on religious experience, told from the perspective of a narrator who is slowly remembering what happened in the political tumult that ensued . . . So while it might be tempting to cynically dismiss Leary's September 1966 founding of The League of Spiritual Discovery, or his 1967 book *Start Your Own Religion* as canny maneuvers to keep his favorite "drug" legal, the fact is that psilocybin, *ayahuasca*, peyote, and the newcomer LSD had always been fundamentally and not accidentally involved in spiritual quests.

Author and mystic Aldous Huxley, Laura's husband and subject of the aforementioned adventure, found that mescaline extracted from peyote enabled an encounter with the Buddha nature and Clear Light of Tibetan Buddhism he had read about for so long, and in correspondence with scientist Humphry Osmond, Huxley tried coining a different label for the compound than *psychotomimetic*, the one it had been saddled with. Huxley penned *phanerothyme*," meaning "manifesting spirit." Protesting that this name was "too beautiful," Osmond countered with *psychedelic* or mind manifesting.

Psychedelic, of course, prevailed and has now been recently joined by *entheogens* and *ecodelics*. It is worth noting that all of these neologisms emphasize the capacity of these plants and compounds to bring forth aspects of our consciousness that had been hidden, repressed, ignored, and forgotten. *Psyche* means both "life" and "mind" in ancient Greek, and it is in this double sense that I want to suggest that we take psychedelics literally as agents for the manifestation of mind and life and see a bit more clearly what was at stake in the first wave of psychedelic integration into a technological society.

A technological society is one that excels at the manipulation of matter. Progress in the human ability to cajole, inform, and transform material conditions is nothing short of breathtaking. Yet the very success of technological models of the objective world has contributed to an atrophied sense of the subjective realm—the world of consciousness where we spend every instant of our lives. Even in those moments when we are manipulating matter on the nanoscale, designing chips, solar cells, or drugs to aid memory, we never leave the realm of consciousness.

Indeed this persistence of subjective states and their resistance to description as "objective phenomena" has led philosopher David Chalmers to frame the relationship between physical mechanisms of the brain and the fundamentally qualitative experience of consciousness as the "hard problem," which he sums up succinctly as "Why should physical processing give rise to a rich inner life at all?" In other words, given the nature of the objective world, how and why is there a subject (each of us) at all? This downright puzzling aspect of subjectivity—the space we inhabit our entire lives, and perhaps after—speaks volumes about the mismatch between our post-modern ability to command the material realm and our bewilderment before our own experiences. Perhaps this bewilderment is due to the fact that consciousness involves more than matter. As Leary learned, it involves the effect of consciousness on itself.

TRIPPING THE BARDO WITH TIMOTHY LEARY

Timothy Leary, at the apex of the era of biological reductionism, discovered with the Harvard Psilocybin Group that while chemicals such as psilocybin enabled the remarkable experiences they were having, they did not strictly *cause* them. Leary discovered, for example, that he could "program" psychedelic experience with different linguistic scripts, music and images, chapels. It was not just matter in the usual sense affecting psychedelic experiences, but *attention*, the focus of consciousness by some conscious being. This opened up an enormous space of investigation—not the objective world of molecules, but the subjective domain of all possible states of mind navigable by a conscious being, the "rich inner life" pondered by Chalmers. It is this realm of the subjective that Timothy Leary stumbled upon when as a young psychologist he ate psilocybin in Cuernavaca, Mexico, and we can sympathize with the astonishment he felt at the *sheer magnitude* of consciousness beyond what Pahnke later called, in his thesis, ego death. From "The Psychedelic Mystical Experience in the Human Encounter With Death" (Psychedelic Review, No. 11, 1971):

> During the mystical experience when the experiencer has lost individuality and become part of a Reality Greater-than-self, paradoxically something of the self remains to record the experience in memory. One of the greatest fears about human death is that personal individual existence and memory will be gone forever. Yet having passed through psychological ego death in the mystical experience, a person still preserves enough self-consciousness so that at least part of the individual memory is not lost.

Given advances in neuroscience, we can now hypothesize that at least part of this "Reality Greater-than-self" that is experienced in ego death was the immensity of the brain itself, freed from the constraints of the relatively meager egoic "narrative mind," what Huxley had labeled the "throttling embrace of the self." We now know that the human brain is even larger in magnitude than Leary's neuroscience had modeled. While Leary marveled at the capacities of a "13 billion cell computer," neuroscientists now map consciousness as (somehow) emerging from 50 *trillion* neuronal connections of the human brain.

JOANNA HARCOURT-SMITH

Astronomers estimate that our entire galaxy contains only 100 billion stars, so the magnitudes involved in the space of all possible consciousness are quite literally astronomical. Of those 50 trillion neuronal connections, neuroscientists estimate that only a fraction are involved with what they call "narrative mind," that portion of conscious experience that involves thought involving the "I." It is this that falls away in ego death, enabling the investigation of the realms beyond thought, likely obscured in human experience since the acquisition of language about 70,000 years ago. Recent data, for example, suggests that the deactivation of the narrative mind by long term meditators—those who have meditated for 10,000 hours or more—is identical to that occurring under the influence of psilocybin.

The re-discovery of the awful splendors of the subjective realm felt downright evolutionary to Leary—as if he were an early mutant amphibian who got more than a glimpse of the stupendous possibilities of land. My own research hypothesizes that *phanerothyme* plants played a crucial role in human evolution through what Darwin called sexual selection—the very vector that brought Leary together with Joanna Harcourt-Smith, complete with romantic foreplay focusing on images of the human brain.

And more recent evolutionary biology would suggest that Leary was not far off in his understanding of the new domain of subjective experience as an evolutionary shift of profound importance. Merlin Donald, for example, has argued for a past shift in the "functional anatomy" of the human brain under the influence of writing as it arrived to form a culture of literacy; and current research is focused on the effects of ubiquitous social media on dopamine levels in the human brain. So Leary's interest in the ability of psychedelics to cleanse the doors of perception and then "imprint" and "program" the astronomical space of subjective reality was, if anything, prescient. Now, years later, if you wish to program your subjective reality, you can download various psychedelic meditation apps for your iPhone, itself designed by a man who used LSD 10 to 15 times during the very period of Leary's exile and imprisonment.

Perhaps the analogies of evolution and space travel favored by Leary were appropriate. Not only did psychedelics consistently and persistently "manifest spirit" and the spiritual quest in many who took them, but so too was this a scientific quest for the nature of and *space* of all possible subjective experiences and the lives that would very much manifest out of them. Psychedelics were at once catalysts for a spiritual quest and new instruments for the pursuit of scientific truth in an astronomically large new frontier: mind. Thousands of scientific papers were published on LSD alone, and theologians debated the merits of enlightenment and revelation enabled by the tools of modern science.

As a new ecological niche in scientific study and modern human experience, early explorers were subjected to downright Darwinian selection. The same year as the Good Friday Experiment, Thomas Kuhn extended Ludwig Fleck's analysis of scientific change in *The Structure of Scientific Revolutions,* concluding that even in science, change required not just new ideas, data and insights, but the collapse of the old regime. When Leary built on the early success of his psychological career—his route to Harvard—and began to incorporate the *space* of subjective investigation into his research, the push back was immense from diverse quarters of the *ancien regime,* and—as this book details—it was often brutal.

Here in *Tripping the Bardo with Timothy Leary: My Psychedelic Love Story,* we find precursors of the contemporary practice of extraordinary rendition, and *from Afghanistan* no less! Leary's lengthy solitary confinement warrants analogies to waterboarding. It is difficult to fathom, in retrospect, that it was a scientist following the data in his research on religious experiences that launched the United States' longest war, but nobody ever said spiritual evolution was going to be easy.

Richard Doyle, aka "mobius," is Liberal Arts Research Professor at Penn State University, where he has taught since 1994. Having read the work of futurist Alvin Toffler at age 12, Doyle has been on a scholarly and personal quest to understand the effects of information technologies (IT) on the evolution of human culture. Since completing a PhD at UC Berkeley and a post-doctoral fellowship at MIT, he has received grants from the National Science Foundation and written a trilogy of scholarly works on IT's effects on human evolution and of language on consciousness. His latest work, Darwin's Pharmacy: Sex, Plants & The Evolution of the Noösphere *(University of Washington Press, 2011), focuses on the co-evolution of humans with psychedelic plants such as psilocybin, cannabis, and ayahuasca.*

PREFACE

The seeds of the Sixties have taken root underground. The blossoming is to come.
   - Timothy Leary, *Neuropolitics*, 1977

The idealistic mind of the Sixties is still at our backs, though, and most people I know who are my age have that ingrained in them forever.
   - Steve Jobs, quoted in Steve Jobs: A Biography by Walter Isaacson, 2011

I.

This is the story that "blew my mind."

Who is Timothy Leary? If you don't remember him, it is no wonder; he's part of the history hardly anyone has taken seriously enough to really write about—yet.

The name Timothy Leary is now little more than a meme, a disembodied brand name conjuring up the vague notion that once upon a time sex, drugs, and rock'n'roll were the hip passport out of the Cold War Fifties box.

Throughout the Sixties, Timothy Leary was the Pied Piper whose psychedelic flute led enchanted flower children over the cliff of what until then had been packaged and sold as consciousness. I followed him off that precipice, and my family, nationality, and sanity were fragmented beyond recognition.

Timothy Leary was crafted into a major media hero, then morphed into a Counterculture scapegoat and Judas. Paradox was both his magic and his nemesis: Dr. Jekyll and Mr. Hyde, Harvard professor and trickster, genius and crackpot, spiritual leader and impostor, adventurer and iconic manipulator, devil and angel, guru and scientist.

Born in 1920 in Springfield, Massachusetts, the superstar of the Sixties was not born into the Counterculture tribe that would most value him. From the beginning, Timothy Leary was destined to be an ideological trafficker threatening the world of white Irish Catholic men he was born into. At 20, he merited the rebellious distinction of being almost court-martialed by the US Military Academy at West Point, then (ironically) finally achieved his bachelor's degree in psychology during World War II while in the United States Army. His PhD in Psychology came from UC Berkeley in 1950. He stayed on at UC Berkeley until 1955 when his wife Marianne committed suicide. From 1955-1958, he directed psychiatric research at the Kaiser Family Foundation in Menlo Park, California, then lectured at Harvard University 1959-1963 until he was dismissed. As Wikipedia puts it, "The decision to dismiss him was allegedly influenced by his role in the popularity of then-legal psychedelic substances among Harvard students and faculty members."

In August 1960, while studying ethnomycologist (and vice president of J.P. Morgan) R. Gordon Wasson and the psychoactive plants of the Mexican Mazatecs, Timothy ate psilocybin mushrooms for the first time in Cuernavaca, Mexico and learned more about psychology and the possibilities of the brain than he'd learned in fifteen years of studying and doing research.

When the three Harvard psychonauts—Timothy, Richard Alpert, and Ralph Metzner—stumbled upon the extraordinary psychological states that LSD (lysergic acid diethylamide) unleashed, they understood that the drug does not *produce* the transcendent state but instead acts as a chemical key to release the nervous system from perceiving only Ordinary or consensus reality.

Their next jump to light speed was to define the LSD experience as a "trip," a journey through a psychological state of existence the Tibetans call the Bardo, a purgatory, limbo, or kamaloca often filled with Dantean nightmare illusions and real danger. Once they had experienced enough "ego death" to map the Bardo's landscape of pitfalls, illusions, Clear Light vistas, road signs, restaurants, and rest stops, they wrote *The Psychedelic Experience: A Manual Based on the Tibetan Book of the*

Dead (1964) to once and for all reject the major Western pitfall that Dr. Carl Jung described in his psychological commentary to the *Bardo Thodol*: "Whenever the Westerner hears the word 'psychological,' it always sounds to him like '*only* psychological'.

    The Bardo was why Timothy took LSD so often—not to "party" or get high, but to learn how to "die" and trail-blaze the final frontier of consciousness. He was dedicated to mapping the Badlands of freakouts that musician Frank Zappa defined as the shedding of tired, old standards and stale cultural maps that no longer reflect the post-Bomb experience. With an up-to-date map, pilgrims could then hold firm, make sense of the chaos, and reset their bearings. Such was the light at the end of the tunnel that drove Timothy Leary, despite all of his foibles and "head trips," despite all of the cops-and-robbers games he became embroiled in, including whatever happened to him in prison that made him who he was when he was finally freed.

    Timothy left the Fifties in the hallowed halls of Harvard, abandoning forever the mindless drudgery that Freud and the Industrial Revolution termed success to leap wholeheartedly into LSD and the Sixties. Poet Allen Ginsberg called TL "Coach Leary"[1] because Timothy was set to create a new religion he wittily called the League of Spiritual Discovery. Seriously, the media didn't label him the Pope of Dope just for the sake of a catchy rhyme: Timothy was the unelected high priest of a new religion he and Allen and many others hoped would change the world. The Age of Aquarius was on its way, just as I heard the Counterculture musical *Hair* sing when it opened in 1968 in London at the Drury Lane one day after the 1968 Theatres Act that abolished theatre censorship.

    The Death of God that French philosopher Jean-Paul Sartre talked about was for Timothy not just the death knell of religion but of psychology, as well. Timothy saw how commodified and objectified men and women had become. As French-Cuban writer Anaïs Nin put it, "Leary talks about games, the disguises, the false life, and that made perfect sense to me" (*The Diary of Anaïs Nin*, Vol. 6, Harcourt Brace Jovanovich, 1977). Ever the intrepid trailblazer, he set out to hack his

---

1 Steve Silberman, "The Plot to Turn On the World: The Leary/Ginsberg Acid Conspiracy," PLOS Blogs Neuro-Tribes, April 21, 2001.

way through the reified jungle of consumerism that Americans had been programmed to define as life. He envisioned a way to a consciousness that would no longer follow others' rules but be committed to discovering what lay behind one's own individual brain.

TL was the magus who opened the mind with a chemical key to free the nervous system. He was both charismatic and catalyzing. In 1966, turned-on Beatles John Lennon and Paul McCarthy wrote "Tomorrow Never Knows" to document the LSD excursion—

> *Turn off your mind relax and float down stream*
> *It is not dying, it is not dying*
> *Lay down all thoughts, surrender to the void,*
> *It is shining, it is shining.*
> *Yet you may see the meaning of within*
> *It is being, it is being*
> *Love is all and love is everyone*
> *It is knowing, it is knowing*
> *And ignorance and hate mourn the dead*
> *It is believing, it is believing*
> *But listen to the colour of your dreams*
> *It is not leaving, it is not leaving*
> *So play the game "Existence" to the end*
> *Of the beginning, of the beginning*

Did you know that it was the CIA that released LSD into the general population to see what would happen? Yes, Swiss scientist Albert Hofmann discovered LSD in 1943, but the CIA was his "problem child's" biggest importer. For millennia, taking *entheogens*[2] had been a privilege reserved for an aristocracy of priests, shamans, initiates, and seers, but for a brief window in time in the 20th century the Counterculture was the first generation in history allowed to steal a democratic peek through what the East calls the Veil. Timothy felt that when the privilege was withdrawn by being criminalized in 1966, it was to keep democratically minded youths from seeing what life and consciousness are really about.

---

2   Coined in 1979 by ethnobotanists and scholars to indicate "spiritualizing" substances (*entheo* = full of the god; *gen* = to come into being).

TRIPPING THE BARDO WITH TIMOTHY LEARY

All the major players wanted a piece of the LSD action, from the hippies who wanted it for their Yellow Submarine into the *terra incognita* of the unconscious, to the military and elite Blue Meanies as a ticket to more political and societal control. Timothy argued that psychedelic substances taken in proper doses in the right *set and setting*[3] could, under the guidance of the right psychologist, alter behavior in a way not easily attained in regular therapy.

On March 11, 1966, the Marihuana Tax Act came down heavy on Timothy two months before he was to testify before the Senate Subcommittee on Juvenile Delinquency. At the Tex-Mex border of Nuevo Laredo, he was arrested for possession of 0.01 grams of marijuana and eventually convicted and sentenced to 30 years, a $30,000 fine, and an order to undergo psychiatric treatment. He immediately appealed the case, claiming the Marihuana Tax Act was unconstitutional.

During the week of May 9-13, 1966, Timothy testified before the Senate Subcommittee on Juvenile Delinquency, having understood early on that if LSD remained in the hands of the government, it would become a powerful brainwashing tool for controlling unsuspecting populations. He begged that LSD be left to the discretion of the medical profession as a prescription drug for certain psychiatric or terminal patients as well as the rehabilitation of criminals. But his impassioned plea was not heard. Five months after the hearings, on October 6, 1966, LSD was classified as a dangerous drug, banned and made illegal in the United States, after which legislated funding for research was cut.

The Counterculture began falling like dominoes. The Summer of Love in 1967 was followed by the Death of the Hippie funeral that tolled the end of "the brief golden age of the Haight psychedelic city-state."[4] Along with Hofmann's "problem child"—

> *[LSD] gave me an inner joy, an open mindedness, a gratefulness, open eyes and an internal sensitivity for the miracles of creation . . . I think that in human evolution it has never been as necessary to*

---

3 Wikipedia: the context for psychoactive and particularly psychedelic drug experiences: one's mindset and the setting in which the user has the experience.
4 Marty Lee and Bruce Shlain, *Acid Dreams: The Complete Social History of LSD: The CIA, The Sixties, and Beyond*, 1985.

have this substance LSD. It is just a tool to turn us into what we are supposed to be.

- Albert Hofmann, World Psychedelic Forum, "LSD – Problem Child and Wonder Drug"; on his 100th birthday in Basel, Switzerland, January 2006

—hard drugs like heroin and cocaine and their derivatives were systematically pumped into the streets by the CIA and its Mob allies. "Bummers" became epidemic—or as Timothy would have framed it, negative spin on the collective set and setting practically preordained that one would end up in a bad-trip Bardo. If one could be properly prepared to navigate the Bardo, liberation from society's games would be at hand. But if the CIA was allowed to continue manipulating the set and setting—well, the story of Cold War scientist Dr. Frank Olson speaks volumes.[5]

Angered by the government's irresponsibility, Timothy ignored the risks that came with even discussing LSD and went on lecture tour, drawing large crowds of young people, seeking to warn them against using LSD recreationally, emphasizing that it *must* be taken under the best of circumstances because it was a powerful spiritual tool, much like peyote in Native American religious ceremonies.

It was the *politicizing* of psychedelics that made Timothy say *Turn on, tune in, drop out*—in other words, don't vote, don't politic, don't petition because you can't do anything about America politically. History claims that Timothy Leary wasn't political, but he was ahead of the game on the silent, covert war of the National Security State versus the people that the Cold War was *really* about. The endless cops-and-robbers Bardo games that would drag him all the way down with the Counterculture he so loved had just begun.

The acid experience is so concrete. It draws a line right across your life—before and after LSD—in the same way you felt that your step into radical politics drew a sharp division. People talked about that, the change you go through, how fast the change could happen on

---

5 Frederic J. Frommer, "Frank Olson Family Sues CIA Over Bioweapons Expert's Mysterious 1953 Death," AP, November 28, 2012.

an individual level and how liberating and glorious it was. Change was seen as survival, as the strategy of health. Nothing could stand for that overall sense of going through profound changes so well as the immediate, powerful and explicit transformation that you went through when you dropped acid. In the same way, bursting through the barricades redefined you as a new person.

– Carl Oglesby, former president of Students for a Democratic Society

In 1968, LSD possession (misdemeanor) and sales (felony) were added to the 1965 Drug Abuse Control Amendments and the Bureau of Narcotics and Dangerous Drugs (BNDD) was created. In 1970, LSD was classified Schedule I by the Food and Drug Administration. Any LSD research that might have been made available to the public then fell under the jurisdiction of need-to-know US Army Intelligence and the CIA. In 1973, the BNDD would merge with the new Drug Enforcement Administration (DEA) as an instrument of the ever-growing police state and Nixon's institution of the so-called War on Drugs.

Timothy was arrested again on December 26, 1968 in Laguna Beach, California for possession of two marijuana roaches (butts) planted in his car by Agent Neal Purcell. On May 19, 1969, the Supreme Court declared the Marihuana Tax Act unconstitutional and quashed Tim's 1965 conviction. That very day, he announced his candidacy for Governor of California against Ronald Reagan, for which John Lennon wrote the song "Come Together."

On January 21, 1970, he was sentenced to ten years for the 1968 bust, with a further ten added for the 1965 bust. When he was administered his own Interpersonal Behavior Test that he'd designed at Harvard, he answered the questions so he would be assigned to the low-security California Men's Colony in San Luis Obispo where he would work as a gardener until his escape in September 1970 with the help of the Weather Underground and Brotherhood of Eternal Love. Fleeing first to Eldridge Cleaver and his Black Panther government-in-exile in Algeria, he then opted for Switzerland which had no extradition. It was there that we would meet in 1972.

JOANNA HARCOURT-SMITH

The truth is that Timothy was punished over and over again as a political prisoner by a nation that still prides itself in not having political prisoners. Timothy's crime was blowing the conditioned minds of youth. In a nation more interested in developing the group or hive mind than in respecting the adventure of developing self and group therapy as a way of life, Timothy was a threat.

II.

Seventy million civilians and military killed during World War Two, 21 million during World War One. Such was the first half of the 20th century punctuated by the atomic bomb.

Being born into the Counterculture generation on the heels of the Bomb in 1945 meant that we shared a passionate desire to affirm life not death, peace not war. But as we came of age, it slowly dawned on us that we were embroiled in machinations of yet another war—not just Vietnam but the secretive Cold War whose victims might not be so carefully tabulated. In America, the new *quiet* war was veiled by economic boom times and deep denial regarding the bombing of Nagasaki and Hiroshima; in England and on the Continent, shock and mourning.

It was America's fate to open Pandora's box through the simultaneous arrival of the Bomb and LSD. Swiss scientist Albert Hofmann discovered lysergic acid diethylamide in 1943; matter was split open on July 16, 1945. Both the atomic bomb and LSD were *implosive* and as important as Christianity when it came to spiritual turning points in Western civilization. Inheritors of the European Renaissance (14th-17th centuries) and Enlightenment (17th-18th centuries) produced both. Such was what the Sixties generation was born into.

When President John F. Kennedy was assassinated in Dallas, Texas on November 22, 1963, I was seventeen and living in Lausanne, Switzerland. After going to the cinema, I had bought a special edition of the Swiss newspaper on the street. As I read the headlines, I was struck to the quick by intense grief. Walking back to my mother's apartment, I realized for the first time that I was sharing grief with all the teenagers of the world. This American event was *world* news. Not five years later, Martin Luther King, Jr. and Robert F. Kennedy would be gunned down on other American streets. *Three strikes and you're out.*

These were the coming-of-age years for the Sixties generation.

The counterweight to our Sixties implosion was the Watergate implosion of the Nixon administration, thanks to the secrecy slowly devouring the last of any moral greatness in the Western world. With radiation silently spreading and Camelot crushed, world consciousness began sliding toward a Mordor state of fractured, imploded disillusionment that is everywhere today. Normalcy was redefined to include the endless war that seamlessly moved from the Cold War to the War on Terror. The Sixties would be recast as sex, drugs, and rock'n'roll *only*. No politics, no consciousness revolution, no explosion of creativity.

My second cousin Dr. Stanislaw Ulam had been pivotal to the implosion known as the Manhattan Project. Physicist Hans Bethe said Stan was the father of the H-bomb, not Edward Teller. Being of the generation that told themselves that such a weapon of destruction would render nuclear war impossible, Stan felt little guilt for having been part of leading humanity to a place at which it could annihilate itself. Such was the reckless, shortsighted thinking that dominated World War One and Two generations.

I often say that my life has a life of its own. Thus life placed me between Stanislaw Ulam and the Bomb, and Timothy and LSD—Leary the Promethean Dionysus, Stanislaw the Pluto of plutonium and Uranus of Uranium, the hot fire of life versus the cold fire of death. Two men as different as you can imagine, two key 20th century imploders—one seeking the free liberation of psychic energy, the other the forced liberation of primordial energy. And there was Stan's brother Adam Bruno Ulam, who also appeared to be well placed as a tenured Kremlinologist at Harvard University, where Timothy had encountered LSD. What did these "coincidences" say about my role in these implosions?

I remember thinking how complex it all was when I brought Timothy and Stan together at the Pink Adobe restaurant in Santa Fe in 1976 after Timothy's final release from prison. Both men were fascinated by fractal perceptions of reality, the world in a grain of sand, solids behaving like liquids, which is exactly how the solid world looks through the psychedelic lens of LSD. *Fluid.*

The Sixties line between fantasy and reality was thin even without acid, which may have been why the mythical, metaphysical, and political merged in our minds as we strove to learn how to become conscious enough to tell ourselves our own story in the implosive wake of the Bomb and LSD. In England, land of Lord Byron and Percy Bysshe Shelley, the LSD scene was more about music, fashion, and beauty. Aesthetic Britain, political USA, and music music music everywhere.

The metaphysical banquet available ranged from Aleister Crowley and John Dee to Merlin and the Holy Grail of LSD, the quest always about the inside of the soul, the true *terra incognita* of Renaissance and Enlightenment inheritors. Karma and reincarnation were daily topics. Cathartic hedonism, promiscuous sexuality, eroticism, drugs, mysticism, radical politics, racial equality, colorful bizarre clothes, long hair like *hipi* Indians, feminism, Buddhist and Hindu mantras and mudras, simple macrobiotic food, homosexuality, androgynous bisexuality, fierce individualism and the longing for community. The cornucopia available took us beyond the confines of both Establishment religion and the quantitative brain.

So how did this volcanic eruption of evolutionary and emancipatory activity end up with more prisons, torture, and surveillance? The answer lies in this book and its Epilogue.

The Sixties generation was the largest generation in Western history, its tribal members rich in unbelievable Renaissance-caliber talent. While President Nixon and his National Security Advisor Henry Kissinger connived and Whitehall in England plotted against the Rolling Stones and Project Phoenix massacred Cambodians and FBI COINTELPRO and CIA Operation CHAOS teams rousted and killed Black Panthers and MKULTRA ripped into people's brains, a culture war for the right to expand individual consciousness raged hot and heavy.

III.

From the moment I awoke in the pink and yellow suite at the Beverly Hills Hotel in Los Angeles the morning after Timothy had been returned to the United States after a cunning re-arrest by DEA agents in Afghanistan, to the day he was finally released 22 federal and state prisons and rural jails later and we broke up, I watched the Clear Light of the magical theatre we had shared degenerate into a B-grade cops-and-robbers rerun. I fell prey to it all, for I was what Timothy called a "heavy game player," someone who would cling to ego at all costs.

Still, once we broke up, I promised myself that I would tell, to the best of my knowledge, what we had been through for two reasons.

First, for myself and my shame at having served as his "guided missile" when he became a prison informant, a role that branded me with the scarlet letter of a Sixties blowback scapegoat; and

Secondly, for my public obligation to tell as much of the truth as I know in an era of lies—to begin to set the record straight about how we became informants for the FBI and DEA, and the role we played together in the history of the demise of the Counterculture, a history that is often misunderstood and purposely distorted. My purpose is not and has never been to discredit Timothy Leary in any way. We were caught in a trap, and it is this trap that my story unravels.

As a European member of what Tim called the "hedonistic elite," I could not fathom his byzantine legal situation nor begin to understand the curious political shell game going on around him. For example, only years later did I realize that some of Timothy's celebrity lawyers who constantly assured me that he might have to spend decades in prison might have been enmeshed with the CIA.

Dope dealers by the thousands were being caught and imprisoned. Drug users were becoming hopeless addicts like me. Some were eventually able to pick up the pieces of their young lives and return to college to prepare to receive the legacy their upper and middle class parents would pass on to them, but all I had was Timothy, my ageing Sixties icon. Being somebody by association was the best I could think of.

Governments have their ways of breaking people. In a country that claims to keep no political prisoners, imagine that your influence is so great that you frighten attorney generals and presidents. In old Russia, you would have been sent to the Gulag, never to be seen again, but in America it's often done with trumped up charges, unjust prison sentences, media manipulation, excessive solitary confinement, drugs, pain, irrational acts with no forewarning such as nocturnal moves from one prison to another, orchestration of cellmates, intimidation, surveillance, deals you can't refuse, buying off lawyers and judges and intimidating the lawyers and judges they can't buy off, veiled threats to loved ones. *Worse,* you're sent to a medical facility for "evaluation" and when you come out, you're not the same man or woman who went in—you've been "adjusted" and are now out of focus. Your sting gone, you are no longer a serious scientist but a vaudevillian who's made an expensive peace with his enemies. Who will ever take you seriously again?

Timothy told a lot of stories after his release in 1976 but never *this* story. Why? Perhaps he couldn't face having turned government informant in order to get out of prison. Or perhaps he simply couldn't *remember* what had been done to him and what he had been coerced into doing. Somewhere between these two possibilities of the devil and the deep blue sea lies the truth.

The man who finally exited the Cinnamon Stick (San Diego Metropolitan Correctional Center) on April 21, 1976 was a different man. During our 49 days of Clear Light in Europe, he had exuded an unbreakable sense of freedom and loving kindness, but when he came out of prison, the man I'd known was no longer free. Timothy had been held with no hope for release by a system that viewed him as a traitor to the Establishment that had reared him as one of its own. Thanks to the fearlessness he had gained from hundreds of LSD trips, his savvy as a psychologist, and the meditative practices he clung to while in solitary confinement, he was able to navigate much of what happened to him during those three and a half years of prison Bardos—but not all.

During those desperate prison years, I'd concentrated on keeping his name alive outside, all the while moving from one prison to another (see Appendix 2), sitting across from him at one prison table after another, our knees and eyes touching but never our hands, skin being forbidden. As his visiting wife, I served as primary witness to the daily and weekly attempts to break and wear him down through solitary confinement. Sometimes, he greeted me with his usual bright-eyed calm and Leary smile, but at other times he was a man in a fog of Thorazine or other medications deemed "necessary," thick-tongued, slurring his words, shaking during our one allowed hug at the beginning and end of visits.

Day and night, I obsessed on freeing him, an impossibly rigged chore that prevented me from perceiving my own state of bondage to drinking, drugging, and sleeping with strangers until I passed out. Timothy and I were trapped in America, land of the free—he deep inside the prison system and I deep inside myself, both of us the unwitting dupes of DEA handlers like Special Agent E. Donald Strange and sorcerer's apprentice Dennis Martino. When Timothy finally succumbed to the proposition to collaborate, I stood by my man with Mata Hari determination and set up whomever he named, all the while clinging to the fantasy that when the Feds finally said it was enough, Timothy and I could ride off into the sunset and live happily ever after.

Despair, alcohol, and drugs blind a person and lead to very dark places. I functioned like the robot I was to destroy the lives of people I had no reason to care about. There would be no way up for years, only down. When you become as morally corrupt as I had been raised to be, there are no limits or boundaries to hang onto, and the solvents of alcohol, cocaine, and heroin leave you as empty as a string puppet.

Long after my bowl was shattered and I was forced to mend myself and my ways, the voltage of my 49 Clear Light days with Timothy in Europe, along with the commitment I made to him during the three and a half years of his imprisonment, have continued to resonate along the fault lines permeating my conception of what a life is for. Now, I attempt the truth for Timothy's sake, for my sake, and for the sake of the generation brought to its knees in those Nixon years.

I trust that many will recognize pieces of their own story in mine and perhaps be able to elicit the courage to tell the truth and thus forgive themselves for whatever roles they played out during the outrageous climax and dénouement of the Counterculture Sixties. *One cannot forgive oneself unless one finally tells the truth.* I have spent the past 28 years learning the difference between illusion and truth so I could write this book about the beginning of law-and-order America that has finally arrived with a vengeance.

Consciousness is our only defense now in the National Security State and what Oliver Stone in his 2012 HBO television series "The Untold History of the United States" calls Capitalism's Invisible Army.

I am one of the very few who survived. Only you can decide which Sixties you believe happened.

PART I

The Wheel of Fortune

Mata Hari, after being unjustly sentenced to death on scant evidence provided by both German and French intelligence that she was a double agent: "I have always lived for love and pleasure."
   Paris, The Palace of Justice, July 24, 1917

Which is better: to be born stupid into an intelligent society or intelligent into an insane one?
   Aldous Huxley, *Island*, 1962

1

TOMMY THE TUMBLING DICE

Fall 1972

"You're not just paranoid," Tommy teased, "you're plain guilty."
    True, I had a couple of grams of cocaine in my wallet, left over from the quarter-ounce we had bought from the Colombians before leaving Geneva. I also had a little vial of Afghani hash oil, and even some acid, Clear Light in six tiny tabs, slipped inside my Chinese journal. It was natural, as I had been born in a hotel and spoke five languages, to feel like an exile in every country. I loved running contraband as a way to defy authorities and border checks by virtue of my inherited sense of entitlement. Besides, outlaws were the future, the only ones who would survive the System. I was sure that when enough people of my generation challenged the order of things, legally or illegally, we would create our own set of rules—after dismissing everyone over thirty, of course. Since I was already 25, it was obvious that the change of order was going to happen within the next five years, or else I would have to be excluded by the terms of my own principles.
    I had a grave little face and porcelain skin, punctuated by many dimples. My mother envied what she called my English complexion, calling me "a Dresden doll," even though she insisted I wasn't especially

pretty. I smiled a lot, finding that it had a seductive effect and kept people from seeing when I was afraid. My body was small and limber; ten years of grueling ballet classes had permanently instilled it with grace and agility, and left me feeling that I was always on display, ready to perform at any moment, depending on who was watching and what I wanted.

At the Olympia Music Hall in Paris, I had attended a concert where the Beatles played the warm-up for Trini Lopez; now, it was the Stones, the Who, the Moody Blues. I wrote poetry in English as I moved through the haunts of the Jet Set, never quite able to resign myself to the crushing boredom of the scene. In the world I was raised in, everything was possible but so little actually happened. I was an Insider by birth and name, but alienated people by acting as if something might really count. Anything was possible, yes, but I knew it was only possible with certain people in certain places. So I kept moving in the hope that the Sixties would lead me, somehow, to the Outside.

Tommy was working out well as my man of the hour. He was tall, with platinum blond hair falling to his shoulders, thick sensuous lips, mocking eyes, and the sleepy, exalted manner of someone who had done a lot of heroin and was always watching for the Man. Intense in the understated manner I could not resist, Tommy was a gifted musician who had traded his art for a life of freestyle decadence, open-ended and amoral, just the way I liked it. Having lately spent several months in the south of France with the Rolling Stones while they were cutting "Exiles on Main Street," he was full of stories about Keith and Anita, Mick and Bianca. From what Tommy told me, I imagined Mick and Bianca's hideaway to be something like the Villa Diodati, Byron's house in Italy where Shelley and his wife Mary and their entourage had created *Frankenstein* in an atmosphere of free love, drugs, mad poetic exuberance, and gothic addiction to the risk of death.

Accompanying us at all times were my two children Lara and Alexis and Tommy's two ragamuffin sons Jake and Charlie. I was touched—and often shocked—by the way he totally included his children in his life. The three of them together made a picture that constantly fascinated me, like a small troupe of nomadic lions with an endearing jungle royalty.

I finally responded to Tommy, searching for the right words. "Sure, but not guilty about anything I've done. It's more the kind of guilt you feel from being accused of something you never did and never being able to show you're innocent." I paused, caught again in the peculiar sensation of being two people, one having the experience, the other trying to understand it, bound together for life like Siamese twins but incapable of coming together to help each other.

Tommy showed me how you can drink longer without passing out if you have enough cocaine with which to sober up; how a touch of heroin loosens the body, making it ready for sweet lingering caresses and wild secrets that last all through the night; and how acid taken in successive doses creates the sensation of jumping into the ocean from cliffs growing higher and higher, like divers I had seen on TV leaping from rocks in Acapulco.

Besides being an alchemist who knew how to mix drugs in devastating combos, Tommy was also a fabulous dancer. He had a way of talking that always started mid-sentence, making whatever he said sound urgent and conspiratorial. As we wandered from Amsterdam to Geneva to Marbella and back to Geneva again, we kept playing "Tommy the Tumbling Dice" from a demo tape of "Exiles on Main Street." Singing along, Tommy moved his hips to the sound, looking as androgynous and enticing as Mick Jagger himself.

Most of all, Tommy inspired me with the forbidden feeling of being out of control. He gave me the freedom to follow the signals LSD was flashing at me too fast to know exactly what they were saying. Since breaking away from my life in the Jet Set, he was my wild escort into the world of rock'n'roll gypsies.

"No, it's not the guilt of taking on a false accusation, that's not right," I went on, watching Tommy lay some lines of coke on a small makeup mirror from my bag. "It's more like the guilt of thinking, 'What's wrong with me that I'm all the time condemned without even a judge or jury?' and knowing I would never have done what I was accused of in the first place . . ."

Tommy looked at me curiously, then shrugged. "Maybe you're a little anxious about meeting the Stones. Here, a line of coke will keep you cool." He held up the mirror with the gesture of a magician totally confident of his next illusion.

My errant thoughts about guilt trailed off without protest into the easy limbo of a thousand unfinished conversations. Tommy was right, of course. I was feeling a little anxious, especially because I was convinced the Rolling Stones had something to tell me. Their music had the reckless drive of my own feelings, violent and tender, playfully and defiantly sexual. I had met Mick at parties a few times and glimpsed the way he continually played people, taunting and testing, darting back and forth across sexual boundaries. He embodied a danger that had attracted me irresistibly, until I found Tommy. It was natural to see myself in "You Can't Always Get What You Want"—

> *I saw her today at the reception*
> *In her glass was a bleeding man*
> *She was practiced at the art of deception*

Tommy and I had come to Switzerland to see Keith Richards at a chalet in Villars. At last, I was discovering people who lived perpetually at the edge, who took every risk as an invitation to live more passionately, even if the risk entailed facing death. Wrecked lives were as common in this set as wrecking 5-star hotel rooms. Brian Jones, Janis, Jimmy, and Morrison were already dead. Early last summer while he was in the south of France, Tommy's wife Ruby Tuesday had died of an overdose, providing Tommy with even more of a desperate edge.

We were ready to leave Geneva after scoring some prized high-grade morphine as a peace offering to Keith Richards. Before gathering up our things and checking out, Tommy laid back, ceremoniously rolled a fat joint, and passed it around.

"Hey kids, only one toke each," he advised Jake and Charlie. When he let the kids smoke like this, I always felt uncomfortable but had to convince myself it was okay.

By leaving with Tommy, I had finally been able to turn my back on my mother and the lifestyle in which I was always the misfit without knowing why. Outside meant another world, a wonderland of new possibilities almost totally unfamiliar to me. I needed a Tommy or somebody better to lead me into the unknown.

2

LARA

Lausanne, 1967

My mother had never talked to me about contraception or pregnancy. She just left me to struggle with my precocious womanhood at the end of the long corridor that separated her room from mine. In the kitchen, lying like a country between us, the servants complained, laughed, and whispered secrets reeking of olive oil and garlic.

Frightened and believing I was going to die, I was eleven when I had my first period—a scrawny little girl with straight scraggly hair in ankle socks and a navy pleated skirt. I went to tell Mummy sitting deep in a bath fragrant with drops of oil of rose geranium from Floris of London. Mummy said "it" was nothing, "it" would go away in a few days, not to worry, unfortunately everyone gets "it." Chewing my lip, I wondered if it had to do with Mummy's tall, dark chauffeur visiting me at night and doing things to me.

At twenty in Lausanne, Switzerland—six years before Tommy—I'd met a Greek named Nico just a few months older than I. Lausanne was familiar to me. I'd stay with my mother in the Palace Hotel or one of the several apartments she had owned there over the years, or settle in with a lover or friend. For years, my family had been coming through

Lausanne en route between Paris and St. Moritz. From Geneva, which could be somewhat exciting for a Swiss city, it was just an hour to Lausanne, which was not exciting at all but was Swiss-pretty with its rolling hills strung with tram lines running down to Lac Leman, and France on the other side of the lake. The town was a well-known tax haven, a sedate bourgeois paradise of posh clinics and top-level international banks.

Nico gave me what I craved: a lot of attention, and most of it in bed. I nicknamed him GT because of the black Ford Cortina Grand Tourismo we drove around in that summer. He drank heavily and liked nightclubs and dancing. He took particularly beautiful black and white photographs of me with his German Leica camera. Though he was going to college in Switzerland, he never attended classes or showed up for exams. He too was from a wealthy family, and his mother sent him money to stay out of her way.

I became pregnant. I told Nico that I could not have an abortion, the doctor in Lausanne said it would be too risky. Besides, my mother was so exasperated with me, I thought she would surely kill me; marrying Nico would mean emancipating myself from her tyranny. So he drove to Paris, where his mother was attending the fall fashion collection, and told her he wanted to do the right thing, that I was from a good family, and that he loved me. We were married in December before a gathering of Jet Set people including William Holden, Yul Brynner, and the Prince and Princess of Monaco. I was 45 minutes late for my wedding at the Greek Orthodox church, hopelessly drunk on Dom Pérignon, and Nico was two hours late, barely recovered from a night of drinking with the boys at a strip joint in Geneva.

We lived together in an apartment provided and decorated by his mother. It was awful for both of us. Our baby moved inside of me, but I had a hard time imagining what it was. The only babies I'd seen were in the movies; I certainly had never held one in my arms. My mother would not speak to me because I had told her friends that I was pregnant before the marriage. Nor did Nico and I speak much, given how terrified we were of our coming responsibility. Neither of us knew anything about communication and had to deny what we could not fathom.

I yelled at Nico as my mother had yelled at me. "Go to the university or your mother will not send us any more money!" and "What are we going to do with this baby since we do not have enough money to hire a nanny?" Some nights, we had terrible arguments, me pounding him with my fists, him pushing and slapping me. Then, panicked about the baby, I would lock myself in the bathroom and fall asleep on the carpet, dried tears on my baby face.

Our little girl was born in Lausanne, Switzerland on May 30, 1967 during the Israeli-Egyptian Six Day War. She was beautiful. Five pounds, a lovely little face like a baby bear cub, a full head of dark brown hair, and tiny little hands that wrapped themselves firmly around my index fingers. The big Swiss doctor said breastfeeding would ruin my breasts and make the baby too dependent, so I was given a shot to dry up my milk and taught how to feed little Lara with a bottle.

Ten days after Lara's birth, I took her to a clinic where experienced nurses took care of babies so she would be safe from Nico's and my helpless screaming and fighting. Mummy had always said that babies were little better than pieces of meat that felt nothing and were no one until much later in life. While my baby was safely locked away among professional caregivers, I would connive a way to divorce Nico, get money, and make a life for myself and my little girl.

When Nico went to Greece for his military service, Mummy hired a Swiss nanny and I brought Lara to live with us in Mummy's house above the lake. When Lara was nine months, we closed the old creaky house on the lake and moved to Marbella, Spain, leaving behind the pain of my first failed marriage. It was March 1968, and the smell of *dama de noche* permeated the air. I would live off and on in Marbella with my mother for years. In the south of Spain, the weather was excellent and the servants cheap.

3

THE DOMAIN OF THE WITCH

Spring 1972

Marbella was a small village of narrow whitewashed streets, geranium pots in the windows, and a main square with two concentric rows of sweet-smelling orange trees where flocks of birds circled at sunset, filling the air with jubilant sounds. In Marbella was a small hotel called La Fonda with a courtyard and fountain, run by a wealthy hippie decorator who kept it filled with rock musicians, clothes designers, and loll-about English actors, all of them chilling from the frantic scene on King's Road in London.

When I'd arrived in Marbella with Mummy and Lara, I looked very straight in my pleated skirt, lamb's wool sweater, and Gucci loafers. But in no time I was smoking dope and slipping into ruffled blouses and gypsy skirts, letting my hair grow and listening to Bob Dylan sing "Like A Rolling Stone" while chain-smoking Gitanes at the local café. Marbella was exciting but sleepy, like a young girl unaware of her charms who would awaken one day to the many things she could not yet imagine. I walked around the village barefoot, chatting with the locals in fluent Spanish, feeling for once happy and at ease.

Eventually, Mummy rented a beautiful house called the Domain of the Witch in the mountains behind the village. Everything about the house was round and the walls a rich pink that turned to glowing burgundy in the setting sun. There was also a huge garden full of different kinds of flowers, filling the air with heady scents ranging from sweet to pungent. I loved the luxuriant and sheltered beauty of the garden, especially the enormous bushes of white daisies surrounding the pool. I spent most of my days sunbathing, riffling through magazines, watching clouds drift across the sky out and over the Mediterranean sparkling like jeweled tapestry in the distance. I'd get up around noon most days and took a good long time recuperating from the previous evening at the Rodeo Club, the fashionable piano bar where Don Carlos, the brother of the Queen of Belgium, played for wide-eyed women of high society. A cup of strong coffee helped, followed by a glass of orange juice and half a dozen little speed pills. By 25, I had taken up collecting men as my main occupation, for which I had to stay thin as possible and therefore got to know every pharmacist in Marbella who would sell me Dexadrine, Valium, or Librium.

None of the men I'd encountered presented the slightest challenge until Tommy came along. Lara was five when I met him. Like Tommy, I too adopted the prevailing hippie style of parenting with Lara constantly by my side, either falling asleep in my arms at a Moody Blues concert or on the sofa beside me during the long nights of being drunk and stoned.

As for Mummy, she was the heiress Marisya Ulam, a tall, slender woman of strong presence and imperious air. Her hair was always impeccably teased and curled, even when she got out of bed. I had never seen her without red nail polish. The only time she seemed to surface from being extremely bored with everything was when she played bridge, usually with the ambassador's wife or an exiled Austro-Hungarian aristocrat. At 53, she had never made a bed or washed a dish in her life. She could neither drive, nor accomplish a simple bank transaction. Like me, she had a lot of time on her hands and very little notion of what to do with it. But sometimes she would chase terrified servants out of the kitchen and take over, cooking up a Polish dish of beef goulash, cabbage, potatoes, and bread dumplings stuffed with juicy plums, dirtying every pan and utensil in the place. When I was small, I often sneaked into the kitchen to watch attentively from a corner as the chef cooked up an elaborate meal. I imagined Mummy doing the same years before in the kitchen of the cold Polish castle in which she had grown up. I imagined, but did not ask.

Mummy was born in Poland in 1910 to a Jewish family of extraordinary wealth and social power, landowners who cut down trees to make cigarette papers. The story goes that my grandmother and grandfather, Leonie Caro and Michael Ulam, had two daughters, my mother and her sister. Anjie was the older, perfect child, beautiful and talented, a piano virtuoso by the age of twelve, whereas my mother was the troublemaker, a drama queen by nature and, worse, an aspiring actress. Anjie's death by appendicitis at fourteen made her the family saint and my mother the family scapegoat. Failing to achieve her dream of becoming an actress, she would play every role offered up by life with total and flawless dedication.

The Ulams fled from Poland to France in the early Thirties, taking with them a hoard of jewelry, securities, and art—a fortune that would establish them in café society on the fringes of the high society to which my grandmother aspired more than anything in the world. As matriarchal heir to the family fortune, she was envious of the aristocracy, even though she had been born of a lineage as ancient as any aristocratic bloodline. Her origins were, in fact, Biblical, and she could claim the Grand Rabbi of Poland as her grandfather. Her ancestors had long been accustomed to the rights of high privilege, and I was often reminded that no one in our family, going back to legendary times, had ever worked for a living. My grandfather was the chief architect of the Polish government and came from a Jewish family of great wealth and intellectual stature, as well.

The Hungarian financier Arpad Plesch had worked for my grandfather as his secretary and business adviser from the time my mother was four years old. After my grandfather's death in 1938 at the Hotel de Paris in Monte Carlo, Plesch married my grandmother Leonie and moved the family to Switzerland, a safe haven for Jews. With him, Leonie would finally acquire what all her money couldn't buy, a tenuous entrée to European aristocracy. They hired several suites at the Palace Hotel in St. Moritz, where I was later born, as their wartime residence, safe from the Holocaust going on just over the border in Germany and beyond in Poland, where the town of my mother's birth had already ceased to exist. Life was glamorous and well organized: candle-lit dinners and Dior gowns, bridge games with members of deposed royal families. The family fortune grew through Plesch's Faustian deals with whoever crossed his path. His genius was for making connections, many of which led to circles within circles of European politics and aristocracy, including movers and shakers in the American government. Plesch would dominate my world as he did my mother's, the man with a mysterious power over everyone and everything.

Leonie died by Plesch stabbing her in the heart with a silver dagger. Mummy often related the story of the night her mother died and how no doctor would issue a death certificate. Finally, one was found for a large sum of money. Mummy also told my first husband Nico of Plesch's rape of her that same devastating night. Once Leonie's fortune passed to my mother, Plesch was ready: within four months, he married my mother. From being Mummy's stepfather, he now became mine. It was June 1952 and I was six years old. A year after their marriage, Mummy and Plesch separated, pending divorce. I was sent back to Gstaad for school, and Mummy returned to the apartment Leonie had owned on avenue Foch, leaving Plesch to manage all her money and dispense it to us as he saw fit. Though an heiress to enormous wealth, she lacked the faintest idea of how to handle money.

The only time the Domain of the Witch lost its calm was when Mummy panicked over money. Observing her, I got the impression that money was like the weather, a mysterious entity you could neither control nor predict. Where it came from, where it went, no one could say. She still depended entirely upon Plesch to dispense her monthly allowance and bail her out with her own inheritance when her allowance fell short, as it usually did. Accustomed to having her own way, she would rage and take it out on me, listing all of the things I had done wrong, foremost of which was being born. She spoke seven languages and in her rage would effortlessly slide from one language to another for words with which to abuse me. Sometimes, even seven languages did not seem to suffice.

4

GEORGE SAND MEETS JEANNE D'ARC

September, 1972

Upon arriving at Villars, Tommy and I didn't see much of Keith Richards or the other Stones. Keith stayed downstairs in the basement most of the time, rehearsing on his electric guitar and piano for a world tour coming up in a few days. It didn't matter, given that I had already decided that his old lady Anita was the one I wanted to get to know, and from the moment Tommy introduced me as "his lady," Anita was eager to know everything about me. In a matter of minutes, we had plunged headlong into conversation at the dining room table while Tommy looked on, rolling joints and pouring drinks, obviously pleased to have been our liaison.

The house was like many old chalets I had seen during my youth in Switzerland, replete with a cook working intently in the kitchen and a nanny looking after Anita's children Dandelion and Marlon and Tommy's and mine as well—all perfectly normal, except for the selection of drugs laid out on the dining room table along with Jack Daniels, an excellent Bordeaux, and lots of Cuervo Gold.

Anita was tall with platinum blond hair—a female version of Tommy. Her manner was quick and animated and she had a habit of almost whispering in an excited way, completely absorbed in the intensity of her own seductive powers. Her voice was husky with a German accent, and her bright blue eyes looked straight through pretenses. On the one hand, she sized me up for the measure of my courage and defiance to see if it matched her own, and on the other took me immediately into her confidence. Being French, I saw her as a George Sand, muse of Chopin and Liszt, one of the first truly modern, liberated women challenging men to their utmost, and she seemed to recognize me as a peer in that art. Brian Jones, the dead Rolling Stone, had loved her madly, and it was rumored she had been with Mick, as well.

"It will be terrible if Nixon is elected again," she insisted with a sharp nod of her head and grave look. "Sure enough, things seem to be heading that way. I mean look, it's close to the end of September, just a month from the elections, and something *huzz* to be done because McGovern has run out of money."

I raised my face from a vanishing line of cocaine, drawn into the deep seriousness of her tone. "How about getting the Stones to donate the profits from their upcoming US tour to the McGovern campaign? I mean, if it's only a question of money."

Anita, who appeared to observe and think even more furiously than I, came back without skipping a beat. "Great! It will be on me to convince the Stones. You and Tommy will make the perfect emissaries to go to the McGovern people and tell them that help is on the way."

We discussed details over brimming shots of tequila. Anita licked the salt off the back of her hand and studied me closely, the tip of her pink cat's tongue showing.

"When you dream, lady, you dream big," she said with a husky laugh. "It's good to meet a woman who really wants to change things. Besides, when George McGovern beats Nixon and becomes president, he'll surely pardon Timothy Leary." An expression came over Anita's face when she said the name, something like awe.

"Who's he?" I asked. *Where had I heard that name?*

"Another exile in Switzerland, like us," she told me, "but with him it's not about taxes, it's far more political. And he's American." Her eyes narrowed as she slowly explained in her amazing German-Cockney accent that Leary was the foremost authority on LSD in the world. "He started out as a psychologist at Harvard, a brilliant mind, avant garde, one of the few people doing serious clinical work on going past the known limits of the mind through LSD and mescaline. Harvard approved and financial support was flowing. But when he and Richard Alpert really started to party, they were thrown out and the project was cancelled. Since then, Leary has been insanely persecuted. That never happened to Aldous Huxley, did it? Well, Tim is the Huxley for our time and a long time to come."

My intuition had been right. There was something the Stones had to tell me and I was hearing it from the Muse Herself. Someone like Aldous Huxley was the most influential man of my generation.

"What does all this have to do with the government, though?" I asked. "You said something about Leary being pardoned."

Leary's personal life had gone bizarre after Harvard. On a trip to Mexico with his wife Rosemary and his two children Jack and Suzy from a former marriage, Rosemary pressed Suzy to conceal a small stash of marijuana in her underwear. At Laredo, they were body-searched, the dope was found, and Leary was charged with smuggling and interstate transportation. After the Texas court handed down a conviction that carried a sentence of ten years, Leary appealed to the Supreme Court and the case was overturned. Then, at the press conference to report his triumph, he announced that he was going to run for governor of California. John Lennon wrote a campaign song for him. Remember 'Come Together'? Well, that also became the campaign slogan: 'Come together, join the party.' A lot of us were into using rock'n'roll as a tool for revolution then, and the Stones got behind it, too. Then came another bust, even more absurd than the first—a plant, pure and simple. Cop pulls him over in Laguna Beach and they 'find' a roach in the ashtray. All hell broke loose. The trial was a media circus, all the hippies in white robes at the courthouse, flowers, incense, the whole show . . . No one was surprised when he was convicted. Not the end of the story, though, uh uh." She stopped and fixed me with her vivid blue eyes. "Do you know the Weather Underground?"

I furrowed my brow. "You mean, the weather under the ground?"

With a quick glint, Anita took me in all over again from head to toe, then smiled. "It's a radical revolutionary group in America out to bring down the System with bombs—the real thing, like the old anarchists in Russia! Anyway, they helped Timothy escape after he'd been locked up for almost a year. Incredible, *n'est-ce pas?* Disguised, he managed to get out of the country. The crazy thing is that he went to Algeria first, to join Eldridge Cleaver—you know, the Black Panther leader—but Cleaver had his men put Tim under house arrest. Finally, he got out and now he's hiding here, in a little chalet just down the road. We've been seeing a lot of him, actually."

"Perhaps we can meet him while we're here," I said in a hushed tone, unable to conceal my anticipation.

"Sure," Anita said casually. "Actually, he's funny and quite attractive. I'll call him later and perhaps we can arrange something."

By now, it was five in the morning. The children had long since crashed in each other's arms on the living room floor, and Tommy was passed out in morphine dreams in front of the glowing fireplace. Up from the basement drifted honky-tonk electric piano—bluesy, driving chords coming fast and hard. Outside, snow fell in thick pastry flakes, throwing up soft polkadot patterns against the velvety backdrop of night.

Anita wandered off to check on her children while I stared across the kitchen at the poster for the Stones' last world tour, an art deco design with an ocean liner and magnificent Bugatti. I was high, my thoughts and emotions exaggerated to wild extremes, pondering my next best move. Should I concentrate on Leary, or head off for America to participate in the Revolution? This outlaw professor sounded like the kind of man I wanted to find: brilliant and adventurous, a man living beyond the rules—a genuine revolutionary, and anyone worth knowing had to be a revolutionary. He was also an infamous fugitive, the hero of a generation, and the one person best qualified to answer all of my questions about LSD and God, as Aldous Huxley would have done . . .

But what felt more important at the moment was to fly to Washington to make the connection between the McGovern people and the Stones before it was too late. It was my first real chance to change things and I was ready. That's what Jeanne d'Arc would have done, at least at first.

5

HUXLEY AND HEINEKEN

Summer 1968

Since childhood, I had viewed life as a kind of treasure hunt, *un jeu de piste*, knowing that if I could just connect the dots, I could understand my place in the often confusing and painful canvas of life. Grownup life didn't seem to be all that different, except that the clues were bought and sold or denied. *Co-incidences* played a role, and the doctrine of karma said the clues were like Golden Oldies played over and over until you got the right answer, or as the Stones put it, *You can't always get what you want, but if you try sometimes, you just might find you get what you need*. The Great Wheel accounted for a lot when it came to *This is like this because that is like that*, but what about all the left-hand turns and zany transformations, or the possibility that I just might *not* get what I needed?

Whatever you called the clues, heading off with Tommy the Tumbling Dice to Washington, DC, I flashed back to four years before and my first trip to America. I was sunbathing topless in a tiny lime-green bikini on the balcony of a lover's house in Lausanne when I received a visit from my tall and lanky English friend Nicky Phillips soon on his way to Argentina to work in a bank. Dressed in pressed blue jeans and a tailored shirt of deep crimson, he sat down in the same wicker chair he had sat in the month before after I returned from the hospital with my wrists bandaged—52 stitches, the *fifth* time I'd tried to kill myself, the first having been at the age of twelve. It was an understatement to say I yearned to be special, to have a life that mattered.

"I'm worried about leaving you here, you are so fragile and unprotected," Nicky said, looking tenderly into my eyes. "Being as beautiful as you are makes you have a lot of doubts, I know. It's hard for you to see where you're going, so remember I love you." He handed me a book entitled *A Timeless Moment*, written by Laura Huxley. "I think you will find what you are looking for in this book," he said softly, then gazed at me in silence.

When he was gone, I opened the book that would set the wheel spinning. Laura Huxley, a young Italian woman cosmopolitan like myself, talked about life with her husband Aldous Huxley, one of the first Establishment people to experiment with and study LSD. They had led an exciting life of travel, meeting bright and fascinating people—just the kind of life I wanted. They also took LSD together.

I turned the pages rapidly, skipping whole paragraphs. Just as I had suspected, they did a lot of daring things in America. No one I knew could get LSD. Magazine articles said it was a growing fad fated to reach dangerous proportions. People were jumping out of windows and chromosomes were being damaged for generations to come, but Laura Huxley described it as neither trivial nor sinister. Instead, she talked about the ecstasy and peace that she and Aldous had experienced on LSD. Her use of the word "God" struck me in a completely new way, as if I had never heard the word before. God in her language sounded like an adventure that could happen between a man and a woman who loved each other very much.

Un jeu de piste-style, Nicky had tucked a Geneva-Buenos Aires plane ticket between two pages. I took it as the sign it was and decided to cash it in for a trip to America.

In the last pages, Aldous asked his wife to give him LSD while he was dying so he could experience death in an altered state. I put down the book and shut my eyes, overcome by sweet, sweeping emotion. This man and woman had achieved a union I too could find. Love, death, LSD—all that I had not found in Europe. Laura Huxley's story confirmed my dream of America. Perhaps there was someone for me, someone who knew all about LSD—a man I could find, marry, and give LSD to when he died.

That same summer in Marbella another friend brought something else I would need for discovering America. Tall and blond, half-Hungarian and half-Italian Egon von Furstenburg was an outrageous young prince who charmed and shocked with equal nonchalance. He had just returned from Paris where a kind of revolution was going on.

"Joanna, young people in the street are throwing cobblestones and demanding that De Gaulle resign," he said excitedly. "I think they're showing solidarity with the Chinese students toting Mao Tse-tung's little red book."

"I wish I was in the Revolution, too," I said enviously. It's so boring with everything always being the same."

"Yes, I know," Egon concurred with a mock sour face, "it's a miracle that we survive the boredom."

Maria set champagne out on the deck table between us. Glass in hand, I gestured to the surroundings. "Marbella is delightful, but it is like the rest of the world with the old people running the show and money leading to nothing but more money. It's so predictable. Sometimes, I think the poor are the only ones having the fun because they're always ready to do something to better their lives. At least they have something to look forward to . . . Why is it they always start the revolutions and not us?"

I caught Egon's wide-eyed look. Of course! For once, the rich must begin the revolution! Taught from the cradle that the rich were powerful and the poor powerless, we could feel only contempt for "the masses." Nothing could be gained by disowning money and power in a naïve spirit of communism. Idealism might be inspiring, but only money and power changed anything. Why, look at what had happened to the American black leader in April.

"Now is definitely the time," Egon said, "and for once it will be us who start the heads rolling." We toasted the revolution, wherever it might occur. For us, considering revolution beside a pool in Marbella was a lark, far from the bread of necessity. In the meantime, we made plans for lunch at the Marbella Beach Club. Egon was in town on holiday and was going to liven up the place, thank God.

After his visit, I bought all the American newspapers I could find to see if the revolution was there yet. I had become bored with the war in Vietnam running like a long serial on Swiss or French TV night after night—Americans walking through the jungle in uniforms shooting Asians and getting blown up by mines. I flipped from channel to channel until I found the Sorbonne students flooding the streets of Paris, holding up their little red Mao books, shouting in unison. I wanted to get into the streets with them, push over barricades and cheer the wild speeches of Daniel Cohn-Bendit. But what could they hope to accomplish without money, the real power in this world?

I picked up the telephone and called Freddie Heineken, busy in Amsterdam clinching a merger between Heineken and Amstel, to tell him my idea about revolution-by-the-rich. Freddy was delighted with the prospect of parodying Mao and his *Little Red Book* and promptly put me in touch with a Dutch professor who would whip my ideas into something called, appropriately enough, *The Little Green Book*, a slim volume of quotations with a strong conservative message paid for by the little green bottle. After scribbling a few aphorisms at the Hotel de l'Europe, 100,000 copies were printed in English, German, Spanish, and French. I then appeared in my green velvet Mao suit, flashed my smile, and finally was shoved down the steps by the Chinese Legation at Portland Place—a moment captured by the London press and plastered all over the world—and almost kidnapped in Bonn.

Whatever the revolutionary impact *The Little Green Book* had in the world at large, in my own world it was a radical event of the first degree. I had worked and been paid for it, something unheard of in my family. Free of financial dependency on Mummy who was desperately dependent upon Arpad Plesch, I would use the money for my first plunge into the American scene.

Who says *un jeu de piste* has no sense of humor?

6

AMERICA WITH A K

November 15, 1969

Egon had given me the name of a friend in the States, Valencio, a South American student at Georgetown University. I converted the ticket Nicky had left me into a roundtrip fare, slipped *A Timeless Moment* into my suitcase, and caught the flight from Geneva to Washington, DC on November 15, 1969.

Valencio was a typical sleek South American with soft eyes, a drooping mustache, and the habit of carrying himself like an overgrown child. To my surprise, he declared with a mysterious smile that we must go immediately to the Washington Monument. Despite the night cold, we took off in his little convertible Fiat down the long straight avenues, top down, the winds of a new world tossing my hair. He passed me a skinny little joint, different from the fat joints my British friends rolled with hashish and tobacco. It was only about the third or fourth time I had smoked marijuana, and this marijuana-only joint was powerful. I liked the pungent taste and wondered if pot would be a good substitute for all the pills I had been taking.

"It's a great day to arrive in America," he declared.

"Any special reason?" I asked.

He shook his head slowly and smiled knowingly. "I guess any day is a great day to arrive in America."

"Sure, because this is where things can really change, right?"

"That's right. You'll see," he said, once again breaking into a mischievous smile.

At last, we parked on the sidewalk between two garishly painted vans. Hundreds of cars were parked close together. I grabbed my camera and we were off into a massive crowd with people mingling and meandering in all directions. This was America, all right, everything on the grand scale I had imagined. At nine o'clock at night I was used to seeing a lot of people in the streets, but never like this. In Spain and France many people, even children, stay out in the street on summer nights talking, drinking coffee, and enjoying the night air—but not in the winter. Here, even the air throbbed with an intensity and excitement I had never felt before.

"I can't believe there are so many young people here," I said to Valencio as he led me through the crowd, seemingly bent on a destination. "If America is dominated by young people, no wonder they're way ahead." I was delighted. Here at last was a place where my under-thirty philosophy really made sense.

Now in the depths of the crowd, hippies were close up and "live." Despite the cold, bare-chested young men with long hair and headbands walked with a lanky, careless stride, emanating the untamed energy of children running wild on a playground. The women wore brightly colored flowing skirts of brilliant oranges and indigo blue and macramé vests over their breasts. Flowered bandanas restrained their long hair, and babies rode easily in slings across their bellies. They reminded me of gypsies in the south of France each spring. Their casual and fearless air was even more striking than their outlandish dress.

Valencio and I were out of breath by the time we reached the esplanade. All around us was an undulating sea of humanity laid out like a crazy quilt, the air full of laughter, songs, shouts, and the murmur of ten thousand conversations. Valencio gestured to a group of people sitting on the grass and we sat down with them. It was as if everyone knew everyone else—no built-in boundaries like in Europe. Knowing that I could talk to anyone about anything that came into my mind intoxicated me, even though I hardly knew yet what to say.

A woman with flowing blond hair in a flowery skirt and embroidered jean jacket offered me an apple, and when the man next to her proffered a joint, it seemed perfectly natural for us to take a toke. I inhaled deeply and smiled with all my warmth at these casual, openhearted strangers. America was just the way I had dreamed it to be, thriving with generous people filled with the spirit of sharing and adventure. No one cared what your name was or where you came from. No one here was going to ask me stupid questions about my family.

"Don't you think Nixon will have to end the war now?" asked the girl who gave me the apple.

"I don't know. I'm European, I just got off the plane."

"Well, your timing is fantastic, sister," the young man at her side said, "today is the Vietnam moratorium."

I thought a moratorium must be some kind of service for all the young men who had been killed in Vietnam, so I composed my face into a somber look. The hippie compressed a toke in his lungs while explaining. "Our gathering here, 500,000 strong, is only one. It's happening all over the country, and it's going to stop the war. We're all staying here until Nixon says it's over."

"No one has ever seen so many people gathered together here," the girl chimed in, gesturing toward a platform far away at the edge of the crowd. " Dylan and Baez are on the stage, Ginsberg's chanting a mantra at the Pentagon. Here, have a hash brownie. War has to end, it's hazardous to little children and flowers." She smiled beatifically.

I was stunned. The very idea of an event on this scale was frightening in some ways, and yet I felt perfectly safe. This circle of strangers and the larger gathering around us stretched all the way up to the stairs of the Lincoln Memorial. People in all directions looked intent and purposeful even while smiling. Off to the left a couple was making love under a blanket by a tree; far away at the edge of the crowd was a podium where Bob Dylan and Joan Baez were talking with black people about freedom and peace, their voices rising and falling, drifting over the murmur of the crowd like foam riding swells.

Policemen were everywhere, too—on motorcycles with helmets and clubs, some waiting in buses in full riot gear. The Days of Rage had just baptized Chicago by fire the month before, six hundred Weathermen armed to the teeth. The Weathermen were one of the most militant

New Left factions sprouting from the dying body of Students for a Democratic Society (SDS); they had taken their name from Bob Dylan's "Subterranean Homesick Blues"—

> *You don't need a weatherman*
> *To know which way the wind blows.*

The Weathermen vowed that only blood flowing in the streets would cleanse white imperialism's sins against the Third World. I could almost see Richard Nixon wringing his hands and pacing back and forth in the Rose Garden. I wished Egon could see me now.

After an hour or so, Valencio took me on a leisurely route through the crowd and then into the streets of Georgetown en route to his friend's apartment. At the corner of 19th and O, some people were scuffling when suddenly blue uniforms were bearing down on the people ahead of us, yelling, "Get out of here! Go home! Enough is enough, get the hell out of here." I took off and ran straight into a melée of people running in all directions as the cops moved in with menacing gestures. A couple was arguing with a cop, then everyone was shoving and shouting, then a sharp *hiss!* and my eyes were burning and tearing. Valencio was beside me, breathing hard and grabbing at my arm.

"Bastards, bastards!" he hissed with a strong Spanish accent. "We've been tear-gassed. Run!"

I felt like I was rooted to the spot, unable to register the meaning of his words. I wanted to stay and see how it all turned out, but Valencio pulled me away from the clouds of gas.

I felt exhilarated, no longer regretting that I had not joined the students in the Latin Quarter in May '68. From my very first moment in the United States, I had become part of the movement demanding change. It was no mistake that I had arrived on this particular day, no mistake that I had been tear-gassed. My christening would commemorate my future participation in the drug revolution and peace movement in America.

Years later, I would learn that nearly one in six demonstrators at any one of the demonstrations in the 1960s and early 1970s was an undercover operative working to subvert those who objected to American policies.

7

ALEXIS

Washington, DC, 1970

By a month after the moratorium, I had rented an apartment on Phelps Place and by spring was running a poker game in the basement. Bartenders came late at night after their shifts and I cooked and dealt cards until about eight o'clock in the morning. I had two rules with my poker partner Guy: no investing my own money in the game, and no sleeping with any of the players.

Then John D'Amecourt arrived—tall, handsome, and a born gambler. From the moment he appeared in our poker den, I was attracted to him. Leaning against the fridge by the stove, he whispered to me, "Why don't you invest some money in the game and later we'll go up to your apartment for a drink?" Without hesitation, I handed him a $100 bill, smiled invitingly, and made him a rare hamburger with extra mayonnaise. By the time winter dawn was struggling through the haze of bureaucratic Washington, we were sitting on my third floor living room rug and he was playing the guitar he'd retrieved from his car, his fingers sensually caressing each string, his rasping, hesitant voice singing Bob Dylan's "Just Like A Woman." He said he worked for a congressman on Capitol Hill. An artist-politician-gambler, he was my kind of man.

He didn't go to work that day, and by late morning we were making love in my unmade brass bed amidst a flurry of discarded clothing. We talked in bed until the harsh sounds of evening rush hour traffic on Connecticut Avenue were intruding. I could tell he was already in love with me; he even showed great interest when I mentioned my daughter Lara in Spain with my mother and how I wanted to bring her to the States. Six weeks later, my three-month visa about to expire, John jumped out of bed stark naked at four in the morning and dropped to his knee on the bare wooden floor.

"Marry me. I'll take care of you and your little girl, and both of you will be legal."

It was a good gamble: I was in love with him, and he wanted me *and* Lara. I joined him on the floor, kissed his face, and said yes. I would call Mummy and tell her that I had a new husband. I was finally on the right track.

My first LSD trip was with John. It was night and from my orange Goodwill sofa I watched him in the armchair near the window, his face in motion, changing every nanosecond, every thought bringing with it a feeling. The possibility that I could look so deeply into another's psyche terrified me because it meant he could see me, too—what a phony I was, worthless and unlovable. I did not want anyone to *see* me. With effort, I got up off the couch and went into the bathroom. In the mirror was the face of someone I could not accept. I felt the deep split in my psyche that I would struggle with for years, followed by the sure thought that my only salvation lay in accepting myself, flaws and all. *All of me was me.*

When I returned to the living room, John was staring at his hands. Out the window behind him was the great pink magnolia tree, beauty in every graceful branch, perfection in each tender leaf. Miraculously, conflict left my mind as gratitude and appreciation for the tree filled my awareness. It was a Buddhist moment in which the observer, the act of observing, and that which is being observed become one. For a timeless moment, I could feel the intricate relationship connecting all of life. The Veil lifted and the simplicity of truth appeared clearly. Later, Timothy would tell me that thoughts are imprinted on the brain much like words are imprinted on paper. *If so, then where do they come from, if not the brain?*

In May, John and I tripped our way into our marriage vows at Criminal Court in downtown DC, then honeymooned at the Domain of the Witch in Marbella. After staying up all night drinking, laughing, and making love, I felt the very moment my son Alexis came into being as a tiny little gamete combo. Pink bougainvillea was blooming outside the window and dandelions were staining the green lawn yellow. I whispered to John, "I am pregnant, I know it, we are going to have a baby nine months from now."

John and Lara had really taken to each other. He sang to her and played the guitar he had brought across the ocean. She shook her long blond hair and danced around him on her brown bare feet. "More, more!" she cried, rolling her R's in the first English word she had learned from her new stepfather. John quit his job in Washington and started a real estate business in Marbella.

But as with Nico, things began to deteriorate. My American knight in shining armor was a mere insecure mortal, torn between the desire to be a hippie in a commune somewhere in America, playing his guitar, smoking dope, and working on his spiritual life, and the desire to be a successful businessman as his mother wanted him to be. His real estate business in Spain was slow in starting, so he spent a lot of time reading Gurdjieff and Blavatsky and playing backgammon with other ex-patriate drifters.

Two nights before our son was born, I dreamed I was about to give birth from atop a tower overlooking the Mediterranean. Behind me, the land was devastated as if by a nuclear bomb. Beneath me, a British warship appeared and the captain called out, "Jump down onto the boat and you and your baby will be safe!" I jumped and delivered a son on board with the crew assembled around me exclaiming that my baby was Admiral Nelson.

The next night, I played poker all night at the local Marbella bar to make enough money to pay for the doctor. By morning, I had made four hundred dollars and insisted that John drive me to the hospital so my labor could be induced before we spent the money on something else. Alexis was born at 10:30 that evening, February 13, 1971. Like Lara, he was a beautiful mystery to me, especially since boys were virtually unknown in our family.

That same night, John collapsed with acute hepatitis and had to be hospitalized in the next room. When he came home two days later, he needed as much care as the baby. In fact, three days after Alexis was born I was at the village market buying salted cod for fish soup and saffron for the rice. The Spanish ladies at the market stalls asked me where my belly was. Smiling, I showed them the small bundle on my arm. Afraid of the food and water in Spain and probably fed up with how committed I was to cultivating the art of self-destruction, John returned to his mother's home in the United States to recuperate.

Mummy paid the rent on a little house overlooking the Mediterranean and found an old gypsy to help me with my son. Lara adored her new little brother and told him long stories in Spanish about hungry cats bristling when nasty stray dogs barked at them, assured Alexis that one little grey kitten could scare away a whole pack of threatening predators. She, the three year old, would keep her brother safe from witches and monsters.

Months passed. Once the early spring sunshine was sparkling on the sea, my daydreams of rejoining my husband on the other side of the vast round pond turned to plans. At the end of the summer, I packed up the kids and flew back to Washington, DC. John and I struggled to live a bourgeois married life in the beautiful brownstone in Georgetown, replete with a Colombian nanny provided by his mother. We spent hours scheming about Spanish real estate deals, but the magic was gone. When I was in Europe, I loved America, and when I was in America, I hated it, losing myself in songs about Woodstock, like "Helplessly Hoping" by Crosby, Stills and Nash—

> *Gasping at glimpses of gentle true spirit*
> *She runs, wishing she could fly*
> *Only to trip at the sound of "Goodbye". . .*

By the following summer, John had raised enough money through his mother's connections to open a real estate office in Marbella, so the four of us set off once more across the Atlantic. But the magic didn't return in Spain, either. Then I met Tommy and it all began.

8

MICHEL

September 1972

Michel-Gustav Hauchard, French swindler extraordinaire, my protector-sponsor in Switzerland, friend of J. Edgar Hoover and admitted CIA contact, used to muse aloud: "The simplest thing would be for them to kill you."
"No," I said, "the technique now is to say the dissenter is crazy. Anyone who opposes the monolithic system must be crazy."

Timothy Leary, *Neuropolitics*, 1977

So Tommy the Tumbling Dice and I were commissioned by Anita and the Rolling Stones to go to America to save McGovern from Nixon. I had only five tickets, all I could afford, for Jake, Charlie, Lara, Tommy, and me, so we took Alexis to Marbella: John D'Amecourt and I had separated that summer and he was living in a village not far from Mummy's Domain.

Before calling John, I sat up most of the night agonizing and crying over Alexis' crib. He looked like a cherub, with his blond curls haloing his forehead, his beautiful full pouty lips, his little body curled under a light cotton sheet. I watched him breathe and imagined taking him with me on this strange journey. His helplessness increased my own. I was afraid for him, afraid that my drinking and daily use of drugs would harm him.

Through the open window, I felt the warm breeze from Africa. It was September and southern Spain was under a heavy heat wave. I touched his warm little hand and whispered, "What will happen to us if I leave you here? Will I lose you forever? Tommy's drinking is often out of control, it is already scary enough to take Lara along."

Archibald my cocker spaniel moaned in his sleep.

"I can't give up going on this journey, and I can't bear to take you with me," I whispered, my voice trembling, "will you ever forgive me?"

Through the window, the first light of dawn was peeking over the Mediterranean. It was time to wake Tommy and the children.

Slowly, I walked into the living room and dialed John's phone number.

"Ya?"

"John, I'm leaving this morning with Lara and Tommy. Please come and get Alexis."

There was a long silence at the other end.

"Don't make this hard, please," I said, "I'll get in touch with you as soon as I know I have some stability."

"Are you sure you aren't going to regret this?" Now wide awake, his voice was grave.

"Please, John, I've got to go, I'm so sorry."

"Okay, I'll be there in a few minutes."

Tommy, the kids, and I arrived in Washington, DC to find that the McGovern people, up to their eyes in political frenzy, were not the least bit interested in our revolutionary proposal. The East Coast manager of Campaign '72 told us with a mixture of relief and disgust that they had already lost the election to Nixon—a mere three years after the Vietnam moratorium I'd witnessed. This was not the America I remembered.

Our adventure dead-ended, we bought a used Lincoln and drove to New York City. As I was running low on money, we ended up on the floor of a Brazilian friend's apartment in the Village in borrowed sleeping bags. The next afternoon, I called Diane von Furstenberg and she invited me to come over immediately. She and Egon were living in the City in a superb duplex on Park Avenue. The bedroom walls were covered in peach silk, and their huge bed had a mink bedspread and sumptuous pillows. As we lounged on the bed gossiping, the two telephones rang constantly—people calling about arrangements for her new fashion collection or details on the organization of next weekend at Fire Island. Once, the phone was even for me.

"*Bonjour, cherie, c'est Michel*," the voice said, "how wonderful that you are here. I am just een New York to sign a contract for a book. Not mine, of course. It ees a book called *Confessions of a Hope Feeend* by Timothy Leary. You remember the name, *non*? I told you some months ago that I own Teem."

It was Michel Hauchard, international gangster extraordinaire. I had met him at Monte Carlo in June 1964 when I was eighteen and facing the inexplicable feat of turning into a woman. I was *une gamine*, as the French say, a woman-child with charms whose implications go far beyond her age. If older women like my mother knew what those implications were, they weren't telling. Mummy just told me to find a man to take me off her hands. I had already had quite a few lovers, refused proposals of marriage and extravagant gifts—even throwing a diamond bracelet into the Mediterranean from a yacht—and knew that men could be crude and impetuous. But the men kept coming, a seemingly endless supply. I got a lot of attention I didn't know how to refuse, while most of my own attention was going toward the fascinations of the era: Bardot with her beehive hair, Charles Aznavour, and Jean-Paul Belmondo.

Michel and I had played gin rummy in the magnificent Art Deco hall of the Hotel de Paris. As with Timothy later, his white hair and elegant looks struck an absent father nerve. I beat him mercilessly, at which he laughed and went to Van Cleef & Arpels to buy me a gold and diamond broach in the shape of a lion's head—my prize for winning, he said, but actually to prove to me that he was a true chevalier. He had been a French Resistance hero of sorts during World War Two and clung to this image of himself whenever he could.

From the start, he courted me like a grand seigneur of the Renaissance. I was inundated with love letters buried in bouquets of dozens of yellow roses and white roses dropped into Mummy's swimming pool from an airplane. He renamed his magnificent Italian speedboat *Joanna*. We often went off with friends to water ski or swim, taking whole days to cruise around the bays and beaches along the Côte d'Azur. In the evenings Michel would give lavish dinner parties at which I was the center of attention, and before leaving me each evening, he would kiss my hand or brush my forehead lightly with his lips, *un geste* I found exceptionally touching, given how unaccustomed I was to any sort of tenderness. No other man had ever been so considerate, though I knew that eventually he would claim his right to make love with me. But in the meantime, our foreplay was absorbing. I was flattered that a man so generous and grand wanted me more than other obviously available women who were older and more sophisticated and paraded around Monte Carlo displaying their elegant charms.

Michel said he was "in business," a thorough enough explanation in my world. To be engaged *dans les affaires* was a mysterious occupation that granted men chauffeurs and Rolls Royces, summers in Monaco and winters in Gstaad, as well as the privilege to acquire and spend money in equally enigmatic and extravagant ways, and of course to enjoy the company of lovely, desirable women. I had seen my mother courted in this way for years, but now she was mostly alone. I was careful not to care whether or not she was jealous of Michel.

There is a term the French share with Americans: *les règles du jeu*, the rules of the game. At eighteen, I still did not know a lot about these rules, but knew enough to see that a code of silence protected the game and talking about how it worked was a serious violation. For example, the richer you are, the less you should mention money. I had lived under the weight of the game's silence all of my life, and had been painfully confused by it. People could talk about each other as long as they didn't give away the secrets, having cultivated a talent for calculating the impact of how much and what they said or to whom they said it—a talent I distinctly lacked. Mummy had raged at me many times, screaming that a liar and a spy was in her house because she expected me to keep secrets without even knowing what they were. I fought back by talking as little as possible until I discovered that I could talk and let others talk but not listen, then it hurt less when people withheld things I wanted to know or told me what I didn't want to know. Often, I could even work out beforehand what people were going to say or even what they were not saying.

With Michel, I sensed a narrow option within the game, a kind of reprieve, even a chance for some freedom and safety. I meant something to him, and he expressed it in a way that gave me a rare sense of power. Like Arpad Plesch, he thought I was special.

"I am the special man for you because I see that there are very few women like you in the world," he would say. "You are what every man in my position hopes to find, though few of them ever do, almost none. Even the most successful man is at a loss without the treasure you can give. Oh yes, you are so very beautiful, young, sweet, erotic—but I don't speak of that now. It's a different thing I mean. It's really indescribable, but sometimes it has been called the blessing of *la dame fortune*."

Lady Luck was indeed important to Michel because he turned out to be not just an international gangster but a heavy gambler. At Monte Carlo, he obtained from the manager of the casino an under-21 exception that granted me access to private salons where all the croupiers knew him by name. He played roulette at outrageous stakes, believing that 8 was his lucky number and covering the numbers 8, 18, and 28 with thousands of francs in glittering chips. With me by his side, Michel's luck improved. One night he won all the money at the table, which almost never happens. I watched with fascination as four valets in red uniforms piped in gold ceremoniously covered the table with a large black cloth to signify that it had "died." All other games came to a standstill as everyone in the casino surrounded us, applauding and toasting, my body swept by the eyes of ladies in Cartier jewels and long evening dresses who looked at Michel with inviting smiles. The men in dinner jackets took their turn looking us over as well, and I found myself looking back. As we passed the cashier's booth on the way out, Michel loudly instructed that I was to be given a large part of the winnings because without me it never would have happened.

But these were not my first days in Monte Carlo. I had gone to a day school there during Mummy and Plesch's brief marriage, when we had lived at our villa La Leonina in Beaulieu on the Mediterranean coast in the south of France. Inside the white villa that looked like a huge birthday cake, sixty servants labored; outside, flawless gardens were kept by eleven gardeners. There, Plesch had received all kinds of people, from emissaries to the Vatican to movie stars like Kirk Douglas. Orson Welles came for lunch, and even Winston Churchill who lived nearby in St.-Jean-Cap-Ferrat. Curious and full of questions, I mingled quite freely with our guests. From the age of four or five, I had the habit of expounding spontaneously on different subjects, usually history or mythological anecdotes as if from an inexhaustible repository of facts and fabulations, declaring with great conviction that I was going to be a famous ambassador when I grew up. Certainly the stream of visitors at La Leonina provided me with good early training for that role.

Visitors were amazed to hear a child speak so boldly. Once, an emissary from the Vatican gravely asked me a question, which I answered by climbing up onto his lap and whispering into his ear. Kirk Douglas, fresh from his enormous success in *20,000 Leagues Under the Sea*, was so struck by my outgoing manner that he promised to come back to France and make a movie of *Le Petit Prince* with me in the starring role and himself as the aviator. I awaited his coming, but he did not keep his promise.

Family secrets were covered under *les règles du jeu*, as well—such as the story that my half-sister Florence's father was a French count with whom our mother had a much celebrated and fashionably scandalous affair when the family arrived in Paris in the mid-Thirties, after which he abandoned her for the Second Great War, etc. I puzzled over this secret for years, especially after Plesch moved my English governess and me into a guesthouse some two hundred meters from the villa while he, my mother, and Floki—our nickname for Florence, who at thirteen was peering through Coca-Cola bottle glasses—remained in the villa. Basically, he adopted Floki and treated her as his own while remaining studiously aloof toward me. It was the *as his own* that made me wonder about my step-grandfather become stepfather.

And yet amidst his preoccupations with business and his collection of botanical and esoteric pornography books, Grandpère Arpi did take a concentrated if not *odd* interest in me. He would observe me closely when I entered the salon to perform for our guests and draw the attention away from talk of politics and money. At other times, he would take me aside and sit me down in the library in front of a microphone attached to a voice recorder, the new invention using wire to capture what people said. He would then ask me questions I don't remember and diligently record my responses. What I said must have been important, I knew, because Grandpère was not interested in anything unless it was important. Meanwhile, at the Monte Carlo school I was not understanding what the teacher said because I had somehow learned to leave my body as soon as an adult started speaking.

A month after Michel had made the Monte Carlo game table die, I joined him for a weekend at the Savoy Hotel in London. We spent the golden September afternoon walking around Knightsbridge hand in hand, followed all the while at the curb by a Rolls Royce Silver Cloud. He bought me cashmere sweaters at Harrods, pleated tartan skirts at the Scotland House, and stuffed animals at the toy shop on Kensington High Street. He was as considerate as ever, leaving me with the impression that he valued my happiness more than I did myself.

That night, after Persian caviar, *blinis*, and cold Russian vodka in our rooms, we made love for the first time. As usual, I did not feel very much but assured him it was the best lovemaking I had ever imagined. After he fell asleep in the huge white bed amidst mounds of down pillows, I slipped on a bathrobe embossed with the Savoy crest and sank into the blue velvet sofa in the salon, musing over a Gauloise. Looking around the splendid room, I thought, *At last here is a man to protect me from my mother, at last I can relax and let down my guard.*

I had been letting men make love to me since I was 14 years old. When they were inside me, where they seemingly found the greatest pleasure and even justification for their manhood, I felt the power of rendering vulnerable these men upon whom I depended for everything—men who withheld or gave money at their will, and who by wanting me or not decided if I was a thing of value or not. Sex was having them at my mercy. With Michel, it was no different.

I yawned and stretched full length on the sofa. On the table beside me was a coral pearl and gold bracelet he had given me earlier. I slipped it onto my wrist and looked at its colors against my skin for a long time. When a man gives jewelry to a woman, it means she is beautiful enough to enhance the luminosity and texture of the precious stones and metals, not the other way around. What I had observed between men and women convinced me that a woman was as important as the money a man was willing to spend on her. But the bracelet felt cold on my arm. Inside, it made me feel lonely and let down. I pulled the robe tight around my body, unfastened the bracelet, and slowly put it back into the Cartier box. The feeling of reassurance and tenderness, so fleeting, had faded as quickly as it had arisen. I took a very hot bath, scented with Floris rose geranium.

So long before Michel Hauchard would become Timothy Leary's handler in Switzerland, he was my very first prisoner. I never saw him in Paris, but once a month he would send a plane ticket and I would join him in Morocco or Portugal. The rest of the time we would talk on the telephone; like a good father, he didn't mind if I called him to talk about anything at all, at least until he was arrested and taken to the awful Prison de la Sant in Paris, a real hellhole. His lawyer was cryptic. "Michel is in for a long time," he sighed, "unless I can prove to the judge that he is insane. I have sent several doctors to the prison to examine him. They will plead that Michel be transferred to a clinic where he can be closely observed and his condition properly treated." He laughed as if he suspected that Michel's "condition" might be one of insanity, after all.

"Can I go and see him?" I asked.

"No, only the immediate family is allowed to visit. But once he is transferred . . ."

"Tell him I will write every day and wait for him as long as it takes," I said with great conviction to make sure he would convey the import of my message.

Soon, Michel wrote that I could live in his apartment in Paris while he was "away." The imprisonment, he insisted, was a foolish mistake (whose, he wasn't telling) and he would explain everything to me in detail when he was released and we were reunited.

I was jubilant. Now nineteen, I had a place to myself for the first time in my life. Michel's lawyer gave me the keys to the apartment and each month money arrived by messenger. I was exhilarated by the freedom I had gained in exchange for Michel's misfortune—another rule of *les règles du jeu*: use everything to your own advantage. Michel was a man and being in jail was part of business; he could handle it. Meanwhile, I would live as I had always dreamed of living, free of Mummy's screaming threats and accusations that I was a spy in her house, a liar, a little whore. I spent nights dancing at Regine's and days wandering about Paris, the city of my very young years on avenue Foch.

Mummy had been a distant figure with impeccable nails and hair living at the other end of our huge apartment. My grandmother, Plesch, and Floki lived in another huge apartment on avenue Foch 32 numbers down from us, away from the Etoile. So I'd turned to my English nanny, a devout Catholic who often insisted that I swear to things I did not understand on a cross under my pillow; she had made English my third language after German and French. Despite our lack of physical contact, Mummy had treated me as her only confidante, often waking me at four in the morning when she returned from a flurry of cocktail and dinner parties to tell me everything that had happened, and if my head nodded, scream at me or shake me. At other times, she threatened to throw me out into the street because I was costing her too much and to remind me that nothing around me was mine, even the elaborate dollhouse Plesch had given me for Christmas. Thus, from Mummy I learned how it felt to be owned but not to own. Mummy did not even choose the clothes she wore; each day her personal maid laid out three sets of clothing for her with matching bags and belts, one of which she must pick.

When I was eleven—the year my father died—my mother took me out of the Marie-Jose boarding school in Gstaad, Switzerland where I had been since I was four and placed me in Le Couvent des Oiseaux, a huge and ancient chateau convent 45 minutes outside of Paris in Verneuil. Le Couvent was night and day from my Marie-Jose. The village Verneuil was the last sight of real life before passing through huge iron gates and taking the dirt road to the chateau. Although situated in the middle of a park that became luxuriant and mysterious in spring, the convent itself was cold even in summer. The classrooms where we were forced to sit for hours were too large to retain the heat exhaled by old clanking radiators, and the dormitory stone walls were always damp to the touch. In the dining room, 300 girls between ten and twenty gathered each evening to eat dry potatoes and tough meat as they talked *ensemble* at the top of their voices. Whether in this din or in the stillness of the dormitory after lights were out, I felt more lonely than I had ever felt. I missed Sophie, my one close friend at Gstaad, a genuine Russian princess who had conspired with me to obtain and conceal our precious contraband of Bazooka bubble gum and the comics they were wrapped in. The one advantage of Le Couvent des Oiseaux was that I could go home on weekends.

But it was on one of those weekends that Mummy's Spanish chauffeur first entered my room on avenue Foch, sliding his hands under my pajamas and touching me all over. Frozen with horror and too sickened to resist, I couldn't find the courage to tell my mother until after he had visited me many times. She scoffed at me, insisting it was just a lie like the one I'd told when I was four about Grandpère Arpi's head gardener Monsieur Gosser and Grandpère had said, "So frightfully young and already seducing men."

"Lies won't get you what you want, Joanna," Mummy said. "Besides, good servants are hard to find."

Turn-of-the-century Vienna's manacles still gripped the minds of my caretakers raised with the mandate that children were born evil and should have their spirits broken as early as possible. I learned early to dissociate, retreating into a fantasy world where my best friends Babar the King of the Elephants, the American Lone Ranger, Pluto the dog, and *le petit prince* would gather around me to protect me when Mummy shouted, "I am going to succeed in breaking your spirit!" instructing her Italian personal maid to hit me so she would not dirty her hands with such a menial task. As the fat hand came down, the Lone Ranger would lift me onto Babar and gallop alongside as Babar whisked me off to the small planet of *le petit prince* somewhere in the Milky Way.

Les soeurs in white headdresses and long black skirts haunted the corridors with their ominous pacing, and the clicking of the heavy rosary beads hanging from their belts were in turn frightening or reassuring. The distant, stately air of these brides of Christ made me feel even more like a helpless victim of an experiment being conducted on an alien planet. Sometimes while gazing at them, I would fantasize plunging into sin and pleasure until fifty, then returning to the cold seclusion of the convent, beyond the reach of human consequences. Becoming a saint sounded interesting, although I wasn't sure what a saint was. I took it to be someone who at least got full credit for their suffering. To *les soeurs*, I was an unusual, deeply spiritual child because many nights they would find me asleep in the chapel. They would then awaken me, give me a cup of hot milk, then lead me solemnly back to my cot. They knew nothing of the chauffeur.

I stayed at Le Couvent des Oiseaux until I was almost fourteen years old, then returned to live with my mother in Paris. Fourteen was a great time of life to be in Paris, a city I truly loved, but I had no friends, and behind our heavy paneled doors I was surrounded by obsequious servants who showed me the pretence of friendliness while firmly protecting their world against my smallest intrusion. Beautiful props—engraved silver, Aubusson carpets, objects of rare and captivating beauty, sculptures by Rodin, paintings by Matisse and Jackson Pollock, Baccarat crystal and Louis XVI furniture—made it clear that people were not as present or important as things. Becoming a beautiful object seemed like the obvious thing to do. Having already exhibited a certain talent for chameleon performing, I aspired to brilliantly please, certain that I would eventually attract the attention of someone extraordinary since I lived in such an extraordinary world.

Now I was ensconced in Michel's apartment without Michel, proud to be living in Paris again. People say it is the most beautiful city in the world and they are right. Everything from the bookstalls along the Seine to the Musée du Louvre, to the crackly croissants from the *boulangerie*, suffused me with elation. To walk through Paris was to walk through history, each building's architecture time travel. I visited Louis XIV and his mistresses Madame de la Vallière and the scheming *empoisonneuse* Madame de Maintenon. In the evening, walking along the Champs-Élysées, idly perusing cafés and cinemas, I felt I owned Paris, perhaps the first time I had ever felt that I owned anything.

At the Place de la Concorde with its gigantic obelisk brought from Egypt by Napoleon, I was comforted by the mad traffic spilling in all directions, even by the insults drivers screamed. At the museum Jeu de Paume on one side of the Place, I would buy a ticket and roam for hours through the cool rooms, gazing at Van Goghs, Cézannes, and Modiglianis. We had had Cézannes at the villa in Beaulieu, but looking at them in the museum was a different experience. Sometimes I would stand for half an hour in front of a painting, waiting for its beauty to sweep over me, waiting for a deep and nourishing force that I knew must be free for the taking, then leaving feeling sad and empty in a way so familiar to me.

After six months of having my own life in Paris, I received a telephone call from Michel.

"It's happened, *cherie*," he announced with elation, "I've been granted a certificate saying I'm crazy and will be transferred to a lovely little clinic outside of Paris, with a police guard at my door 24 hours a day. Come and see me quickly, my precious one."

"Of course," I said as a sinking feeling came over me. "But Michel, will I still be keeping your apartment for you while you're at the clinic?"

"Of course, of course," he reassured me, "and by the way, *cherie*, when you come bring some *paté*, some Camembert, croissants and raspberry jelly, a good bottle of wine, and don't forget some of the cigars in the box on my desk, right by the large amber vase."

Suddenly, I was no longer alone. Michel was right there in the apartment with me, reaching for his cigars. When I hung up, I felt angry and resentful. I was not in the habit of thinking about this man anymore, and now he was intruding on my good life. The next thing I knew, he was going to want his apartment back and I would be forced to go back to Mummy.

For the next few days I brooded intensely, trying without much success to come up with a clear plan of action. Whatever happened, I desperately wanted to remain independent. I needed more time to find my bearings, to get a sense of what it was like to have a life on my own, to see if events would lead me to discover the world on the Outside. I could easily go and see Grandpère Arki right there in Paris, but enormous pain welled up when he even crossed my mind—the *other* father who had abandoned me.

During the brief year he had been married to Mummy and we had all lived at Beaulieu, Grandpère had taken me on walks around the magnificent grounds, pointing out the exotic passion fruit flowers, the blooming mimosa trees, calling out the names of plants in Latin. I would listen to everything he said with every fiber of my being, given that the world did as Arpad Plesch commanded. Even while listening to the radio, I could detect his voice speaking through other voices, like a ventriloquist, his words reaching my ears and even touching my body, to the point that it made me a little suspicious without wanting to be. *Why was it that Grandpère was so interested in me, asking me questions, recording my answers?* I wondered. *Was it because he was involved in something evil?*

Most of the time, he was there only as a powerful and distant name to be evoked. Then he would physically appear and give me encouragement and praise—the only love I ever knew and I would hold onto it as if my life depended on it, which it did.

"Have you thought about what to do with yourself when you grow up? It is very important that you understand what is required to develop your gifts." His manner was a little stern, yet I was thrilled to be taken so seriously at the age of eight.

"Well, I used to want to become an ambassador, remember?"

"Yes, when we were in Beaulieu you always said that."

"But now I want to be an actress," I told him proudly as we sat down on a bench to rest and take a little coolness in the shade of a big rubber tree.

"This is not a good plan, Joanna. It's the same thing your mother wanted to become and her parents discouraged her, which was right. I must say the same to you. There are much better things for you in life—to become a landscape architect, for instance, or a stock market analyst. You have the mind for something like that. An intelligence as rare as yours must not be wasted."

"Yes, Grandpère," I would say meekly, "but being an actress would be so exciting, and the people I— "

"No, little one," he would interrupt, "you must think about what I say. How can I take care of you and Mummy, as I've promised to do, if you don't do what is best for yourself in this world? Being an actress would be a vulgar thing to do and would ruin the family reputation."

After the divorce, Floki had stayed with him while Mummy and I returned to Paris. For years, I was haunted by a memory of Floki in her Coke bottle glasses sitting at the dinner table staring down into her blue Limoges plate and never looking up. When Plesch came to see Mummy and me in Paris, it was only for family business. During the divorce proceedings, he had somehow persuaded my mother to sign over to him not just responsibility for her fortune but most of the fortune itself. I remember her writing him a check for a million dollars, which puzzled me, given that Mummy was always in a rage about scraping together a few hundred francs to do this or that, like to buy me a coat or cover her bridge game losses. The truth was that Plesch had managed to appropriate our entire family fortune while increasing it.

In my last year at the chalet Marie-Jose boarding school in Gstaad, he married a Hungarian aristocrat with a noble title but little else. Mummy went insane, going so far as to have the bride arrested at their honeymoon suite in the Grand Hotel in Zurich. The police explained with some embarrassment that a charge of embezzlement compelled them to lead Plesch's new bride off to jail. To this, Plesch had responded in a soft, marveling tone, "It's amazing what poverty will drive some people to do." He had promised to take care of Mummy, Florence, and me after his remarriage, but my allowance being issued through my mother, I rarely saw any of it. I was outraged but not surprised, viewing it as yet another puzzling instance of *les règles du jeu*.

When Michel was finally released from the clinic, it was understood that we would take up our life together where we had left off and that now things would be even better. On the first night of his freedom, we celebrated with dinner at Maxim's with a number of his old cronies.

"A good thing for my career, actually," he told me en route, referring to his internment, "it gave enough time for some new developments to mature. Now, *cherie*, I will be acting as the middle man between the French government and heads of some of these newly formed African countries. My job will be to provide them with whatever they need, from grain for bread to submarines for war." He laughed and I glimpsed the chevalier who had initially attracted me. "I will earn a lot of money conferring with those black kings and presidents," he boasted.

"That is wonderful, Michel," I answered, beaming my best congratulatory smile. "Will you be keeping your apartment in Paris under this new arrangement?"

"Of course, but it will also be necessary for us to live in Switzerland, so I have someone looking for an apartment there as well. I'm sure you will like it there, *cherie*. You are somewhat Swiss, after all." He was as charming and playful as I had ever seen him.

But he was wrong about Switzerland. I stayed home all day in the new apartment, infuriated to find myself cast again in the role of Michel's sole and exclusive possession. I knew a lot about being owned, and I hated every moment of it. Michel for his part proved to have a blunt and inexhaustible appetite for my charms, treating me more and more like a daughter, even to insisting that I braid my hair and wear ankle socks. He wanted sex every day, but I had come to detest his too soft, too white, and too old body. Soon, I was back in a familiar limbo, oscillating between extreme boredom and dangerous risks. Michel found out that I was having liaisons with other men and had me followed, even following me himself a couple of times.

Finally, one afternoon when we were drinking champagne at home, he lost his temper, jumped on me, put his hands around my neck, and pressed his thumbs down until my eyes bulged. "You are mine, you little whore! All mine! I will kill you rather than let you go," he screamed in my face.

I managed to pull myself clear and stood up. I gave him a look of cold contempt, my eyes glinting with the knife edge of cruelty I had seen demonstrated so many times by Mummy when she raged at Plesch or me. "If you kill me, you will go to prison for real, forever." At the moment, it was all I could think of.

Now, far from being safe with Michel, I was in familiar danger once again. I stayed with him a little longer, keeping to myself as much as possible. Finally, it was a choice between a mother who had wanted to kill me just to get rid of me, and a daddy who wanted to kill me if I tried to go. There was nowhere to go but back to the less dangerous of the two. One of the rules of the game, I saw, was that nothing is ever really over; everything comes back one way or another.

Fortunate for me, Michel soon took up with another eighteen-year-old who was as docile and submissive as I had never been. It was depressing to think of living without the constant stream of clothes and jewelry and expensive hotels, but I had to leave in order to survive. After I left, Michel curiously returned to his original attitude toward me, from a distance playing the gallant, pursuing his obsession with me because, I surmised, it sustained his fantasy of the perfect post-War romance for a post-Resistance hero. In any event, he was not the kind of hero I needed.

9

HOPE FIENDS ABOUND

New York City, Fall 1972

Now seven years later, here was Michel once again, this time relaying information about Timothy Leary. My first impulse was not to believe him, but then I vaguely recalled receiving a phone call from Michel in Marbella not long after I'd met Tommy. He had sounded particularly mischievous.

"There is a man who is called the Pope of LSD," he said. "He lives in Switzerland now, due to some trouble with the American authorities, which is really no great matter. I have been able to assist him and now own him, of course. If you come back to me, you can meet him, eh?"

How suspicious it all had sounded. The Pope of LSD was not the kind of character I expected Michel to collect. Michel was, after all, a self-righteous, self-made swindler whose tastes ran to young girls, Crystal champagne, and the best Cuban cigars. Drugs and international fugitives were not on his agenda. It was so typical of Michel to play on my love of intrigue, a trait we unfortunately had in common. But now in New York I was listening to his enticements in a totally different way. It seemed that *un jeu de piste* was on the move.

"Michel, your timing is excellent, as usual," I purred, "let's get together for a drink at the St. Regis at six o'clock."

He could tell I was really intrigued this time. Diane loaned me a black and white silk jersey dress from her collection—sleek and bold, perfect for the occasion.

The hotel bar was dark and comforting. Michel looked crisp and commanding in his usual Savile Row suit and Hermes tie. Clearly, he was still obsessed with me. He stood up while I seated myself, then leaned down and kissed me lingeringly on both cheeks before taking his seat. We spoke in French and as usual Michel got right to the point so there would be no doubt as to who was in control.

"Look what I have here," he said, indicating a large shopping bag on the floor by my chair, full of perhaps thirty paperback books of various sizes.

I gave his prize the mere flick of a glance as I held a Gauloise for him to light. "What's the good of that, Michel," I said, "you don't even read English."

He took it in stride, lighting my cigarette with care, then settled back to study me for a moment. "But, *cherie*, that is of no importance. Why read books when you can own them? These books are from the president of Bantam to show me his gratitude. I have been helping them with a little arrangement which concerns Teemothy Leary, the Pope of LSD, you remember? His book is called *Confessions of a Hope Fiend*, and because of my assistance it will be published soon with a huge promotion. Interesting, *non*?"

I smiled and casually looked around the bar. With Michel it was always helpful not to look too attentive. "I'm not so sure publishing is your forté, Michel," I said, keeping my gaze across the room.

"Of course, it's just a little diversion," he said, reaching into his inside pocket and withdrawing a long envelope, "but not an unrewarding one." He extracted a check from the envelope and held it up in front of my eyes—from Bantam Books, made out to Michel Hauchard: *Pay to the Bearer $86,000*. Michel watched my face for a moment, then laid the check on the table and slid it halfway over to me.

I was momentarily speechless, unable to disguise my shock at the figure. Michel kept me closely fixed in his sights as he poured more champagne. "And that's just the first installment," he said quietly, brimming with understatement. "There's more to come. Leary's book sold for an advance of $125,000."

"This Leary must be important," I mused aloud, recalling what Anita had said about him.

"Well, he's a strange man, actually," Michel noted rather dismissively, drawing back and striking a pose of shameless casual confidence, as was his habit when everything was clearly on his terms. "Kind of a gentleman but always on drugs, you see. But you know me, ready to lend a hand if someone worthy is in a fix. I made a few inquiries when I heard that Leary was coming to Switzerland as a fugitive from prison in the States. When the Swiss government almost arrested him and put him at risk of extradition, I became alarmed, and yet there was nothing I could do to keep him from stewing for a couple of months in prison, right there in Lausanne, while I tried to work out a way with the CIA to get him off. Finally, I went to see him in prison and told him that if anyone could get him political asylum in Switzerland, it was I. He was very grateful, given that he's been refused in any number of countries. In exchange, he offered to write a book about his escape from the prison in the States, and his adventures in Algeria—all that has happened since he fled—and sign over the copyright to me in exchange for whatever I could do."

"*Bien sur*," I said, giving him my most winning smile.

What Michel was really saying was that "lending a hand" meant he saw something to gain; his "alarm" at Leary's arrest meant he was probably the one who alerted the Swiss police to arrest Leary and, since Leary wasn't extradited, Michel hadn't managed to cut a sweet enough deal with the CIA and was left with Leary in the hands of the Swiss authorities and no apparent way to make a killing on the man. But then, why not make the best of a rotten situation? Leary in jail generously rescued by Michel translated into Michel extorting Leary to get him out of the jam he'd created for him in the first place. It was how business was done and Michel always extracted the maximum price for his "services." No doubt he had intimidated Leary into signing over full book rights and God knows what else, against the promise of springing him.

We had finished the first bottle of Crystal and another magically appeared. "He accepted, of course," Michel said, smiling graciously as he topped us off. "After that, it was quite easy. Fortunately, I have friends who saw the futility of holding him without charge."

This meant that Michel had arranged with the Swiss authorities to keep an eye on Leary in case he did anything really worth being jailed for. A very tight and tidy arrangement, leaving Michel the option of having Leary re-arrested at any time for any reason or accusation he might devise, at the same time keeping the Swiss authorities off his back. I wondered to whom Michel was pondering to sell this man next.

"Leary has been writing since I had him released and I have been supporting him." He paused to inspect the tip of his Davidoff cigar, then looked at me with a faint smile and raised eyebrows. "You can meet this Leary anytime you like, and he will do for you whatever I say, of course. Now tell me, will you live with me again? You know you are my favorite little girl."

My head was swimming, and not just from the Crystal champagne we were putting away. Here I was in one of my usual situations, with one of the usual players in the life I had lived so far, but something different was in the air, strains of an alien music playing into my old soundtrack, capturing my attention. Every time the name "Leary" came up, something stirred. It was as if the mention of his name was shifting my reality. Timothy Leary was in trouble and needed to be rescued from his would-be rescuer, a fiend indeed—Michel Hauchard, of all people.

I couldn't think clearly and didn't want to talk anymore. Michel was on the verge of ordering another bottle of Crystal when I made to leave. He saw my expression and, before I could stand up, slipped the check across the table and under my hand. I saw a familiar look on his face and suddenly felt alone and afraid. Our affair had been stormy, and I knew he was capable of dangerous moves. Instinct told me he was making one now, so with enormous effort I pushed away the check, got up, and left.

10

UN JEU DE PISTE, FOR REAL

November 1972

A week after Richard Nixon's re-election, Tommy, Jake, Charlie, Lara and I boarded a Swissair flight to re-cross the Atlantic. The children colored in coloring books in the row ahead of us while we did the obvious and customary thing one does on an airplane: drank Black Russians, sneaked into the first class bathroom, and made love with me sitting on the basin.

In Geneva, we rented a car and Tommy drove us the forty miles to Lausanne. We were heading for the Palace Hotel, but I routed us past Michel's villa on a hill facing town and rang the doorbell. Michel's Moroccan butler opened it—a magnificent man, very dark in a white headdress and long white caftan, looking more like an Arabian wizard than a butler.

"Hello, Miss Joanna," he said with surprise, "I am sorry, but Monsieur Hauchard is in New York."

"That's okay, Mohammed," I said, managing a look of disappointment, "I'll just come inside and write him a note."

Led by Mohammed, the five of us entered the elegant living room. As Tommy offered hashish to Mohammed, I moved quickly toward

Michel's study. What I was looking for was right there on the polished top of the mahogany writing desk next to the telephone: Michel's wine-colored leather-bound address book with five numbers under "Leary." Carefully, I copied them onto a page of Michel's embossed linen stationery while pretending to write him a note. When I returned to the salon, Mohammed and Tommy were sitting on the velvet sofa, laughing amidst a thick cloud of hashish smoke.

At dinnertime, our little pride of lions checked into the Palace Hotel where Mummy said I'd learned to take my first steps. The receptionist gave us the best suite in the house, top floor, two bedrooms, two bathrooms, and a living room. As usual, there was no discussion as to how our stay would be paid for. I had no idea how much money was left in my bag, but whatever it was, it was all I had. Tommy and I never talked about money, as per *les règles du jeu* that said it was rude and that everyone had plenty of it so there was nothing to discuss. Having lived for years with the chaotic finances of my mother, I had come to develop my own ways of getting by without ever facing the subject in a direct way. The main trick consisted in believing that money arrived and vanished magically, and in assuming that someone always paid in the end so there would be no scandal. Most of the time, men bought me things, sexual adventures being a constant means of commerce, the most reliable I knew.

We made ourselves comfortable and time slipped by at its usual drug-induced, indecipherable pace. After only a day, the suite looked like a Moroccan bazaar, with silk cushions scattered over the floor and my red Spanish shawl thrown on top of a tall Chinese lamp so that it cast eerie patterns on the walls. Tommy stayed drunk and refused to get dressed, parading about like a pasha in a blue satin bedspread, at moments becoming defiant and touchy, making an issue of small things that normally would pass without comment.

I kept calling the five numbers for Timothy Leary, but each time I got through someone would say he had just left or was due to arrive soon. The codes for the numbers corresponded to different Swiss cantons, perhaps various hideouts shadowed by underworld creeps working for Michel. At last, after a couple of dozen attempts, a low, tentative voice said, "This is Timothy Leary, who are you?"

My heart was beating fast and hard, and my cheeks were burning. In all the hours of waiting I had not prepared what to say. "It's Joanna, a friend of Michel's. I just saw him in New York. I want to meet you as soon as possible to tell you all about it." I was dreadfully afraid he would not take me seriously.

There was a ten-second pause on the line, then the voice asked, "What kind of drugs are you on?"

"Every one I can find, but especially psychedelics," I said. It seemed like the appropriate response, leaving things wide open. I wondered what he was going to ask me next.

"Michel told me about you. Yes, it's a good idea for us to meet. How about tomorrow at the Kunsterhalle in Lucerne, the big beer and sausage restaurant at the amusement fair?"

"Yes, sure," I answered, a bit surprised by his brevity and directness. Then it struck me that if he was not inclined to chat, he must have good reason, maybe a tapped phone. "Tomorrow is fine. Seven o'clock, then." I was pleased that it was turning out to be so simple.

I put down the telephone and danced around the room, shouting, "At last, at last, something exciting is happening."

Tommy was standing in the doorway to the bedroom, still draped in his pasha's robe. He looked upset. Petulant, he threw himself onto the sofa. "Come here," he said brusquely. "What do you want from that man, anyway? He's a has-been. He's not worth the ride. He'll just drag us down into his cops and robbers problems."

I sat on his lap and ran my fingers through his golden hair. "Don't worry," I reassured him, taking a sip of scotch from the glass on the carpet. "I know exactly what I'll do. We'll get him to find some money and buy a big sailboat. You and I will go to Amsterdam and score the ideal craft, smuggle Leary into Holland, and we'll all get on the boat and sail to Jamaica. Keith and Anita will be going there soon with the band, remember? Well, we can join them and add Leary to the party."

"Hmm," Tommy mused, stroking my thigh, "I've always wanted to sail around the Caribbean. There are some islands there that have barely been discovered yet. And the music there is really wild."

"Our boat will be our own country and no one will be able to get us or Timothy Leary. We can start a radio station on board, maybe even a

TV station, financed by the Stones, and we'll broadcast revolutionary messages all around the world."

Tommy must have genuinely liked the idea because he stopped sulking and resumed being playful. I was relieved that we were not going to disagree over Leary. Something big was happening to me, I knew, but I couldn't stand the thought of losing Tommy in the process. I hated tradeoffs.

Tommy ordered dinner and drinks from room service, then made room for me in his pasha's robe. "While we're waiting, close the door on the kids and come over here," he crooned, "I'll show you how a good woman feels good."

I was as excited as I had rarely been in my life. The treasure hunt was finally going to pay off. It was difficult to wait out the 24 hours until our rendezvous, so I obsessed. *Was I really ready to capture this man? What would it require?* The question posed itself in my mind as if someone else were thinking it through me. First, to capture a man you must appear irresistible. It is helpful to be involved with another man, so that the new man has to lure you away with his charm, intelligence, and sexual powers. Second, you have to be self-contained, *sang froid*, looking as though you need no one and nothing. You have your drugs, your music and favorite songs, all of it enclosing and protecting you. You do not need him, but you could be persuaded to choose him if he proves to be stronger and more attractive than any of the other men who might be available. Third, he has to know he is really getting the prize. All kinds of signs and insinuations must show him this. Love is like that, a jungle contest where animals fight for the best of the female lot.

I pondered furiously, ranging about the suite chain-smoking Gauloises, detached from Tommy and the kids. My heart was nagging me, contradicting the exercise in stealth and calculation that I was carrying out involuntarily like a prepared script someone had thrust into my hands. But I had stopped dialoguing with my heart long before. The wheel of fortune was spinning before my eyes, like the roulette wheel had spun for Michel, and it was all I could do to follow its dazzling whirl.

11

THE UNIVERSAL SOLVENT

The next day the kids and I walked down the street to a balloon stand and bought out the vendor's entire inventory of multicolored helium balloons. As the amber winter sun touched the white mountain snowfields, Tommy and I piled kids, balloons, and ourselves into the car and headed for Lucerne.

The Kunsterhalle was a huge, boisterous beer hall and by eight in the evening was packed with large, jolly Swiss-Germans drinking beer from huge grey stone mugs like medieval relics, gobbling bratwurst and swapping stories as they unwound from a long day of work at one of the banks or pharmaceutical companies for which the land was famous. The scene was brash and jarring, a sports event under the glaring lights of an operating room, yet the ambience was festive—appropriate for the moment to come.

The five of us sat at a round table, tied our helium balloons to the backs of our chairs, then ordered schnapps and beer for adults and Coca Cola for children. The drive had taken about three hours, during which Tommy and I had smoked quite a lot of dope and talked very little. Despite the tension that had been building between us all day, my head was swimming pleasantly as I imagined us as lions surrounded by hulking but harmless Swiss-German rhinoceroses snorting, spatting, and feeding in a strange game preserve.

I kept my eyes riveted on the entrance until a lithe, jaunty figure appeared in the doorway. My pulse jumped a couple of octaves as I registered the flashing grin and caught his eyes, then he was heading straight for us, directly into my eyes, not walking, really, but bouncing from one footfall to the next. He was wearing a blue shirt and beige cashmere sweater under a white parka, grey slacks, and dazzling white Adidas with blue stripes. His hair was straight and fine, a silver-grey mix, cut rather short. The thin-rimmed glasses he wore made him look vulnerable. There was something indefinably comforting and relieving about his appearance.

Tommy and I stood up, teetering a little, and introduced ourselves. Leary smiled radiantly and sat down so close to me that we were almost touching shoulders.

"I love the balloons," he laughed, his blue-grey eyes twinkling, "a great touch, though I would have found you, anyway. I feel like this is a celebration of a long-awaited reunion, even though we've never met before. You and I have a lot in common, Joanna. We're both *personae non gratae* in several countries, for one thing."

I wondered how he knew that about me. Michel must have told him about *The Little Green Book*.

"I have great admiration for a woman who can make a scandal and a statement at the same time," he said.

"It comes naturally," I said.

Looking subdued and on edge at the same time, Tommy asked, "Sounds like most of your life, too, doesn't it, Tim?"

I threw Tommy a reassuring glance.

Leary smiled wistfully and nodded. "Yes, but not always by intention."

We ordered more schnapps and beer. Timothy was restless and vigilant, glancing furtively around the room, and yet when he talked, he immediately relaxed, though his words betrayed the urgent tone of someone who had a lot to confide and no one to confide in. Again, he spoke about me.

"Michel talked a lot about you, Joanna—all the time, in fact. He said your life has been full of adventures. I can relate to that. Things have a way of happening around me, and not always to my advantage. You carry the same kind of energy. It comes with being a catalyst."

He sipped his beer and fell silent.

Hesitantly, I said, "Michel has been in my life for a while, but he could never really see what I wanted."

"What does woman want?" Timothy asked with a soft chuckle. "It's a question Freud asked, the best question he ever asked, I think, though he wasn't able to answer it. I see it as a great title for a book I'll write someday. Perhaps you can write it with me?"

Little did I know then that I would borrow $25,000 to publish that very book in 1976, just before his release from his last prison.

"First, I'll get what I want, then I'll write about it," I replied, lighting a Gitane and placing the pack on the table. Timothy took a Gitane from the pack and I lit it.

"Fair enough. I know something about how to do that. The real trick is not giving away too much in the process. You know . . . settling for a bad tradeoff?"

I smiled uneasily and glanced at Tommy.

"That's where love comes in," Timothy continued, "the love the alchemists called the universal solvent. It's the highest biochemical state. All the other chemicals, the sacramental drugs especially, the psychedelics and neurotransmitters, are just ways of accessing it. I can tell you're ready for that ultimate state. There's a way people look when they're ready."

"Love is what it's about, all right," I said weakly, "it must be powerful because it seems to be more forbidden than drugs."

"Yes, you would know about that, wouldn't you?" Timothy said, reaching out and touching my arm. "Michel said you gave your virginity for a love in Egypt, to the son of the Egyptian Minister of Culture in Cairo—that it happened beside the pyramids on your fourteenth birthday. You were ready then, but the world wasn't. Then Interpol and soldiers with machine guns escorted you to the airport and put you on a plane." He finished quietly. "Separating you forever from your first love."

It was mesmerizing to hear him tell my story, yet I shook inside with rage that I was allowed no secrets in this world and yet was expected to keep them all. The old, excruciating confusion. But it was Timothy

Leary talking to me now, describing my past as if it deeply mattered to him, as if my suffering counted in a way he and he alone could appreciate, as if he knew how much I had longed for kindness and had finally had to settle for sex.

Cairo, Christmas 1959. I could almost smell it as I smelled it that day Mummy and I disembarked in Alexandria—the scent of cardamom, tobacco, almonds, and mangoes drifting heavily across the port. Mahmoud was nineteen, sleek and confident for his age, so handsome with his dark copper skin, thick lips, and mysterious look—inherited, I learned, from his Sudanese grandfather. On my fourteenth birthday, he claimed me as I mentally compared his caresses with those of Mummy's Spanish chauffeur. But this time my body was trembling as my legs spread on the white sheets, then the sharp pain, my eyes open and lingering on his dark muscular back and buttocks—and after, when I asked, "Are you all right?" and there was no response, no noise other than heavy breathing and beyond the shutters children calling in Arabic.

And a few months later in Paris, how daring of me to steal money from Mummy in order to return to my young love so we could hide at hotels and feed on our brew of passion, ideal love, and sense of impending doom of Interpol crashing into our room and heavily armed Egyptian soldiers driving us to the airport in Cairo. I could see the garish scene as if it were yesterday, everything transpiring in slow motion like an acid flashback: Mahmoud snatched away and locked inside a car his father had sent, its tinted windows closed—me looking over my shoulder as that 14-year-old me was escorted onto the plane. We had been so close, closer than anything I had ever known, and then there was only the razor-like glint of gun metal in the merciless Middle Eastern sun. I never saw him again.

Timothy was gently squeezing my arm. Tommy had eased back from the table and assumed a distracted air, nursing a schnapps, leaning over occasionally to whisper to his kids. Only Leary and I were talking now.

"I heard that . . . Mahmoud later became a psychologist," I faltered, "because he was so fascinated by the workings of the mind."

"I don't dabble in psychology, anymore," Timothy said, nodding to Tommy as if to make sure he'd also heard. "It's too literal, too limiting.

For me psychology is obsolete, ever since I discovered that it's possible to re-imprint the mind by deleting old experiences and taking on new information while on LSD."

"I can see the possibility of what you're saying," I said. "If we can change how we think and feel, then we can perceive a whole other universe."

"Universes," Timothy responded, pronouncing the word with a stunning grin, "like Giordano Bruno said and they burned him at the stake for it. We just seem to be confined to this one world because this is where we have to start looking."

"Fabulous. Let's start looking, then." I looked at Tommy, grinning, then back at Timothy, meaning I was eager to leave the Kunsterhalle.

Timothy shrugged. "Why wait? I couldn't agree more." He dug in his pocket for money. "If there's anything I've learned from sitting it out in a few prison cells, it's that there's nothing to wait for. Come on, let's go to my house, it's just a few kilometers away on the lake."

We paid and left. For me, things couldn't happen fast enough now. I wanted the next level of our encounter to start unfolding and never stop.

The boys hopped into Timothy's 911 Porsche Targa, taking their balloons with them, while Tommy, Lara and I followed in our rented car. I could see their blond heads bobbing up and down through the back window as Timothy drove ahead with careless ease. Balloons played out on their long strings on both sides of the little car, thrashing in the slipstream.

12

EVERYTHING

It was nine when we got to Timothy's digs, a chalet of wood and stone at the edge of Lake Zug. Several casual and open people were living there with Timothy under close, undefined terms: a redheaded Englishman named Bryan Barritt, co-author of *Confessions of a Hope Fiend,* his wife Liz and their six-year-old son. Next, we met Dennis Martino, a seedy-looking American not much taller than I, wiry, with intense brown eyes; his girlfriend Robin was taking a nap in one of the bedrooms. Enigmatically, Timothy referred to Dennis as the sorcerer's apprentice, and it turned out that Dennis' twin brother David had had two children with Timothy's daughter Susan, and Dennis and Timothy's then-wife Rosemary had both lived at the Brotherhood of Eternal Love (BEL) commune in Palm Springs when Dennis was dealing dope for them. Dennis was also tight with Billy Mellon Hitchcock who owned the Millbrook mansion in Duchess County, New York where Timothy had carried out LSD research.

As we entered the living room, Timothy confided that Dennis had served six months in prison, then jumped bail pending appeal for a drug-smuggling charge to join Timothy and Rosemary in Algeria. I didn't show it, but I was immediately displeased by the implied closeness between Timothy and this seedy-looking character. Little did I know what all of Dennis' connections meant.

The living room occupied most of the ground floor with a large deck outside facing onto the lake. There was a roaring fire in the hearth and almost no furniture. I counted five mattresses on the floor, loosely covered with pieces of fabric, saris, and Bolivian blankets. Pillows were scattered everywhere. We all sat in a semicircle around the fire, talking at random. I was disappointed that Timothy and I were not taking ourselves away from the gathering but expected we would soon enough.

Dennis dominated the conversation. "I'm a triple Gemini," he said, looking straight at me. "Tim says that makes me dangerous, but this whole game is dangerous, isn't it?" He laughed. Timothy just smiled and nodded. "Like the other day," Dennis continued, "we were all high on acid, right here in this room, all of us peaking at about the same time. I got into playing my Moog synthesizer and there were these strange sounds coming from it, like the keyboard was haunted or something. I just kept playing them as I heard them. Janet was four months pregnant —she doesn't live here anymore—and, well, miscarried during the trip. It just happened. We rushed her to the hospital in Bern, but it was too late."

There was an awkward silence that no one felt inclined to break. In the hallway, the kids were talking excitedly with Bryan and Liz's son. A chill came over me to hear this man speak so callously about the death of an unborn child. Again, to my surprise, Timothy made no comment.

Dennis sighed. "Later, we figured the music might have been an omen. She didn't want the baby and somehow I think it got the message from the music that it should find another way in." His face transformed into a map of lines that made him look ancient and sinister.

At last, Timothy asked if anyone had any LSD. Dennis jumped to his feet, saying he would get some from upstairs. As soon as he left, I pulled my Chinese diary out of my bag, caught Timothy's eye, and held up the two tabs of Clear Light I had left.

"Great," Timothy announced to the others, "Joanna and I will get started with these, since we're celebrating the meeting of true minds."

On the stone bench by the hearth was a tray of glasses and several bottles of wine. While I held the two tiny tabs of Clear Light between my fingers like pinches of spice, Timothy poured two glasses of white wine. We then walked over to the tall windows facing the lake and stepped into the blazing fire reflections in the glass panes as if utterly willing to be consumed by the flames.

With a sip of wine, I swallowed one of the tabs, toasting Timothy with the words, "Who loves me will come with me."

He sucked the other tab from the tip of my thumb, lifted his glass and drank slowly, then toasted me. "To you, beautiful woman. Just tell me what you want."

I looked deeply into his eyes and said, "Everything."

13

ACID QUEEN

We returned to the circle where the others were taking the acid Dennis had fetched. Everyone shifted on their cushions and talked sporadically, reticence increasing as the acid came on.

As so often happened when I took LSD, I was split between a need to concentrate and a struggle with the exhausting tension of overconcentration. Sometimes, I would fall into a trance of total ease and absorption that allowed me to see the beauty and perfection of the world around me—a realm of pure and perfect appearance—and I would feel fluid, aimless, and congruent with everything. At other times, there would be no beauty to behold, only a Cinerama screen flooded with murky memories from my childhood: Nanny forcing me to sleep with a crucifix under my pillow for sins she said I could not know I had committed; my mother wielding her black leather belt studded with rubies and emeralds, laying stroke after pitiless stroke across my legs—visions I couldn't stop so long as I could not break the concentration. Usually, I could only surrender and spin away into a limbo of aching loneliness, mute, my throat gripped by a hot vise of shame, then curl into the fetal position for hours on end.

How to concentrate and relax at the same time? This was my question. I kept stealing glances at Timothy, expecting him to take over, to guide me and tell me what it was all about. He was the High Priest of LSD, and there was so much I needed to know about how to navigate the inner dimensions that LSD exposed. But he simply sat and stared into the fire as we were all climbing into the LSD stratosphere with no definite sense of where we were going.

Detecting a hitch in the action, I took the lead and began reeling off autobiographical stories to maintain some control as the acid peaked. I talked about my first trip to America in the middle of the Vietnam moratorium and everyone was spellbound, Timothy dazzled. When I paused to catch my breath, he encouraged me to continue. I shifted to a vivid account of some of Mummy's bad habits, then to the escape plan I had in mind for Timothy, at which point everyone got involved but especially Dennis.

We tripped until the fire died out and we were left in darkness, each one setting his or her own bearings for the downside of the trip. From another room I heard the Eagles singing, *I'm looking for a lover who won't blow my cover and that's a hard thing to find* . . . Bodies were sprawled here and there on mattresses. Someone had lit a couple of large candles and set them on the mantle. The faces reflecting candlelight looked as soft as masks of wet clay.

Next to me was Tommy, his arm around my shoulders, gazing into the middle distance with peace and resignation in his eyes and on his face. I wanted to say something to him, but we were both too stoned to talk. We nestled down together under a red blanket.

Across the room, Timothy was still sitting in front of the fire, his knees drawn up under his chin, his eyes slowly scanning the room. When our eyes met, I had the sensation of leaving my body and drifting toward him. Without moving, he too drifted out and met me halfway. We connected in midair like birds, my body flooded with intense sexual longing and— something else, something I couldn't name but knew without question, the way a child knows with unfathomable certainty not yet accessible to words. I knew he would have the words for it, and he would tell them to me soon. Disembodied and dancing, we swirled together in the middle of the room, murmuring to each other in a secret language all our own.

14

WHEEL OF FORTUNE, TURN ROUND, ROUND

The next morning, I managed to get moving early. I dug out my American flag bell-bottoms, combed my honey-colored hair, put on a touch of blush, and went outside. The lake was calm; only a few ripples fanned out from majestic swans gliding past the lawn. One of them turned and swam toward me, coming close enough for me to caress his long, sinuous neck, something I had never done before, even though there had been plenty of swans around when I was growing up. Suddenly, he ducked and came around to savagely nip me. I jumped back, shocked, sucking the blood from my finger. It alarmed me that something so beautiful could be so brutal.

A voice with an unfamiliar lilt called my name. Timothy was coming across the lawn. "Will you come and have breakfast with me in the village?" he asked. "I checked on the others and they're still sleeping. It's a good time for us to get away."

He looked amazingly refreshed. Something in his eyes told me he was still a bit stoned. For a man of his age—somewhere well over fifty,

I guessed—he managed to look young and innocent, emitting an exuberance like no one I had ever met, no Jet Set charmer or international star. His magic called to the child in me, awakening my sense of wonder.

I went inside and retrieved the Russian lamb coat Michel had given me years before, then we struck off down the driveway and climbed into the Porsche, Timothy holding the door for me. I slipped on a Janis Joplin tape as we sped into town.

At the restaurant we ordered eggs and ham sprinkled with Gruyere cheese, two cappuccinos and two aquavits. As we were waiting for the food, Timothy asked me, "Do you know the Tarot, the ancient divination cards?"

"Yes," I said, "I always carry the Crowley deck with me."

"Well," he said, taking on a conspiratorial tone, "I see you as the Wheel of Fortune—the card showing a circular wheel with two creatures, a baboon and a jackal, going up one side and down the other, watched over by a sphinx representing the risk and reversal of circumstances involved in any adventure or change."

Michel calling me *la dame fortune* flashed through my mind. "I'm ready for some risk," I said, "and I know what you mean. For a while, I've felt like I'm standing on the edge of a cliff and have to jump."

"Hold my hand and we'll jump together," Timothy said, taking my hand.

Now we are getting somewhere, I thought. He was reassuring, just as I had expected him to be. He was confident and serene, as if he knew all the answers, knew where all the clues led.

Food arrived. He dug in with voracious gusto, but I realized I was still too stoned to eat. I had slept little and was still flying high. The sight of eggs made me start hallucinating all over again.

"If you understand the Wheel of Fortune, you know how the whole game works," he told me between bites. "It's not a matter of providence, you see. It's not chance, it's change. Fortune is not something that works on us from outside. Taking it for a cosmic influence is totally wrong, it's more like an integral in mathematical terms, a kind of law of energy, a thermodynamic principle. At any one time there is so much going on in the system—the world game, you could say—and what makes the wheel spin is that different people in different roles keep exchanging positions. Baboon goes up, jackal goes down, or vice versa. It happens because our lives become, uh, transposed, one person trading places with another." He paused to savor his cappuccino and his thought. "Yeah, that's it. But the game is always the same unless you know the way out to the higher circuits."

I was overwhelmed by what he was saying. I wanted only to hear more, to listen to him talk and talk endlessly, and to respond endlessly in turn. Already I detected that we had a similar way of using language. As if reading my mind, he spoke again.

"Yes, I know you can understand. You are looking for a way out of the decadent aristocratic game, the limbo of Jet Set desperados. Your intelligence has always told you there is something more. I'll show you the way. We can really make the wheel spin, you and I, so that we spin off into other circuits. There's a whole lot of universes out there, and every one of them is fascinating." He grinned as if at a private joke. "Old Bruno, there. You know, it's a good thing the world has changed a little in 372 years, so it won't be necessary to play that script again."

He joked with the waitress as he paid the bill, all the while explaining to me in a whispered aside that Giordano Bruno had been an Italian heretic burned at the stake in 1600 for teaching the existence of infinite worlds. I was amazed by Timothy's ability to do ordinary and extraordinary things at the same time. While I could barely keep up a conventional front on acid, he could obviously out-normal normal people, and go right on with his casual feats of cosmic conversation.

Outside, he took my hand and we walked across the road to sit on a bench facing Lake Zug. Fanning out his arms, he said, "I'm tired of all this. Switzerland is so small, and not just geographically. It's just another prison. Extremely well kept, but still a prison. First, I spent almost a year between Orange County Jail and the California Men's Colony in San Luis Obispo. When I didn't get bail pending appeal or parole on the trumped up charges against me, I escaped by sliding down a telephone wire that stretched from a window to the main road outside the gates. I still have the scars on my palms." He held out his hands. I touched the long calluses lightly.

"Rosemary helped to set up the escape, then went with me to join Eldridge Cleaver in Algeria. We were appalled by his Marxist power trip, so he placed us under house arrest. After a while, we managed to get exit visas so I could go and give a lecture in Sweden, but thanks to Michel Hauchard we flew to Switzerland instead to throw the CIA off the trail. Now, Rosemary is gone and I'm Michel's prisoner."

He threw me a telling glance, as if the mere mention of Michel's name was enough to evoke enormous sympathy, which it was. "Now, I can't leave Switzerland or I could be extradited and returned to prison in California. An Algerian CIA connection assures me that Nixon wants me captured and returned to prison for his second inauguration headlines. I want my freedom. I'm tired of this merry-go-round, these jackal and baboon games."

Tears gathered in my eyes. I wanted to tell him that I too knew the feeling of being locked in prison for crimes I had not committed, but instead I said, "I'll help you. I have come to free you." *Where had those words come from?*

He looked into my eyes. "I know. I knew it from the start. I was waiting for the most intelligent woman in Europe, and now you're here. You've been so bored and lonely. It comes from having a brain all dressed up and nowhere to go."

We looked at each other for a long time, his expression tender and inviting, his eyes full of trust and trustworthiness. The ambient noises receded—footsteps crunching in the snow, an electrical hum, the delicate lapping of the lake—and we were a world unto ourselves.

When we returned to the house, Timothy greeted everyone with a huge smile and announced, "Joanna has come to free me. It's a miracle." He hugged Tommy and thanked him for bringing me into his life.

Tommy and I spent the rest of the morning talking with Timothy and Dennis about the sailboat escape plan. Timothy loved the idea of becoming a revolutionary pirate—the perfect solution to his international flight dilemma. Tommy, the kids, and I would go back to the Palace Hotel in Lausanne, check out, and return directly to Lake Zug for the next steps.

At noon, when we were getting into our rental car, Timothy took me aside and whispered in my ear, "Don't worry, Joanna, my love will chase away all the old lovers, the boring Greeks with moustaches, the hypercritical Arabs, the lustful idiots and desperate one-night stands. Our love is the Perfect Love. I was going to star in a film about Hesse's book *Steppenwolf*, but I would much rather live the story with you."

I was astonished and deeply touched. I had no idea how he knew all of these things about me—my former affairs, my brief broken marriages—but I knew he had taken over five hundred LSD trips and had special navigational skills, so perhaps he could sweep through people's minds and memories like sonar. With him, I would be finished with *les règles du jeu* secrets. Another kind of power was waiting for me, inviting me to discover it in this man's glittering blue-grey eyes.

I had to take the risk, to be brave enough to let go and allow the myth to begin.

15

THE BILL

When Tommy, the kids and I returned to our suite at the Palace Hotel, there was an envelope sitting conspicuously on the table where fruit and flowers of welcome were usually displayed. The bill came to the equivalent of $4,000 and I didn't have to count to know I didn't have the money or anything close to it. After smoking a few Gitanes, I casually asked Tommy how his money was looking. He had borrowed $500 from his sister, he said laconically, and gave it to me with a shrug and a smile, no questions asked.

The waiting envelope was not the way things were customarily done, nor had we given management word that we were leaving. I was even more surprised when I took Tommy's cash down to the cashier and she said, "I'm sorry, Mademoiselle Harcourt-Smith, but you must pay the entire sum today. Five hundred dollars is certainly not enough and there is no question of discussing arrangements. Already, we have been given orders that room service is not to serve you anymore."

So I sat in the corner of the main salon, smoking and thinking for a long time, my anger swallowed up in a keen sinking feeling in the pit of my stomach. I watched Giorgio the concierge ardently attend to a guest and wondered if I should approach him, but thought better of it. Giorgio had been the concierge at the Palace Hotel ever since I could remember. He was well-known among the international set as the wizard who could direct you to the best abortion clinic, command an instant appointment with any medical specialist in Switzerland, recommend you to one of the directors of the Credit Suisse, or conjure up tickets to any show in New York, even in December. Some said he knew the best call girls in Geneva as well as the hour of departure and arrival of every train in Switzerland. He was a permanent and reliable fixture in the world I knew.

More than that, Giorgio had been an ally. He and I had a long, humorous complicity. He had often covered for me when I spent nights in the Palace Hotel with a variety of men. If Mummy telephoned to ask if he'd seen me, he would tell her no, then ring my room and respectfully inform me that he was ordering a taxi so I could go home. Giorgio was, no doubt, the best of his kind in the world. I was so used to counting on his impeccable service that it never occurred to me it might someday be withdrawn. But the sinking feeling in my gut told me it was now happening.

I was about to go back upstairs to cool out with Tommy and try to forget the situation for a while, when I flashed on Michel. Maybe I could play on the grand seigneur one more time. I called him and suggested that we meet at the restaurant of the Chateau d'Ouchy, an old haunt of ours that overlooked Lac Leman. I fortified myself with Valium and cocaine—one to calm me down and put me in control, the other to make me intelligent and quick. The combination had always worked and I really needed it now. It allowed me to have no feelings except sheer, ruthless determination.

"I'm so surprised to find you here, *cherie*," he crooned ironically after we had lightly kissed each other's cheeks. "November is not the best month for Lausanne. It's a bit grey, don't you think?"

"Michel, I have been to see Timothy Leary. He and I found we have a lot in common. We are talking now about many things we are going to do, so all of his activities in the future will depend upon me. This is important, Michel, and you can come along for the ride or be left out." I didn't pause to see how he would react, but lowered my voice an octave. "Right now, I am facing a little problem. I have to pay my bill at the

Palace Hotel. Once that is clear, I can go on with my plans for Timothy Leary. This could be of great benefit to you, if you stay on my side. I want you to pay the hotel for me, or else I will take away your pope, which means that you will lose the goose who lays the golden eggs."

Michel looked at me with studied contempt, a look I knew well. I had seen it on many faces over the years, a permanent feature in circles where contempt and cruelty enforce boundaries that keep the powerful in power. I had used it myself many times, initially against my mother from whom I had learned it in the first place.

"You are a little slut," Michel replied, spitting out the words with typical French vehemence by placing full stress on the vowels. "That hippie character Tommy is very bad for you. How dare you ask me to pay for your drug addict gigolo to lounge around and do nothing. As far as Timothy Leary is concerned, I don't believe you, you are making it up. Oh, it is sad, Joanna, this is always your problem, telling lies, making things up. You have not met him and you will not, unless I make it possible for you. You only want to support that awful lover of yours." His voice was cold and hard, as I well remembered it being on many occasions in the past.

"I'll leave Tommy if you pay the hotel bill," I said, keeping my voice low. "There. Does that prove to you that I'm telling the truth?"

Michel shook his head and finished his drink. He looked around for the waiter, as if I were not even there.

"Okay, be rude. It just proves you can't argue with what I'm saying." I was on very shaky ground, but had to go ahead full bore. "Anyway," I added in a casual tone, "Tommy will have to be disposed of in one way or another so I can be with Timothy, and this will be to your advantage, Michel. Don't be a fool. Otherwise, you will lose him. He's too important for your sordid little games. I'm your only insurance now that Timothy Leary will still be available to you."

"No, no, no, I'm not doing anything for you. You should have stayed with me, Joanna," Michel protested, waving his hand as if to dismiss the option forever, which I knew he could never do. "I was so good to you, a good daddy and a good lover. If you let yourself remember, you will see it's true. I can make life good for you, not that disgusting hippie Englishman or even Monsieur le Professeur Timothy Leary."

Suddenly, I noticed something odd in Michel's tone of voice. We had argued many times before, sometimes as pure banter, more often in violence. Every time, we both brought all our intensity and skills to the contest. Now, his argument sounded flat, as if he was not convinced of what he was saying. I realized he no longer cared how it went between us. What hit me even harder was seeing that my own argument was just as flat, even as unconvincing. *Enfin*, I cared as little as he did, even less.

I sat bolt upright in my seat and pushed my drink away. I shot Michel an intense look of hatred, fixing my stare on the skin sagging around his neck, the lines under his eyes, the silver-white hair I had once so admired, and said, "You are really revolting." The force of my words shocked even me as something inside snapped. I was finally through with Michel, through with his demands, his favors, through with bargaining then and there.

I stormed out.

16

SUITS

Under the Napoleonic Code as observed in Switzerland, the police cannot arrest a suspect during the night. Early winter evening had fallen while I was with Michel, so it was quite dark when I returned to the Palace. Crossing the lobby, I caught sight of Giorgio, who looked at me disapprovingly, then turned aside. The cashier threw me a scornful glance, and the bellboy did not even hold the elevator door open. Feeling naked and vulnerable, I could not help seeing my gesture of entering the lift and closing the gate as furtive and shame-ridden. *How easily it all collapses*, I thought as the elevator creaked upwards, *the grand façade of appearances, the slick game of privilege and obligation*. Something was shifting in the world that was fast becoming my world no longer. Was it happening because at last there was a powerful enough force in my life, in the form of a man, to counteract the tyranny of the old rules?

Tommy and I made up some sandwiches of smoked ham and bread I had bought at a grocery and drank two bottles of wine in silence, watching the kids play enigmatic card games on the floor.

"I'm sure the cops will be here in the morning," I told Tommy when the kids had gone to bed. "They'll arrest me, not you, because I'm responsible. It's my reputation that got us this suite."

"Yeah, everything I like gives me a bad reputation," Tommy said caustically. He caught my expression and explained, "It's a quote from someone, I can't remember who."

"I see," I said, though I didn't, "perhaps a quote from me?"

"It certainly suits you, darling," he sneered with an irony I could appreciate but barely.

"Well, it's about time I found something worth losing my reputation for," I returned. I sat back against the sofa and fished in my bag for my Gitanes, at the same time making a rough inventory of what pills I had on hand. "If they put me in jail, I'll be out very soon," I assured him. "You'll just have to wait for me at Timothy's. Take Lara with you and I'll rejoin all of you, soon." I beamed a bravado I scarcely felt.

At 6:42 a.m. I awoke and put on my jeans and purple cashmere sweater. After a moment of reflection, I added a strand of pearls and my mink coat. It was still dark when I entered the lobby. Two maids were vacuuming the huge empty hall, a sight I had never seen before. The lights of the great crystal chandelier were dimmed, but I could see the two figures, predictably in trench coats, standing on each side of the entrance beside the matching brown velvet Louis XV armchairs. I smiled politely and glided past them on my smile, down the entry stairs to cross the street to the most expensive grocery store in town. The industrious Swiss would be open at seven promptly; already the manager and clerk were getting things ready. Once inside, I would have another half hour before it was light enough to be officially day. There was plenty of time.

Digging for the last cash in my bag, I bought some melon and strawberries, fresh baguettes, cheese of several kinds, champagne, red wine, and cognac. The sky outside was turning apple green as I made my way back across the street to the Palace. It was comforting, even in this mess, to count on the Swiss sense of order and punctuality.

On the way in, I passed the two men in trench coats with a nod of acknowledgment. They remained at their posts, showing not the least sign of urgency. Upstairs, I left the repast and a note for Tommy and the kids, telling them to have a wonderful picnic on the balcony and to think of me. Then I swallowed three Valium tens, put five more in my pocket, added a Hermes scarf to my outfit, and returned to the lobby just as the cathedral clock struck 7:30.

One of the men stepped toward me and said, "Mademoiselle, you are under arrest. We are going to take you to the police station where we will interrogate you."

I looked at his neatly trimmed grey moustache and matching grey eyes and nodded, putting my hands behind me so they could apply the handcuffs. "But there is really nothing to talk about. I did not pay the bill for the moment, but it will be paid in due time. You'll see." Defiantly, I added a cold, menacing touch. "You'll see how all this goes when my family learns of your stupidities." I felt odd and empty saying the words. No one in my family knew what was happening, nor would they unless I informed them. Nor would they care.

The detectives escorted me to their Peugeot and we drove over the cobblestones through the narrow medieval streets to the courtyard of the main police station. Walking in an orderly Swiss way on either side of me, the two cops led me into a plush room with thick wall-to-wall carpet and a large conference table. Monsieur Mayer of the moustache gingerly removed my handcuffs. The Valium was coming on fast now, putting me into a state of indifference, cushioned and remote, no doubt obvious to Monsieur Mayer.

"So, mademoiselle, why would you want to check into a hotel without having a penny to pay the bill?" Mayer asked after I had tucked myself into a nice conference chair with thick padding and high armrests. "Perhaps there is something else behind all this. Having no money to pay a hotel bill is not something we would expect from you."

I laughed and narrowed my eyes scornfully. "Don't be silly, there's no secret. My family will pay. I have other things on my mind, and so naturally it doesn't concern me. You should know that. My family does not like problems or scandals," I went on, assuming a calm, deadpan attitude, which wasn't hard to do behind the Valium. "But that does not concern me now. Listen, I'm sleepy, I didn't get much rest last night. Leave me alone. None of this is worth talking about."

The cops looked at each other and then again at me, as if hoping to stare me down. I couldn't imagine why and didn't care. Already, I was starting to nod off right before their eyes.

The next thing I knew the other detective, looking very stern, was shaking me by the shoulder. I jerked awake in time to hear him say, "— doing at Timothy Leary's house last night?"

The mention of Timothy Leary came as a shock, jarring me momentarily out of my Valium-induced cocoon. "Lucerne police reported seeing you there," he said. "We know everything, don't try to fool us."

"So what if I was there?" I replied with as much defiance as I could muster. "I am going to write a book with Dr. Leary and I will certainly write about this pathetic little episode— although, come to think of it, it would not be worth including in any book, that's for sure." I was pleased with the Dr. Leary touch but frightened to discover that Timothy and I had been under surveillance.

The cops again looked at each other in silence, then back at me. "Okay, if you want to be that way," Mayer spoke now, standing back and eyeing me harshly, "but you are making a big mistake, mademoiselle. We are leaving to arrest your friend Tommy since we can't get any answers out of you. We know he was also involved. Maybe he will be more sensible."

Before I could protest, they left the room, locking the door behind them. I didn't like the idea of them going to get Tommy or Lara but was powerless over the situation, so I swallowed another Valium, crawled up on the long oval table, pulled my mink coat over myself, and went to sleep.

A couple of hours later, I was awakened by two other policemen in uniform. I could see that they were plainly astounded that I had been sleeping, and on the conference table, but they showed no suspicion that I might be on something. They led me through a series of rooms into the chambers of a judge whom I recognized as the good-looking man who used to play bridge with my mother at her club and had made a couple of passes at me when I was sixteen. Now, I had to stand there and listen to him lecture me on how ashamed I ought to be for doing things that might tarnish my family's reputation.

I smiled back, impervious. When he was finished scolding me, I said, "Well, you're welcome to pay the bill for me, monsieur," then gave him a little wink. He blushed under his winter sports tan.

"Mademoiselle Harcourt-Smith," he said firmly, "I have no choice but to send you to the women's prison for defying me."

17

ESCAPE

On the way to the prison of Boi-Mermet, I began to feel excited, thinking, *It is so paradoxical that one has to go to prison to finally get free.*

Fortunately, I was not searched when they checked me in. I still had enough Valium on me to insure a good night of oblivion, but I needed to do some hard thinking first. They said I was allowed one call, but whom could I call?

The cell was narrow, with a high ceiling and window with bars like in the movies. In fact, thanks to the Valium, it felt more like a movie set jail than a real jail. The bed was carefully made up with white sheets and grey blankets, the room well heated, and on a chair there was a stack of recent magazines. I threw my mink on the bed and stretched out, trying to ignore the awful irritation of harsh overhead lighting.

Calling Mummy now was certainly out of the question. Besides, I doubted that she had any money. I could call Plesch directly. Maybe it would give him a way to come back on my side again. All the talk in the family about my dangerous behavior, my inability to follow the rules, my defiance and constant lies, amounted to a big case against me, but

I was not certain that Plesch had the same interpretation. However, thinking about Plesch left me feeling angry and depressed.

I passed out again, sleeping through lunch. When I awoke, it was close to four o'clock. I banged on the door and insisted on having something to eat. The response was rapid and cordial. A female guard brought me a tray of steaming café au lait and two slices of wheat bread, butter and jam. As I had suspected, the Swiss provided decent room service even in jail. I ate and drank slowly so as to contain an inexplicable sense of exhilaration that I finally realized had to do with the fact that a few months earlier Timothy must have been confined somewhere close to where I was now but on the men's side. We'd talked about it over our breakfast together.

"Michel said the Swiss threw you in jail when you first arrived while they made up their minds what to do with you," I said, without adding that I suspected Michel was responsible for the arrest in the first place. "Of course, what they really wanted was to do nothing at all."

"Ah yes, the neutral Swiss," Timothy reflected with a smile. "It was in Lausanne. The worst part was the language barrier. It was only for a couple of months, though."

"How can you bear something like that, even for two months?" I asked.

"Oh, I'm quite used to it by now. I've seen a lot of prison walls and corridors and iron bars. In prison, I go inside and become like a monk or hermit. I spent a lot of my time meditating." He smiled radiantly at me as he leaned forward and stroked my hand. "Yes, meditation is how I found you."

"What?" I wasn't sure I had heard him right.

"That's how I found you," he repeated evenly, "or really I shouldn't say found you but *created* you, in my cell in San Luis Obispo, before I went over the wall."

My body went tense, then limp, and I felt life drain out of it for an instant. Before I had time to register fright, a new sense of power surged in instead of fear. I gazed deeply into his eyes, matching my sparkle to his. "You mean you had a vision of me before you met me."

"Sure, but a vision I intentionally created, not just one that happened to arise," he said confidently. "It's a trick from the East. The Tibetans do it really well, and I did it with the specific desire to find the Perfect Love, because I knew she would be the only one who could free me. The woman I invented was you. You resemble her in every way, with all of her qualifications. All the women who came before were just pointing to you."

I took in every word and let his voice take me over. Arpad Plesch flashed into my mind, the dark, looming figure who had spoken this way, too, so deeply and powerfully that his *voice* invaded my body. The way Timothy spoke then was just as powerful, but tender. I had not known that such loving expression could come from a man to a woman that was not foreplay.

"Don't say anything, you don't have to," Timothy added, "not right now. You don't have to tell me you feel as I do because I know that. It's the full miracle, the complete alchemical connection. You're the one I created and you know it, which proves you're the one, doesn't it?"

There was nothing more to say. We stared at each other until I turned to watch the swans gliding blissfully in tandem on the lake, remembering how one of them had nipped me.

"Now that I've found you in this so-called real world, we can do anything we imagine." His voice was practically a whisper. "In San Luis Obispo I needed to escape, but not just from where they were keeping me—that was the easy part, purely mundane. You and I are capable of other kinds of escape."

"You mean the boat we're going to—"

"No, not just that," he interrupted, "escape to other levels, other worlds. Perfect Love is about the ultimate freedom."

"So we will become free together," I said.

"Yes. There is so much to tell you—about the circuits, about the way we're made and how we're getting to the next evolutionary stage. Some of us, anyway."

Holding his hands, I again traced the scars in his palms.

Now in a cell near the cell he had been in, I looked down at my own scars, the unsightly red ridges across both wrists. *Escape.* Yes, I knew something about how difficult it was to escape. I had never seen anyone escape the world of Mummy and Plesch, except through death. Even though I felt like an Outsider, I had found no way out. Many times, I thought I would die in that world. To kill myself had seemed like an act of dignity affirming the little freedom I had.

But with Timothy in my life, it would all be different. I had a chance for true escape, a cosmic proposition on the Wheel of Fortune. We two needed each other in order to escape together. The Perfect Love, he called it. He had imagined it all by himself, yet without the counterpart it could not be actualized.

The counterpart, the true paramour, was me.

Early the next morning, the jail was noisy with gates slamming and shouts resounding down the long corridors. At six, the guard told me to go upstairs with the other women for a medical checkup. Although I hated it in one way, it was novel and somehow comforting to be in an environment where everything was decided for me, not so different from years of boarding school.

Over a dozen women were waiting for the doctor to call them up, most of them Spanish or Italian. When the doctor peeked around the door to call his next patient, he found me chatting away in three languages with four women at once and immediately asked me to act as an interpreter. So for the next three hours I assisted him, after which he arranged for me to have lunch in his office before being taken back to my cell. The next morning at nine I assisted him again. Word soon got around that I was due special treatment.

Security was minimal at Bois-Mermet. Just outside the doctor's office and down the hall was the door to a parking lot for visitors and for deliveries to the infirmary, and the guard on duty at the door was often occupied elsewhere in the wing. By the time I was returned again to my cell, I was brimming with determination. There was no one I could call and no need to call anyone: I would get out without help. *Escape*. It was the perfect way for me to show Timothy that we were the perfect match. It was so clear, striking me like the best acid. There was a symbolic aspect to life, as I had always suspected. Timothy knew all about it and would teach me; all I had to do was get out of here.

That night I felt savage satisfaction as I lay on my little cot, visualizing the cells and locked rooms and barred corridors of the prison. Yes, life is symbolic, but freedom is real. I felt real myself, not as I had felt for many years in Mummy and Plesch's world. Tomorrow, I would make my move. Far from needing their help, I was ready to show them I had finally gone beyond their reach.

But then at 9:15 the next morning, the guard appeared at the door of the doctor's office and told me I must come downstairs to see the judge again. This hitch in my plans upset me, but I didn't show it. I suspected they had brought Tommy in and we would have to go through an asinine interrogation. Well, they wouldn't get far with that and it didn't matter, anyway, because I was sticking to my plan to escape at the first opportunity.

It was the same judge as before and Tommy was nowhere to be seen. Assuming a detached air, as if to relay that personally he couldn't care less, the judge informed me that a gentleman who wished to remain anonymous had paid the hotel bill, and as the charges had been lifted, I was free to go.

18

THE SOUP THICKENS

It was early evening when Tommy, the kids, and I returned to Timothy's chalet. The light on the lake was deep and still, as inviting as a mirror you could touch and enter. The mountains blanketed with new-fallen snow were turning vivid pink. I felt a keen and breathless anticipation until Dennis opened the door with his peculiar intensity and monkey-like intelligence that never stopped weaving and probing. *Why does his presence repel me so much?* I wondered, noting that Tommy immediately distanced himself. Timothy had gone to Bern for dinner with Michel Hauchard, confirming my suspicion that Michel had paid the bill at the Palace Hotel as if playing a casino chip.

To give the English family a little privacy, we went to the upstairs living room. Tommy bedded the kids down among the requisite cushions on the carpeted floor. Other than a wooden table and a couple of chairs, there was only a small bureau with a portable typewriter, a heap of carbons, and an extra pair of glasses folded on a book—obviously where Timothy did his writing. I noticed that Tommy had fallen asleep among the children, distancing himself from more than Dennis.

"Timothy comes and goes among three houses in Switzerland," Dennis explained to me, "and though the Swiss have refused to extradite him to the States, he's not out of the woods yet. though." He fixed his uncanny gaze on me. "The Swiss have been playing a cat-and-mouse game to keep him on the move so he never stays in one canton long enough to attract much attention. Apparently, there are only twenty-four hippies in the entire country, most of whom are the sons and daughters of well-known families."

"That is so Swiss," I said with amusement. "Take everything slow so as not to upset their sense of order. Next thing you know, they'll be making a park where the kids can go and get stoned."

"Yeah, well, Tim is a powerful catalyst, and once people start questioning, it's all over. He doesn't even have to do anything, he just draws it out of people. That kind of magnetism is dangerous to the powers that be. Check this out."

As we moved into the kitchen to scrounge up some dinner, Dennis explained that Leary's situation in the States was still very serious: 19 indictments were recently issued against him in Orange County alone. He flashed the December 21, 1972 *Rolling Stone* with the article "The Strange Case of the Hippie Mafia" by Joe Eszterhas citing the government's claim that Timothy Leary had been masterminding all the drug traffic in California for the past five years. The State of California had slapped 26 indictments for drug trafficking and a $76 million tax lien on him. Nixon's second rise to power had gone as well as it had because of the hunt for drug users and dealers, and now DEA fishing nets were closing in on the Brotherhood of Eternal Love.

"That must make him look a lot more dangerous to the Swiss than a simple conviction for having some marijuana," I said as I poured white wine in our glasses.

Dennis shook his head. "A bad scene. Tim's attorney has been calling every other day and warning us that the Swiss authorities will soon be kicking him out of the country. Politely, of course, but definitely out."

"But where can he go?" I asked.

Dennis looked pensive. "It's a turning point in Tim's life. Maybe that's why you're here. He seems to think so." I sensed an edge of envy. "For the past couple of months he's been detoxing from the heroin he did after Rosemary left him for a younger member of the BEL . . . I don't know if you were aware of that." He paused and eyed me for my response. "Anyway, I don't think Tim has really been ready to make a move until now. We've been looking at a list of socialist countries that have no extradition treaty with the US. Hold on, I'll get it for you."

All of these complications about Leary's plight were hard to digest, and I distrusted Dennis for what I thought was his taste for melodrama, conspiracy, and cloak-and-dagger stories—the stuff of James Bond movies, which I despised. What did it have to do with the man I was getting to know? At breakfast four days earlier, Timothy had said that he was a fugitive and had the scars to prove it, but said it in a humble way that was deeply attractive. Timothy was in some kind of trouble, no doubt, especially given that Michel Hauchard was involved. I had never met a truly powerful man who was humble—or was it that Timothy exuded a chameleon *inner emptiness* that put an exuberant, positive face on everything?

I changed into a long fuscia silk Indian shirt. In jail I had painted my toes a deep red, deciding to go barefoot when I could so they would show. Around my neck was my gold necklace strung with fifty-two rings I had been given by friends and lovers over the years, each metal and stone and color reminding me of a different adventure. Puffing at a Gauloise, I hoped that Timothy and I would have some time to ourselves so I could forget about Dennis and everything he had said. If there really were terrible forces pitted against Timothy, he would tell me in his own time, in his own words. After all, he had created me, the one who could free him, and so it was only natural that he would tell me what had to be done.

But whatever was going down, I didn't think I should subject Lara to it. Bolstering my courage with the rest of my glass of wine, I picked up the telephone and called her father Nico in Greece to arrange for him to fly to Switzerland the next day to pick up Lara, explaining to him that Timothy and I had to get out of this scene.

Once we rang off, I stared into the darkness beyond the window, pondering where Timothy would be safe. The answer came easily: it seemed obvious and cosmically correct that the place to start from was the place from which I had started.

19

LIGHTNING STRIKES TWICE

Gstaad, 1957

When the War was over and it was time for my family to come out of exile, they could not leave Switzerland to return to France as they were Polish and Poland was no longer a free country. Plesch, longing to get back to his affairs outside of Switzerland, asked a friend in British intelligence to find an Englishman willing to serve his country by marrying my mother Marisya so she and my half-sister Floki could become British citizens and have family properties transferred to their names. So Marisya was introduced to Cecyl Harcourt-Smith, a tall, stately, silver-haired Etonian aristocrat whose father had co-founded the Victoria and Albert Museum in London, and had been a commander in the Royal Navy, serving British intelligence as a spy. In May 1945, Cecyl and Marisya were married in a Swiss village on Lake Constance near Hermann Hesse's house. The marriage was to serve purely for convenience, but, like the cherry blossoms and tulips exploding into bloom around them, Marisya and Cecyl consummated it.

In June, Cecyl was called back to England while my soon-to-be mother remained behind, pregnant and afraid, trying everything she knew to miscarry. She lay for hours in hot baths, took quinine pills, rode motorcycles on bumpy roads, had deep, penetrating massages, pushed hard on her tummy, even (in sheer desperation) jumped up and down vigorously whenever it occurred to her to do so. Later she would tell me, "You must have really wanted to come, so you held on hard to make sure you did."

On the Sunday I was born, a snowstorm was raging and Mummy was playing bridge in the main salon of the Palace Hotel in St. Moritz. Dressed in a black taffeta Givenchy dress, she was about to execute a grand slam when her waters broke. With some annoyance she excused herself, went up to her room, and after forty-three hours of more annoyance I was born premature. Since it was Sunday, no doctors were on call, nor did any hospitals in the area have an incubator, so the famous British jockey Sir Gordon Richards was asked to be a good sport and vacate his suite adjoining Mummy's for the new arrival. Hastily, the heat was turned up to the maximum against the piercing January cold and my little pink body placed in a linen basket in Sir Gordan's suite.

I was just under three pounds and as perfect and petite as a prawn ornamented with full-grown eyelashes and rice paper nails. Screaming my lungs out for human contact in Sir Gordon's suite-turned-incubator, I was finally put under the care of an Italian wet nurse procured by the ever-accommodating concierge Giorgio while my mother got her dressmaker to squeeze her back into her evening dresses, appearances being crucial in her quest to find another man and forget the shame of another abandonment, my father having left her with nothing but a passport and an official birth certificate for me. Many times, my mother told me that I was a mistake from the moment I was conceived, never making it exactly clear whose mistake. A few weeks later, she would have me baptized Catholic in a Zurich church, due to her terror of being Jewish. Even in those early months of 1946, my father was afraid of being associated with a Jewish family. In that I was Jewish and a girl, I was an instant throwaway for him.

While I was at the chalet Marie-Jose in Gstaad, Mummy came to take me out of school for an excursion. I remember being dressed in blue organdy and my hair being curled and secured with blue satin ribbons. Mummy and I then went to meet the Channel train at Calais where I watched an impossibly tall silver-haired man walk towards us across the quay. He bent over and put his face down close to mine, so close that I caught the force of his mocking blue eyes. With a terrible English accent, he said, "Parleeez-vous anglais?" I was extremely offended, having practiced my English to perfection with Nanny. But it didn't matter: Daddy had nothing else to say to me.

Seven years later in Gstaad, Marta the maid approached me during dinner and whispered that I had a telephone call. Over the receiver in Madame Racine's small *directrice* office, I heard Mummy's voice say abruptly, "Joanna, your father has died."

At exactly that moment, through the tall, dark rectangular window, a huge zigzag of lightning electrified the mountains. I jolted as if there were nothing more frightening in the world.

"Did you hear what I said?" Mummy's voice came again over the line, hard and distant.

"Yes, Mummy. Daddy is dead," I repeated.

"Tomorrow, your sister and I will go to the funeral in England."

"Can't I come, too?" I begged in a tiny, faltering voice, my eyes suddenly so large that I might fall through them into a bottomless chasm.

"No, you are too young," she said.

Again, lightning hit the mountains, imprinting an emblazoned afterimage on the window. I began to cry in short, shallow gasps.

"Don't cry," Mummy said, "you didn't even know him."

I was eleven and not getting on very well at school. Word soon got around to the other children that I had been lying all along when I said that my father had died before I was born.

20

THE WHITE SCARF

November 1972

Having made the painful arrangements with Nico on the phone, I found Tommy sitting listlessly at the kitchen table nursing a bottle of tequila, and Dennis perched on a stool at the counter, ignoring Tommy completely but ready to monopolize my attention again.

Suddenly, we heard the roar of the Targa. A minute later, Timothy burst through the front door and rushed straight for me. Pulling me toward him, he cradled my face in his hands. "I just left Michel, he talks of nothing but you," he said effusively.

"What do you mean?" I was puzzled and embarrassed. We all gathered at the round table in the dining room. I fingered my gold necklace and stared at Timothy.

"After we talked about my situation, which didn't take long, it was nothing but you for the rest of the evening." He poured wine around and toasted in my direction. "He asked me if I had met you, if I knew where you were, and I just smiled and smiled."

I blushed as my stomach lurched. I wanted to cry, scream, and shout, all at the same time. Instead, I fingered my rings and beamed at them all.

"Here's two thousand," Timothy said, placing an envelope on the table in front of Dennis. "It's from Michel for the escape yacht you're going to get us in Amsterdam. He doesn't know that, of course. Now we can really get going."

Dennis picked up the envelope, gave it a quick glance, then handed it nonchalantly to Tommy. "Yeah, man, it'll be a snap," Dennis said, looking at Timothy with his head cocked to one side. "I'll have to stay here in case your lawyer asks for any special arrangements. Tommy can take his kids and go to Amsterdam to find us a boat. I've been checking some leads and I don't think it will be too difficult to find exactly what we need."

"Right," Timothy concurred, "Joanna will stay here with me until we hear from my lawyer that it's safe for us to drive out of Switzerland through Belgium." He beamed at Tommy with his usual smile of exuberant good will. "Then, we'll join up with Tommy in Holland and sail away."

Tommy looked at the envelope, at me, then shrugged. We all toasted to the success of our plan.

Nico arrived early the next morning, bringing Lara a box of Caran d'Ache pencils and three Frigor chocolate bars. She was delighted. Then everything happened very quickly. Nico insisted on getting it over with, so I leaned down, crying fast and hard and trying not to, pulling a wisp of her sunflower hair back from her sea-blue eyes.

"You're going to Greece for a while to stay with Daddy and Granny. I am going to be very busy, too busy for a little girl, and I can't take you with me where I am going. Not now, but later, I hope . . ." I swallowed. "I am worried because you don't speak Greek."

In her little voice, she reassured me. "Don't cry, Mummy, I can talk all I want with puppies and babies."

My last picture of Lara is of her walking to the car with her father, my tiny five year old girl with huge blue eyes and thick platinum blond hair in her brown corduroy *salopette* and woolen sweater, clutching her Caron d'Ache box and coloring book. Little did I know that I would not be allowed to see her until she was fifteen years old. Thinking of Alexis in Washington, DC, I was devastated by the tradeoffs.

As they drove away, Timothy slipped his hand gently into mine and squeezed it.

Later in the morning, I helped Tommy put his few things into the car. It was a bright, crisp day, the air almost searing, making everything look sharp-edged and final. My eyes kept wandering to the eternal mountains for support. Tommy was wearing a white silk scarf that belonged to me. I hoped he would forget it was mine and just take it. I knew if I had to tell him to take it, I might never stop crying.

"I will see you very soon," I said to him, kissing the lips that always reminded me of a woman's lips, so soft and surrendering. I savored my last taste of his mouth. "It won't be long before we join you in Amsterdam. Find us a good place to stay. Maybe we can go to the gypsy caravan you showed me—you know, the one just outside of town where those English people gather before they head overland to India. I'll bet some of your friends are still there. There might even be a place for us to stay in one of the vacant wagons." I slurred over the ambiguity of *us*.

Though I longed to be with Timothy and feel protected by his strength, I was already missing Tommy's androgynous charm. His children were antsy, obviously ready to go and have their father to themselves for a change. I hugged them both and gave them a big smile, hoping they had liked me a little. What a strange stepmother I must have been.

Timothy came up to the car and put his arm around me as Tommy started the engine and looked up at us, saying, "I'll send you dead flowers through the mail," code for the marijuana he was going to score for us in Amsterdam. We had lifted the line from a Stones song, yet I couldn't help but hear an ominous message in it. My hands went cold.

Then they too were off and down the driveway, swallowed by blinding, snowbound light.

21

THE PLAY'S THE THING

I hadn't forgotten my plan to get Timothy to Gstaad, but the next few days were a blur of LSD and incessant talk while driving around in the yellow Porsche from one rendezvous to the next. I was surprised by how many contacts Timothy had, most of them involved with making the *Steppenwolf* film in which he would play the lead role of Harry Haller.

"Hesse's idea of 'magic theatre' is really where it's at," Timothy explained in a café outside of Geneva while we were waiting for one of the cameramen to call us. The November sun was almost white, skimming low over the city in the distance.

"Magic theatre is not just a metaphor, it's a way of experiencing the world once the neural pathways have been opened up by psychedelics. Actually, the term is redundant. True theatre *is* magic, and magic makes theatre. Look around and you might think this is a perfectly ordinary scene," he gestured to everything around us, "but nothing is ordinary, really. 'Ordinary' is a way of referring to our lack of perception, a dead zone in the sensory field. Once the neural pathways open, the curtain goes up and nothing is ordinary anymore, it's magic theatre."

I listened carefully so as to absorb everything he had to say about the psychedelic experience. So far, I had plunged blindly into LSD, often getting lost, but I knew that with his guidance it would be different. My neural pathways were certainly open and everything seemed minted in technicolor precision, yet I wasn't sure if it was "ordinary" or not. Timothy's ability to act perfectly normal on acid was a marvel, and he was telling and showing me how to do the same: to act ordinary but know otherwise. I knew a lot about appearances, so maybe it required nothing more than turning up a more intense concentration on how I customarily concentrated on looking good and pretending to be in control of all circumstances.

On the way to a special dinner at the Deer Hostel in Basel, Timothy entertained me with tales of Freud, Paracelsus, and Lenin—famous previous residents of Basel with whom he felt strongly connected, especially with the alchemist Paracelsus. When we arrived, it was exactly like a stage setting with film people acting like characters from the novel they were adapting to film, and at the next table were three of the top directors of Sandoz Laboratories, manufacturers of LSD. Topping our acid off with champagne, throughout the dinner I took every cue I could read and turned it into high theatre, including sitting on the lap of one of the Sandoz chiefs, whose embarrassment became an occasion for more extraordinary moments in our magic act. Timothy played along, applauding my every move, and everyone else was rendered speechless.

"We're all involved in magic theatre, even though we don't all know it," Timothy commented slyly as we drove back to Lake Zug. "It's like Lao Tzu: those who know don't say, and those who say don't know. This is the Tao."

He'd dropped down to a whisper, and it was as if he could read my thoughts or think them for me—like when I used to hear Plesch's voice on the radio. On acid, the radio was now in my head.

I settled back in the bucket seat, trying to get comfortable with the steel grip of the acid on my spine. I had certainly done some theatre of my own—not magical, but it had often gotten me what I wanted. Like a psychoanalyst, Timothy had a boundless appetite for my confessions and laughed a lot while asking for more, listening as if what I told him was confirming something in his mind. Thus every *histoire* I recounted proved that I had done the problem right.

"I think I see how magic theatre can really trick people," I said tentatively. Through my sunglasses, the darkness outside the car windows looked like black mesh laid over the snow. Inside the speeding glass and metal shell, we were embraced in another *softer* kind of darkness, like being behind stage when the lights are down and the curtains closed.

"Go on," Timothy said in a slightly distant voice, dreaming and drifting at will yet still attentive.

"Well, in magic theatre there can be no audience, right?"

"Absolutely right."

"But some people think they are watching as if they were audience only, while all the time they don't know that they're part of the performance, too." Still blasted on LSD, every word seemed pregnant with multilayered meanings, huge ripples spreading around a stone thrown into the lake of my mind, receding ever outward and away. "That's why they probably feel awkward seeing us come and go. I mean, they have the impression there's a performance happening, maybe you and I are the main part of it, and so they act like people in an audience expecting the performance to start and stop somewhere, so it begins when we show up and ends when we leave. But that's completely false."

"Yes, it's ongoing," Timothy replied. "That's the whole secret of what I'm trying to show people." He glanced appreciatively at me. "I knew you would understand. Everything I've heard about you and everything you tell me prove I was right. You are the most intelligent woman in Europe. In your mind, the extraordinary comes first, you grasp it naturally. How difficult it must have been for you to make sense of the ordinary realm." He leaned toward me to whisper, "By remaining an 'audience,' people think that everything they can't see is controlled."

"By the performers?"

"Right, but the trick is—"

"The trick is," I finished for him, "the performers aren't controlling anything."

"Of course, they're not," Timothy agreed, flashing me a complicit grin, "even if they look like they are. Just consider a group of actors on stage. They're not controlling the story, they didn't write it. They're just *performing* it, while the people in the audience watching them are performing another script exactly in the same way but without knowing it."

Words swirled around me. I noticed that if I stared out the window for too long, I lost all sense of velocity.

"So who is writing the script?" I heard myself ask.

Timothy hesitated, relishing the moment. I heard his intense whisper and another curtain went up. "DNA."

We had reached the drive to the chalet. A few lights were burning. As Timothy turned off the engine, our conversation switched off, too. I felt inspired, yet heard a tiny unformed cry of alarm from a Greek chorus offstage. The power released by magic theatre confused me. Create a sensational impact and then move on with no segue: the LSD acting method. I dared not ask, dared not even wonder where such a script might take us, but in some way I could not put my finger on, it bothered me that he involved everyone in his act, titillating them with his ideas and plans—like committing to do *Steppenwolf* while on the run—and yet was ready to leave Amsterdam at the first sign that the coast was clear.

22

LOVE CIRCUITS

A couple of days later we went to see a publisher in Zurich who wanted Timothy to write a book about his life in Switzerland. I dressed the part: a blue silk shirt unbuttoned to offer occasional glimpses of my breasts, tight hip-hugger bellbottoms (*pattes d'elephant* in France), high-heeled platforms, multicolored beaded necklaces and rings on every finger, a brown felt fedora tipped on my head.

In the publisher's plush, book-lined office, we drank whiskey while Timothy explained at length how everyone in Switzerland was stuck in fourth gear. Again and again, he used machine and computer metaphors like "gears" or "circuits" to refer to human parts and behaviors. At the time, it was his own language—a jaunty, brilliant way of putting things now become common currency.

"What we need is an owner's manual for our nervous system," Timothy told the publisher. I couldn't help smiling at the thought that if anyone could appreciate the concept of a manual explaining how to run ourselves, it would be a Swiss. "It is the most misused, under-used instrument in the world. You see, the brain is like a car engine with several gears—eight, to be exact. Between infancy and death are turning points when you just have to put the clutch in and shift gears. Then, you can move to another level of consciousness and see the world from a different angle."

He paused to see if we were following him. I smiled radiantly. I wanted to elaborate on his words to show the publisher I knew just as much as Timothy did, but I wasn't quite ready to do that, so I flicked back my hair enticingly and poured the man another drink.

"Fourth gear is the one running Switzerland," Timothy continued. "I call the fourth circuit of the human neurological system the socio-sexual circuit, basically the gear for cruising through adolescence, no more. Look, the whole country here has a bee hive mentality—a beautiful control system, no question about that, a watchmaker's paradise where everything runs on time. A lot of nice benefits. But fourth gear keeps us preoccupied with sexual conquest, hung up on power for survival purposes, maintaining social order, and manipulating for top-of-the-heap status. And I don't mean only the straights, either—the everyday people who follow the rules. No. Politicians and gangsters are regular denizens of this circuit." He nodded knowingly to me and grinned. I knew exactly who he meant. "Sure, fourth gear is great, but we can't remain teenagers all our lives. The nervous system is an instrument of untried potentials. There is so much more to know. LSD shows that intelligence is infinite. After the fourth circuit, there are still four more to go."

The publisher straightened his tie and squinted with serious intent. "Fascinating," he said, looking at my silk blouse.

"But meeting in the fifth circuit," Timothy assumed a look of warmth and complicity as he caught my gaze, "is what I call the rapture circuit. Joanna understands perfectly because it's the proper milieu of the sons and daughters of the European elite, the aristocracy. On this circuit, life is devoted to pleasure of body and mind, beauty in all its forms, the joys of intelligence, elegance and aesthetics, even the hedonistic arts, sensuality for its own sake."

While Timothy waxed euphoric, I waited in the wings for my magical theatre cue.

"Look at her," Timothy said, his eyes lingering on me, "a living embodiment of what I'm saying. A perfect flower of the hedonic elite that has always existed in small, privileged circles down through the ages, appreciating that life can be a matter of pure aesthetics, like a religion of beauty practiced day after day. In the East this has been called the Tantric Path. Perfect Love is a fifth circuit experience. On the lower levels it doesn't exist, because everything from fourth gear down involves competition and acquisition, but at the fifth sexual passion becomes mystical and makes it possible for a man and woman to merge into a perfect unity, one entity that never dies. I've known about this for a long time and I've been wanting to write a book about it for years." He looked into my eyes as if the publisher were mere furniture. "Let's do it together."

Sitting at the edge of my seat, I was astounded at the speed things were opening up and drank in his words with the publisher's Chivas Regal. Timothy was enthusiasm, brilliance, and tenderness, a combination I had only dreamed of. This must really be the Perfect Love he was describing, one entity in two people, because he and I were becoming completely transposable. At moments, I even saw myself becoming him.

As we were leaving, I told the publisher, "Timothy can change people's minds and I don't mean their mere opinions. You will become famous for getting his ideas to people. It's the most revolutionary message in the world. He and I will write it together, and I'll do the French translation. Once people understand what we're saying, the world will never be the same again. You'll see."

I was still reeling from my own words as we drove over to the bar at the Bernerhof Hotel and ordered champagne cocktails with little red cherries. We toasted each other, tears brimming in our eyes.

"To the fifth circuit where we meet, and the sixth where we're bound," Timothy whispered, "the ecstasy circuit beyond rapture. I've been waiting all my life to activate that circuit and now we're going to do it together."

His language permeated me as if attached to electrodes wired directly to my brain. Anita had not misled me: Timothy Leary was a true philosopher like Aldous Huxley with a message for the world he couldn't get out by himself. Dennis may have been right about trouble brewing, but it didn't matter now. The message would come through the two of us. My background, my breeding, even my family genetics had prepared me for this.

And I was very drunk, far too drunk to be scared or doubt or ask questions. It was enough to know that Timothy needed me, and the proof was that he was telling me all these things in the most intense and intimate way. As we sat in the bar, he talked incessantly about circuits and imprinting, and I knew it was all about me even though he wasn't referring to me personally. In fact, other than praising my lineage, beauty, and intelligence, he rarely said anything personal that I could apply to my own life, which was odd. Already, a part of me was bewildered, shocked, and disappointed, while the other parts didn't admit it, it being natural for a philosopher to put everything in technical, impersonal terms.

"The sixth circuit—this is where we're going, my beauty, and it's happening fast," Timothy whispered, beaming at me.

"Fast and slow at the same time, like galaxies colliding," I slurred.

"Eroticization of electronics, psy-phi love, tantric high-fidelity . . ."

Words and more words spilled out, shifting to a frequency hotwired to my brain. I smiled my broadest smile, the one that made my face look Chinese, stroked his hand, and whispered softly, drunkenly, "Whatever you want, whenever you want. I want to be with you forever."

23

A TELEPHONE CONVERSATION

That night at the chalet it was unusually quiet. I was no longer disturbed by the presence of other people in the house, now that Timothy and I were defining our own space. We settled ourselves in a corner of the house that he chose at random. "I don't have a particular room here," he explained. Already, I had noticed Timothy's curious habit of avoiding habits: ordering different kinds of drinks, taking detours and irregular routes between familiar places. Initially, I thought it was because he was a fugitive, but finally understood that it had to do with his spiritual practice and observing his own brain processes. I also noticed that for someone on the run, he slept extremely well: a few minutes after we bedded down, he was sound asleep, while I in my usual fashion plunged into an insomniac trance that kept me restless and wide-eyed until almost dawn.

The next day I called my mother. It was lunchtime and the right time to call, given that I knew her schedule by heart. Return to the villa around ten in the evening after her bridge game at the Marbella Club. Switch on an American serial, "Mannix" or "Bonanza," dubbed in guttural Mexican Spanish. Sit in the salon smoking and reading her fortune cards, sighing as she shuffled them, asking them the questions that tormented her: *Will my daughter marry a powerful man? Will I get the money from Plesch to pay for my trip to Paris?* now and then caressing Ben, the beige Labrador she believed was my father's reincarnation. At last, she would go to bed around four in the morning, and around eleven in the morning, the maid would bring her croissant and café au lait, after which she would be available to receive phone calls and guests.

When I lived with her and came home in the wee hours, I would often find her painting little scenes of everyday life that she could picture but never enter in her naïve style on panes of glass with nail polishes. We would sit and talk, our roles now reversed as I confided my nocturnal adventures. If it were in the morning, we might chat a little if she had a minute off the telephone, sitting up in bed in her satin and lace nightgown, croissant crumbs on her chest and stuck to the corners of a mouth still smudged with lipstick of the previous evening. Like everything else about her, the talk on the phone was predictable: long discussions about last night's card game, what to wear to the luncheon at the club.

As usual, the phone rang twice before she deigned to answer in her smoker's Marlene Dietrich voice. "'Allo?"

"Mummy, *c'est moi*," I intoned, looking across the sunlit room to where Timothy was sitting cross-legged, smoking a Marlboro, gazing contentedly at Lake Zug.

"Where are you?" Mummy sounded annoyed. "Your sister called and said you have done very bad things in Lausanne. I've been wondering where to find you. Are you creating *histoires* again?"

I then started to tell her about being with Timothy Leary, but of course she already knew all about him and wanted to talk to him.

A knot tightened in the pit of my stomach. "Timothy, my mother wants to talk to you," I said softly, smiling and trying to look pleased as I offered him the receiver.

"Sure," he said, flashing me a confident look.

The minute he began to speak, it was as if I went underwater. I heard him say how intelligent I was, how fortunate he was to have met me among all the young women in Europe because I was the one best prepared to understand him, and then go silent, nodding and listening to what I knew was Mummy's long rant about me.

"Oh yes, I know she is intelligent, but what good is such intelligence if it's used for telling lies and *histoires*? Joanna has many problems, Dr. Leary, beginning when she was so young. She can't tell truth from what she imagines. Even as a small child, her imagination was too strong. She is unable to follow the most simple agreements about how things are done."

She would adjust what she had to say for the listener, probably appealing to Timothy the psychologist. Mummy always knew how to talk to people.

"She is crazy, Dr. Leary, living in a dream world and never taking life seriously. It is really wonderful, *vraiment formidable*, for her to finally meet a man of your gifts. I hope you can help her, Dr. Leary, show her what is wrong with the workings of her mind. Perhaps you can explain why she sleeps with every man she meets, and what her mind is doing. She has caused her family nothing but trouble, but I know you must understand young people and why they make such trouble . . ."

She talked on and on while Timothy said very little. A huge wave of exhaustion crashed over my head. Concentrating on the winter sun's warmth pouring through the window onto my body, I stood, eyes closed, tears sliding from under the lids. Let her talk all she liked, writing my script as she always had. In fact, it was good she was saying all those things to Timothy: he would know and it would all be different after he heard it.

Grandpère Plesch's image rose out of the void and flitted past me, his huge dark wing brushing my shoulder. I shuddered, remembering his silver hair and calm, inquisitive voice. He had secrets, some regarding me, and they were part of his plan. Every powerful man has a plan. Timothy had a plan, too, and now I was with him. Hadn't he told me that he had created me in his cell in California? He did that because I was part of his plan. As yet, I didn't know a lot about it, but I was learning fast; and besides, some things do not need to be said. We were already living his plan, and he needed me to appear before he could live it out. Now, he would lead me into another life, show me the way to see myself beyond how Mummy saw me. I had never counted for her. Timothy would hear her empty words and dismiss them, and then I would be accepted, safe, and loved.

Only hindsight would show how naïve my hope really was.

24

ALONE TOGETHER

December 1972

The next morning I proposed that we go off by ourselves to Gstaad to ski. I had packed up all my clothes, my tape player and tapes, my hope being that we would not be returning to Lake Zug. From Gstaad I thought we might go on to St. Moritz to see some friends of mine, then easily swing back via Lucerne and Basel into France, then through Belgium to Holland when the word came through from Timothy's lawyer.

It was the beginning of December and the mountains were dazzling in the high, clear light, and snow was fresh. Skiing was a way of being out of control that I loved—gliding down the mountain, free of gravity, the wind rushing past my face as I wove recklessly across and down the slope. Perhaps being out of control in this familiar way would ease my anxiety. So much that was happening now seemed sudden and unfamiliar, although it was what I wanted to happen more than anything in the world.

"I've skied every winter since I can remember," I told Timothy as we left the chalet.

Securing his Rossignol skis and poles on the rack of the yellow Porsche, he said he had been practicing skiing the past two winters he'd been in Switzerland. "I view it as an interesting form of yoga, like life itself—the faster you can go, the less likely you are to get hurt," he said cheerfully.

Gstaad was a ski resort town nestled at about 3,000 feet in mountains known for their postcard silhouettes and fabulous slopes. Its elevation was low enough for wealthy people of all ages and high enough for excellent snow. The village had changed very little since my boarding school days, when Mummy and Plesch had separated. The main street was lined with tidy shops selling expensive cameras, cashmere sweaters, and fancy ski gear. My favorite of all was Cadeneau's, the *papeterie* with neat stacks of notebooks, folders, portfolios, and an endless variety of pens and pencils. Though no one in my family had worked for generations, I often thought of having my own *papeterie*, a place where I could happily work while pretending not to.

At the top of the hill was the Palace Hotel, a veritable castle with turrets, flags, red carpets, and a wide, billowing canopy over the main entrance. If Gstaad was the ski resort of the fashionable elite, then this was the fairy tale castle in which they resided.

We arrived in late afternoon. When Timothy turned down the main street into the village, I told him to pull over at Charlie's, the tea parlor close to the skating rink where my best friend, the real Russian princess Sophie Trubetskoi, and I used to drink hot chocolate.

In the tearoom Mrs. Charlie greeted me warmly and showed us to a round table by the windows. The place was packed with skiers and boarding school kids wearing braces and talking up a storm about their blossoming love lives. Charlie's was where you always came around four-thirty after a day on the slopes to drink hot chocolate with lots of whipped cream and eat jelly donuts or flaky *mille-feuille* while making plans for the evening. Outside in the huge skating rink, nannies in thick sweaters watched children in lumpy snowsuits skate, fall, and pick themselves up in endless repetitions, uncannily orchestrated by the tinny sound of Strauss waltzes pouring from loudspeakers at the four corners of the rink. It was nice that some things didn't change—or was it? I had changed, and was still changing fast.

Timothy and I were in the mellow phase of the LSD we had taken that morning. He insisted we take acid every single day, and I went along without protest, assuming I would eventually learn why. As usual, he was looking amazingly natural in his emerald green cable sweater, grey flannel pants, and moon boots—a college professor on sabbatical, the picture of perfect conservative ease. I, on the other hand, was wearing my playful blue denim overalls, pink long-sleeved t-shirt, and pink kid boots to match.

"How come you lost touch with Sophie?" Timothy asked after I told him about the old days at Charlie's.

"Oh, I don't know. Contact is funny in the world I come from. It's as if there are huge currents keeping people apart or throwing them together—overpowering currents. You can only keep contact with the people moving in the same current, and even then it's usually not that close, not like we are. I guess Sophie and I were really together, too, but . . ."

The festive mood of Gstaad was so familiar and welcoming, and yet I couldn't absorb it. Timothy must have sensed that I was talked out, so we drank our cappuccinos and watched the skating rink in silence.

"Let's spend the night at the Palace Hotel," he suggested. "This will be our first night alone and I want us to be comfortable and close. I like this place. It was a good idea to come here."

Having just come through the trauma of the unpaid bill at another Palace Hotel, I must have looked worried. I wanted to ask if Timothy had any money, but it was too vulgar. As usual, he read my mind, just as I had always wanted the right man to do.

"Don't worry. I have enough money to take care of us for right now and that's all that counts."

So I sat and smoked while he went off to call the hotel. Fortunately for us, they had a suite, the receptionist was as friendly as ever, and suddenly I was back in the familiar world of luxury and seclusion. The suite had two rooms. The large one had two writing tables and a television, a velvet sofa with rose-colored pillows, a round glass table graced by a fruit basket filled with red pears, shiny green apples, and a variety of cheeses from all over Switzerland. Next to the basket was a bottle of Veuve Clicquot in a silver bucket filled with ice. On the table was also a card from management that read, *Welcome Mr. and Mrs. Leary*. I showed Timothy the card and we laughed, then kissed for a long time, our tongues eagerly searching out each other.

Arm in arm, we inspected the bedroom, a corner room with two huge windows overlooking the town, hung with heavy satin drapes cascading to the floor. We gazed at the village spread below us, its lights glimmering. The texture of the huge orange moon rising over the mountains reminded me of an old coin.

I put on Pink Floyd's "Dark Side of the Moon," then ran a bath with a large dose of Badedas. While the tub was filling, I sat on Timothy's lap in the living room. He was drinking champagne and staring at a couple of purple tablets he had placed in a silver tray on the side table. Earlier, while sitting in Charlie's, I had just begun to feel some relief from the intensity of all the acid we had been taking, and now there was more. Resigned, I chided myself that it was a special night and I could hardly refuse.

I emerged from my bath feeling calm and entranced. At nine, we went downstairs to dinner. It was as if everything was floating. I had always loved the impeccable starched white of tablecloths in expensive hotels. Tonight, ours looked like liquid ivory, and the waiter's hands dripped the same ivory to the wrists. I couldn't help staring at the transformed hotel I thought I knew well, so as usual Timothy's consummate ease covered for me so I could completely relax. As the Eagles put it, *I'm looking for a lover who won't blow my cover.*

He chose a 1946 Chassagne Montrachet. "It's fitting to celebrate with a wine bottled in the year you were born," he said.

We began with a light turtle soup, followed by fresh trout from the nearby river Saanen. Between courses we were quiet, holding hands and gazing around, but we barely managed to contain our giggles at the pomposity of the wine steward. Dessert was fresh raspberries flown in from California, coffee, and cognac.

I was feeling high and euphoric, the wine alchemically mixing nicely with the LSD. "You have the eyes of a Ceylonese poet," I said as I fed him a raspberry dripping with crème fraiche, "combined with the soft skin of a Tibetan, and the hands of an old monk who has written down spiritual teachings with pen and ink in the 11th century."

"Let's leave Switzerland and go to Ceylon on our escape yacht," he suggested suddenly. "We can live on the beach with sand between our toes and flowers in our hair. Let's never talk to anyone but each other." Gazing out the window at a horse and sleigh gliding over the snow, filled with people in fur coats laughing and singing, he added thoughtfully, "I've done everything I want to do in America. Everything I *can* do. They weren't ready to hear about LSD there, the message of radical change. I tried to tell them, you know." His voice was quiet, calm, resigned.

I didn't know but nodded as if I did. I had just begun to understand what Timothy had been saying to people, but as yet I knew nothing of how they had responded. Obviously, not all Americans were as open-minded as I imagined.

"I told the US Senate that LSD is not like marijuana or cocaine. It should be made legal and monitored in clinical settings. It has enormous potential for medicine and psychiatry. I warned that if they did not make it legal, it would go underground and then they would be faced with a huge illicit market, a complete nightmare, out of control and impossible to handle." He paused to kiss my palm. "All that seems so far away now, so unimportant. As I look at you sitting there bathed in candlelight, I see one of the Three Graces painted by Botticelli, and the next instant you are Renoir's young girl with milky skin and long wavy hair held back by a red velvet ribbon. If we go to Ceylon, you will become a Gauguin."

Peace and mischief emanated from him. In fleeting moments, I could also see fear glinting behind his blue-grey eyes.

"We are caterpillars sharing a chrysalis. During this magical night, we will become two butterflies with brilliant powdered wings."

I heard the words, not sure if it was he or I who said them.

25

TWO WINGS ARE BETTER THAN ONE

In the bedroom I opened the drapes closed by the maid in customary fashion while we were at dinner. Moonlight poured in, a silver-white torrent so thick and palpable I felt I could plunge my hands into it. It even stained the maroon satin bedspread with a huge wet patch of scarlet. I lit candles on the night tables and poured more champagne.

Timothy took out his brown Samsonite briefcase, incongruous in this setting, then knelt at the base of the window in the full moonlight and opened it with two sharp clicks. He took out a small Buddha sculpted in jade, a round ceremonial mat, then something that looked like a scepter with intricate figures carved into it and four claws at each end, and finally a string of wooden prayer beads. He arranged everything on the mat, adding the Crowley Tarot deck designed by Crowley's mistress Lady Frieda Harris. Then, he added a gold ring encircled by a man and woman entwined in a sexual embrace given him by Hermann Hesse's nephew. The magical ease of his gestures fascinated me.

Finally from his magician's briefcase, he took out a copy of *Life* magazine and opened to a two-page spread of something like a landscape of an alien world glowing with intricate tunnels and coral-like vegetation. Reverently, he laid it in the very center of the mat.

I took off my clothes and slipped into a sleek robe of purple silk embroidered with tiny pink rosebuds. I opened my jewelry box and chose two necklaces, one of lapis lazuli, the other of round jade beads. The jewels felt cool on my skin. I imagined I was becoming the images in the magazine, porous and translucent. I added a string of pearls, white and incandescent, each little moon capturing and holding the light of the greater moon. Finally, silver and gold bracelets on my ankles and wrists. Immediately, every ornament became part of my body. Mysterious and open, I pulsed like a creature woven of delicate filaments.

Timothy gestured for me to join him in the moonlight. He indicated the magazine images at the center of the altar. I saw rivers and trees suspended in a landscape of soft white matter.

"These are pictures of the inside of the human brain," he whispered reverently. "Look at them carefully so you will know that when I make love to you, I am caressing you in the innermost way, touching you everywhere, in every precious river and valley of your brain." He looked me over closely, taking in the array of jewels. "You are the goddess Lakshmi who brings wealth and abundance, consort of Vishnu who dreams the world. I promise you that I dreamed and created you just as you are now before me, covered with jewels, in this room, in this light of this moon. I am Vishnu the World Dreamer. Our lovemaking will be the union of god and goddess making us free in all the worlds."

I ran my fingers through his silver hair. One by one, he slowly removed the rings from my fingers, then placed the gold ring from the altar on my index finger, saying, "This is a tantric ring for a tantric marriage." He kissed my hand tenderly and I dove straight through his eyes.

For the rest of the night we merged and melted, and I felt not only pleasure but release from the pain I hadn't realized I was in. He was as strong and eager as a young man, his body lithe and thin, a good match to mine. Finally, we lay together in the second, greater intimacy of lovemaking: spent, in a conversation without words.

Early in the morning he fell asleep in my arms. I was too happy to sleep, so I lay there and listened to him breathe. My skin tingled from the sweet texture of the fresh linen sheets.

26

MOONFIELDS

I awoke around eleven to find that Timothy had ordered breakfast from room service, croissants and café au lait. I lit a Gitane and Timothy had his first Camel of the day.

"I just spoke to Dennis," he said, "I called him to see how it was going with my lawyer, about us being able to drive to Amsterdam."

"What did he say?"

"That it's not safe for me to go to Holland and there's no telling when it will be safe. But Dennis says Austria has no extradition arrangement with the US and his CIA source says there are some film people in Vienna who want me to do an anti-heroin film with them—good propaganda for the Austrian government. Dennis has a friend there who may be able to get Chancellor Kreisky to grant me asylum. It's a real chance to break away, but it means the plan for getting a boat in Amsterdam is off. He's already talked to Tommy in Amsterdam, letting him know we're not coming. We'll meet Dennis in Vienna."

This sudden news went through me like a knife, so sharp it met no resistance at all. We were going to Austria.

After breakfast, Timothy stretched out on a sofa by the window for a while, listening to the noises of the village. "I feel wonderful," he announced, "let's go skiing while it's still early enough. We can take along some hashish and smoke it on the way up the lift."

"I have a better idea," I said, "let's eat some now so when we put on our skis we'll really be ready to fly."

We left the hotel around one and drove in the glorious warmth of the sun to the lifts. New-fallen snow was dropping in huge clumps from fir branches lining the sides of the road. Going up on the lift, I had the impression that all the moonlight of last night had congealed on the mountains and changed its texture from molten ivory to glistening crystalline powder.

As soon as we hit the slopes, it was obvious that Timothy was a downhill beginner. Nevertheless, I ruthlessly took him through all the more difficult runs on the Wassengrat, making frequent turns and stops to wait for him. I was touched by his sheer courage and determination, qualities he brought to every situation. Time and again, he threw himself down the hill with a huge smile on his face and came up smiling when he tumbled. Once, I was alarmed and called out, "Are you all right?" He just looked up at me with that irrepressible smile, hair full of snow, eyes glinting behind his glasses, and said, "Sure am, let's go. Let's have some fun."

Seeing him fall and get back to his feet over and over again in that boundless, blinding field of crystallized moonlight in the middle of the day blew my mind.

27

NO ROOM AT THE INN

Christmas 1972

The following night after dinner we drove off in the light of a full moon. Gstaad to St. Moritz—my place of true beginnings—would take about nine hours, a leisurely drive through mountain passes and bedded-down villages. We were snug inside the Porsche, like two aliens in our very own spaceship. I laid back, lit cigarettes for us, and imagined we were driving backwards in time, back to the imaginary land of my childhood. Through the sunroof, I followed a time-lapse procession of stars and clouds. Ever since meeting Timothy, I had stepped out of ordinary time. Now, taking LSD, sleeping only when we were tired day or night, we had entered an endless drift of ebb and flow from clocks, the Porsche our Yellow Submarine, our mobile time capsule, its black bucket seats impregnated with the smell of our bodies, its air saturated with our special codes.

At five in the morning we wound down the mountain pass leading to St. Moritz to the Eagles' refrain, *Take it easy, take it easy, don't let the sound of your own wheels drive you crazy.* As always, I was traveling with a lot of music. For years I had lived like a model on a runway, every move in tempo to my music—the Stones, the Eagles, Janis Joplin, Dylan, Beethoven, Haydn, flamenco, Pink Floyd, Vivaldi. Timothy liked it all.

St. Moritz rose before us in the misty dawn, each of its six lakes unveiled by the sunlight like facets of a flashing diamond. We stopped the car at an overlook and got out. How beautiful was the place where I was born! Now, I had returned to be born again. As the last stars faded, we hugged each other in the exhilarating air of 6,000 feet. Timothy felt so warm in my arms, his blood and skin sharing with mine the pulse of our new life form.

We drove slowly into the sleepy town past the shop where Mummy bought my first skis when I was two years old, past Hanselman, the tearoom where I had spent so many afternoons, stopping at last in front of the Palace Hotel. The one and only Palace Baby had arrived.

Walking through the deserted hall toward the dining room, we were sunk in the wordless state of LSD telepathic communication. The *maître d'* seated us at a table overlooking one of the lakes where I had taken endless skating lessons as a child, shivering in my white tutu. At four, I had hoped to become an acclaimed ballerina. Now, I was becoming a dancer of another sort.

We had café au lait and croissants, chewing dreamily as the sun rose huge and pale gold over the mountains, happy and a little awkward, vulnerable as children, as if we had just landed on Planet Earth and were not familiar with its local customs. Inside, memories and feelings of separation or shame enticed and menaced me, a sucking undertow drawing me toward an edge over which I dared not look. Only when I looked at Timothy would I stabilize.

Then the director of the hotel Herr Müller was standing by our table, his cheeks closely shaved and unnaturally rosy, his shirt starched and ironed to a startling stiffness. Even his grey, pin-striped suit with cuffs on the legs and his smell of Dior aftershave did not belie the fact that he was an obsequious someone who had become the director by working his way up from bellboy.

"I am so glad you are here, Joanna," I heard him say from a distance, "it has been a while since you've come to see us. You are still the only person ever born in this hotel—even the sons of the owner were born in the nearby hospital. I remember seeing you when you were just a few hours old—very tiny, so small you cannot imagine. You have turned into quite a charming woman." He paused, all cordiality and smiles, waiting for me to respond. When I just looked at him uncertainly, he asked, "Will you be staying with us for a while, and would you and Herr Leary like to have a room prepared?"

He knew who Timothy was, of course. The Swiss are so thorough. I thought of the two trench coat detectives in Lausanne and wondered what else Herr Mü ller knew.

I managed a polite smile, but his appearance had brought me down. "No, thank you, Herr M üller. Dr. Leary and I will be staying at Chalet von Opel where we are expected this morning." *Can he tell we are on drugs?* I was terrified he might have us thrown out.

But he only smiled and said, "Too bad you won't be staying with us this time, but have a good stay in St. Moritz and be sure to come and see us again soon." He bowed slightly and withdrew.

A curtain went up, a façade dropped away, and I saw Timothy and myself in a light very different from the moonlight of the past few days. My jeans had patches, my platform boots were caked with mud, our clothes were rumpled, our fingers yellow with tobacco stains, and we both had deep circles under our eyes from yet another sleepless night on cocaine and LSD. We were a couple of impostors posing as blasé Jetsetters. Once again, I was in defiance of the realm of appearances, even as I sought refuge in it.

"Let's leave," I said urgently, holding back the wave breaking over me, the overwhelming feeling this place called up. All I had ever felt in this hotel since the day I was born was loneliness, and it hurt all the more because it was such a contradiction to what I had now. All my life I had envied "love" depicted on the big screen and played out in the affairs of the many people I had known in these rooms, like characters in the swirling salons of Durrell's *Alexandria Quartet*. All my life I had dreamed of having my turn, and now thought I saw in the gentle eyes of the man across the table from me the love I had always sought. As sweet and fulfilling as all love is, it also cuts like a knife as it pries at places in me that have yet to see the light of day. I vaguely suspected that being re-born might be as painful as being born in the first place. For me, the

Palace Hotel had stored up years of unspoken pain and now gave it all back, intact, in a single dose.

As we left the dining room in silence, Timothy took my hand. Inside the safety of the Porsche, I was finally engulfed by my terrible childhood loss and rejection while Timothy was watching with the tenderest eyes I had ever known.

28

CHRISTMAS EVE WITH WARHOL

St. Moritz, December 1972

After leaving the Palace Hotel, we drove over to see my friend Christina von Opel, whom I called Putzi. All was quiet when we arrived at her chalet above the village on the road to the Suvretta House. She and her brother had long since gone to bed. Lona, the Austrian woman who had worked for Putzi for as long as I could remember, first as a nanny and then as a housekeeper, showed us to the guest room on the third floor and made us promise to come down for lunch at one o'clock. I ran a hot bath for Timothy, playfully stripped him and marched him into the bathroom. He lay in the tub looking incredibly young, blissfully dipping a huge sponge and squeezing the water over his head.

The few days we spent at Chalet von Opel were luxurious and safe. Lona baked *apfel strudel* and fresh batches of Austrian Christmas cookies. Putzi and Timothy had a strong simpatico. He was delighted with her continuous stream of questions. They talked until all hours about Jung's work and pored over Putzi's limited edition of his *Red Notebook*. Usually, I chose not to include myself in their conversations, instead going off to ski and enjoy the slopes alone. Pretending I wasn't interested in what they were saying meant I wouldn't be judged for asking stupid questions, my aloofness saying that my power over Timothy was not threatened by mere chatter. But the truth was that I felt intimidated by Putzi's ability to have such impassioned and impersonal conversations with this fascinating man.

I called my mother in Spain to tell her how things were going and she ended up having another long and intimate conversation with Timothy that again made me feel excluded and angry. Obviously, Mummy had a huge crush on Timothy who was only six years her junior, even though they had never met. *All the better,* I fumed, puffing my Gauloise: she would be humiliated when she found out how devoted he was to me and me alone.

On Christmas Eve, Andy Warhol and some of his friends showed up at the chalet, all in tuxedos, the women in matching Chanel outfits. Timothy and I stood around in our ski clothes, eyeing them awkwardly. Finally, Timothy and Andy sat down on the sofa, their tail feathers up and alert, waiting to see which one would outsmart the other.

"There are only three real geniuses in America," Timothy said with his usual endearing grin, "you and me and the third one changes all the time."

Warhol said nothing, transmitting his usual silent message of dire import by emanating a pale and hungry air. His distancing reminded me of Mummy and made me uncomfortable. Perhaps noticing my discomfort, Timothy nodded in my direction and said to Warhol, "This is the most beautiful woman in the world and I love her."

Warhol glanced sharply at me, then turned immediately to a woman with a pageboy haircut in a red and gold Chanel suit standing nearby and snapped his fingers, at which she pulled a bundle of 45 rpm's from her handbag and dropped one onto the machine. The voice of Ricky Nelson oozed through the speakers as Warhol stood up and asked me to dance. Laughing, Putzi pulled back the Persian rug and we stepped onto the parquet floor. I just managed to hold onto his cold, clammy hand as he flung me around the living room with surprising force, while Timothy, Ricky von Opel, and the others clapped to the beat—Warhol transforming me into a malleable doll while he, that pale stickman, infused himself with energy for as long as a dance.

29

THE SACRED WATERS OF THE GANGES

Vienna, New Year's 1973

From St. Moritz we made for Vienna by way of an exhausting all-night drive over excruciating back roads to avoid crossing the border into Germany. I couldn't understand why Timothy was traveling under his own passport and not the false documents he'd escaped with, nor where and how he'd obtained it. We stoked ourselves with cocaine and hashish to ballast the LSD and conversation poured through us in long waves, rolling and breaking like surf. Now I felt we were really on our own, finding our own grooves and cutting them deep. I loved Timothy's brilliance and was thrilled to at last trust someone's intelligence and be entertained by it at the same time. His enthusiasm, his free-wheeling, unattached spirit, his sense of wonder and adventure were all my own qualities, although the endearment they had earned me from people of my former world was superficial and left me feeling that I didn't matter. Now it was as if everything mattered.

He talked endlessly about his current passions and problems: the *Steppenwolf* film in which he still hoped to play the lead role; the

"Seven-Up" album he'd made with Tangerine Dream; his interest in Crowley and the code system of the Thoth Tarot deck; his previous incarnation as Renaissance magician and astrologer John Dee and his uncanny sense that Bryan had been Edward Kelley, the low-life highwayman who had scryed for Dee's magical incantations of Enochian spirits; his deal with Michel for *Confessions of A Hope Fiend* and the $70,000 Michel had taken from the advance, leaving Timothy with $10,000; his struggle with heroin addiction before we met; the "hedonic elite" super-intelligentsia forming the vanguard of a global elite who would eventually be the pioneers of space colonization; his sense of being a "change agent" and refugee caught in time; etc. I listened, taking it in through my pores. Our connection made magnificent sense, especially when I added connections from my own background, such as my second cousin Stan Ulam being the mathematician father of the A-bomb. For the first time I was discovering what it meant to know someone profoundly. We had been together night and day for almost six weeks.

In Vienna, we settled in a hotel and made contact with the Austrian filmmakers. We were already on edge when we got to their studio because I had left our little cocaine stash on the table at breakfast. Fortunately, I was able to retrieve it before the waiter did, but the edge was still with us when we discovered that the film commune wanted Timothy to *endorse* drugs. Dennis' CIA source had misled us—why? Perhaps to get Timothy out of Switzerland? When Timothy agreed to do the film anyway but left the terms vague, I was more confused than ever. On the way back to the hotel, he seemed demoralized but said nothing.

That's when Dennis showed up. I was getting used to him always showing up, but I still didn't like it. His fast-talking, conspiratorial manner irritated me less now, but his limber, manic moves reminded me of Mickey Mouse in *Fantasia*. Dennis the sorcerer's apprentice. He listened impassively to our story about the filmmakers' co-op but shrugged it off as a bum lead. Just before leaving Switzerland, he'd received a call from Susan Leary, Tim's only daughter, to say that she would be in Vienna on her way back from India. So the next evening we all drove to the Bahnhof to pick Suzy up. All the way there, I wondered about the "bum lead" and if Dennis had cooked up this erratic meeting, too, then berated myself for being unduly paranoid about the minor players in the *magic theatre* that Timothy and I kept falling into.

Suzy stepped off the train looking a complete fright, eight months pregnant, holding her one-year-old by the hand. We took her to a hotel near the station as a temporary refuge until Timothy and I could find a house to rent, given that we'd decided to lay low in Vienna for a while. As we were leaving the hotel, Suzy tugged at my arm and produced a small bottle from her canvas pack.

"It's holy water from the Ganges," she said in a taut, stringy voice. "I filled it myself three weeks ago when I was in Benares. It's miraculous stuff, it will make all your dreams come true." She proffered the bottle with a hint of the O'Leary smile.

Thinking of Alice in Wonderland and the bottle saying *Drink me*, I took a swig to please Suzy. Nanny had made me drink water from Lourdes when I had the whooping cough, saying it was healing water that worked on paraplegics and other sufferers who came to pray to the Virgin of Lourdes in the grotto where she had appeared to two French peasant girls.

Needless to say, all my dreams didn't come true.

30

THE YELLOW PERIL

New Year's 1973

During the next few weeks, I slid into a kind of exhausting game that kept Timothy and me continually in limbo. Dennis tripped with us most of the time, and we all stayed stoked on the cocaine being generously supplied by a member of the abortive filmmaker commune.

Timothy's enormous doses of LSD daily made me feel that I had to do the same to impress him and show him I had the courage to keep up with his intensity. During the trips, we kept running around, in and out of taxis, in and out of restaurants and discos, rubbing shoulders with an endless stream of hippies, students, and revolutionary types. I had to be at his side looking cool and coherent, even though all I wanted to do was lie down and surrender to the internal currents and images swarming through my body. I had resorted to cutting the tabs to minimize the dosage, or just licking the tab and tossing it away when he wasn't looking. Unlike him, I was not able to absorb unlimited quantities of LSD; a little too much and I felt myself being sucked down by a fearful undertow of something I had no name for and wanted to go fetal. Instead, I fought to keep my style going and keep up with him. He offered not one word of direction or advice on how to navigate the LSD experience, and I was too hurt and confused to ask.

The first week in January, Dennis borrowed the Porsche and totaled it. I couldn't believe it. I screamed him out of sight. The Porsche had been my one touchstone of freedom. Now, without the style the Porsche had provided, I felt horribly trapped. Getting entree anywhere was possible, as long as you had the style to pull it off. Style was the one indispensable gift of survival my upbringing had given me. With dawning panic, I realized what the loss of the Porsche meant and wondered if Dennis knew, too.

The next morning I looked in the mirror and gasped. My eyes and skin had turned a livid orange. I screamed in alarm and ran to get Timothy, who could scarcely believe his eyes. After a brief, chaotic discussion, we dressed and flung ourselves into a taxi. "To the medical school, quick," I said in my tentative German. As we sped along, I talked nonstop. "Maybe it's all this LSD we've been taking, maybe the doses are too strong for me. I think it might be endangering my life, but I don't want to see a doctor. I want the head of the medical school to examine me." Desperate, I trembled with fear and determination.

"I love your attitude," Timothy replied shakily. "Let's go to the top. Sure thing. Always. Now put your head on my shoulder."

We charged up the huge marble stairway and into the building where Freud and Jung had spent countless hours discussing the mysteries of the human psyche. In the imposing hallway, I asked the clerk where was the Dean of the Medical Faculty. Professor Doktor Kraus was presently lecturing on anatomy in the main amphitheater before 1,200 students. I grabbed Timothy's arm and pulled him along the dark corridors and up another flight of stairs until we came to the double doors of the amphitheater.

Bursting through the doors, I headed straight for Doktor Krauss, who was standing on an elevated stage with a lacerated cadaver laid out beside him on a marble slab. "Look at me!" I shouted in German, my voice amplified by the magnificent acoustics. "Look at me! I'm more important than a dead person, but I might be dead soon, too. I am sick and I want you to tell me what's wrong."

As I spoke, I threw off my coat and olive green silk shirt and stood naked to the waist. The entire class stared at me, as did the astounded professor. No one even dared to breathe. From the corner of my eye, I could see Timothy lingering under the double doors archway, taking in the scene with obvious fascination. Silence rang from the dome, then turned to thunder as the students rose in a single body to give me a standing ovation, cheering and whistling.

Regaining his composure, Professor Kraus silenced the students and turned to me without batting an eyelash. In grand academic tones, he pronounced, "Observe, class, a classical case of jaundice due to hepatitis." He moved his fingers from my shoulder and along my arm in a comforting gesture, shifting to English in a slow reassuring voice with a melodious Austrian accent. "Put your clothes back on, *fräulein*, and I will personally take you to the lab and order some tests for you."

As we marched to the lab, Timothy whispered, his eyes twinkling with delight, "You have great talent for making a scandal."

31

THE SHADOW OF DEATH

January 11, 1973

I was indeed very ill with a serious case of hepatitis. The doctor insisted that I be hospitalized immediately or I might die.

Not once did the sacred waters of the Ganges cross my mind.

That night Timothy, Dennis, and I took LSD together in the hotel room and spent a long time talking about what to do next. As usual, Dennis had ideas. He had been to Afghanistan several times to buy hashish from a rich merchant named Rayatollah who had always wanted to meet Timothy Leary. Rayatollah had become a millionaire by trading hashish for televisions, record players, and toasters, and admired Timothy almost more than anyone in the world.

Reclining in a plush red armchair and sipping clear broth I'd ordered from room service to justify to myself that I was attending to my condition, I continued wondering about Dennis and the Porsche, and now Afghanistan.

Timothy tried to comfort me. "You'll be well soon. What you need is peace and lots of it. Peace, rest, sunshine, and good air. We'll find it all in Kabul. Rayatollah will give us a beautiful house, and I will lay you down on satin cushions, make love to you, and feed you light and exquisite foods. We'll have all the Afghani hash we want, and the King will visit us and treat you like a royal princess. After you're well, we can fly to Ceylon and join Christina at her house on the beach. You'll write poetry and I'll watch over you night and day."

I looked at him adoringly, convinced that he really did want to look after me as no one ever had before. I didn't want to go into a hospital. I was so exhausted from the struggle to keep tripping without being overwhelmed that Timothy's vision sounded positively paradisiacal. I rummaged in my bag for some Quaaludes as we discussed Kabul, needing to slide into that smooth dreamtime that made decisions come easy. In any case, I had no alternative to suggest.

I floated to the bathroom, there being no more gravity because love had cancelled it so I would not die. *No gravity, no graves*, I thought, struck by the brilliant simplicity of it, the grave being where gravity deposits us when we give in to it . . . From the bathroom I could see Timothy and Dennis laying out all their money on the dark brown velvet bedspread. Dollars, shillings, francs, a crazy quilt of currencies. I would be safe in such a quilt, beyond the reach of gravity.

When I shut the bathroom door, the mirror swung around and I saw myself full length. The woman before me looked as if she had been cultivating a terrific tan, except something was wrong with the color, and there were no bikini lines. I was dark orange all over, even my palms, even what formerly were the whites of my eyes. I remembered the cadaver on the slab in the amphitheater and suddenly the bathroom was too cold to bear. My Quaalude-LSD mind struggled for a name—someone who had died on LSD like me . . .

My eyes locked onto the mirror. A girl twelve years old, a fat little chunk with braids at the Couvent des Oiseaux outside of Paris, and the movie magazines under my mattress, along with the candy and Swiss dark chocolate I always craved. In the latest magazine were photos of Brigitte Bardot, her long bleached blond hair teased and piled on her head in a beehive, her thick and pouty lips. But in this picture of her she was leaving a hospital outside Paris looking distraught in her dark glasses, begging the press to leave her alone, her wrists heavily bandaged. I decided to never go to a hospital because terrible things happened there.

On weekends when I returned to Paris, I spent long nights alone in the apartment after the servants had gone to bed and Mummy was out, feeling like I wanted to die. If I couldn't grow up to be like Brigitte Bardot, beautiful and adored by all, then what could I do? Grandpère Plesch insisted that I had some talents Brigitte Bardot didn't have, but I had been shown many times that for women only beauty and sex counted in the world in which I had to survive.

One weekend I searched for a razor to see if I could slash my wrists. At least Brigitte always had a man around, and where there were men there were nice little packets of razors wrapped in blue paper. There was no man in our house, so in exasperation I pulled the black 45 rpm off the white vinyl record player right in the middle of Paul Anka singing "Lonely Boy," broke it into three jagged pieces, chose the sharpest, and dragged it savagely across the pale skin of my right wrist. Only after much effort did I succeed in drawing blood. I remember feeling pleased, smug even, with an odd sense of power as I sat there bleeding in my pink flannel nightgown and bunny rabbit slippers, my latest Babar book next to me on the floor. *My life is my own!* I longed to shout. Adults would regret the bad things they had done to me, though I needed to stay alive to enjoy their regret . . .

Timothy opened the bathroom door without knocking and pulled me into a tight embrace. The rugged yet soft texture of his lambswool sweater brought me back to the present, and his familiar smell laced with the acrid smoke of Camels infused me with life.

"You were in here so long, I got worried," he said. "I just called the airport and confirmed our plane reservations, Vienna to Kabul. The flight leaves at 6:50 in the morning via Beirut. We'll stop there and spend your birthday on the Mediterranean, just like I promised you, then go on to Kabul. The only catch is that we need your money with ours for the plane fare—and we won't be able to pay the hotel bill." A shadow fell over his face.

From the other room, Dennis laughed diabolically. "Hey, where we're going you won't need all these winter clothes you've been toting around. Velvet pants, high boots, cashmere sweaters—you won't need any of it. We'll ask Rayatollah to bring us to the best seamstress in Kabul and she'll make you new clothes, breezy dresses, and cool summery skirts. You'll be the best dressed woman in Afghanistan."

Too staggered to argue, I put on my coolest air. "Yes, that's how we'll do it—leave everything, my Pentax camera and lenses, Timothy's skis and ski boots, our binoculars and astronomy books, my coat and shoes. I'll write a note to the concierge explaining that we are in a life and death situation and have to flee. I'll tell him to keep all our things as a guarantee that we will pay when we can."

My heart quaked at every word. *First my style, then my health, and now my word.* We had been at the hotel for almost three weeks, my word and name a guarantee for impeccable service and hospitality, despite the bill incident in Lausanne. The thought of betraying the confidence of the people who served me was almost unbearable.

I wrote the note in French with careful and courteous phrasing, and three hours later, in the yellow-grey of dawn, slowly packed the few things I wasn't leaving into a brown leather carry-on: black cashmere sweater, toilet kit, cosmetics, cassette tapes, journal, my stuffed dog Arthur that Mummy had given me after my first abortion at fourteen, and my little pillow. I took one last look around the room, my eyes heavy with sadness as I surveyed the elegant bed with the mink coat spread over it, the ten pairs of shoes and boots on the floor of the open closet. While checking to make sure I had my passport, a supply of Gauloise and my Cricket lighter, I came across the green card that had been wangled for me by a diplomatic friend on my first trip to the States. The photograph was of a young woman very *comme il faut*, wearing a St. Laurent silk blouse with a tidy bow. Without hesitation, I set the card on fire in the ashtray and stood there for a moment hallucinating in the play of the flames.

Bardo Express

PART II

The Turnkey

"The greater a man's talents, the greater his power to lead astray. It is better that one should suffer than that many should be corrupted. Consider the matter dispassionately, Mr. Foster, and you will see that no offense is so heinous as unorthodoxy of behavior. Murder kills only the individual—and, after all, what is an individual?"
   Aldous Huxley, *Brave New World*, 1932

32

PRESTOMICO

Beirut, January 16, 1973

En route to Beirut, I regaled Timothy with my experience there in 1962 when I was sixteen, two years after Mahmoud in Egypt. Mummy and I had gone to live in Hamra, the chic section of Beirut. When I wasn't in school, I would wander the Paris of the Middle East, and at night, if Mummy didn't have a date, would go with her and her friends to the disco Les Caves du Roi at the Hotel St. Georges where Levantine men would ogle my porcelain doll face with its high forehead, wide-set eyes, and when I smiled, astounding dimples.

Once Mummy began pursuing her philosophy of having to have three lovers—a banker for the cheque, a diplomat for the chic, and a gigolo for the shock—I was often left alone in our empty elegant rooms, at least until she acquired one of the three, a young travel agent who came to join her late at night to wrest sighs and moans from her that embarrassingly filtered into my room. After him, she occupied herself with the ex-president of the Republic. In the late afternoon, his long black Cadillac limo would pull up in front of our house amidst a horde of Arab children begging for money. When the doorman buzzed our apartment, Mummy would walk down the corridor in one of her elegant cocktail dresses and satin high heels, kiss me on the cheek, and say, "Tomorrow when you go to school, don't put on those short white socks the nuns make you wear. What a provocative sight! Wear stockings and tell the nuns I told you to do it."

One night, while I was watching the quiz show *Who Is Lying?* on Tele Beirut, smoking Mummy's Chesterfields, and sipping warm whiskey—I hated the taste but loved the soothing rush—I got the number of the station from information, dialed, and asked to speak to the producer of the show. In no time, a masculine voice answered in French.

Thanks to the whiskey, I said, "I'm Joanna and I'm sixteen years old. I know all the answers to your questions and want to be a contestant on your show next week."

"It so happens we have a cancellation,," the man purred, "so why don't you come? Be here next Wednesday at four o'clock."

The next week, I was there with heavy mascara, dyed blond hair piled high Bardot-style, a black velvet miniskirt, knee-high socks, and black suede moccasins. Under the hot studio lights and the implacable eyes of three cameras, I was unable to answer one question. I'd been wrong about my miraculous influence. I had no charm, no magic. What I had were a lot of good reasons to hate myself and an exclusive address to do it at.

But then the program director approached and hired me on the spot for my own weekly show, *The Teenager's Club*.

Timothy laughed.

"*C'est vrai*, Timothy," I said. "In a few months, I was known all over Lebanon. I stopped going to school and devoted myself to rehearsals and broadcasting, posed for magazine covers—I even made a poetic film about the Baalbek ruins shown that year at the Cannes television festival. I had affairs with most of the directors at the station who then found parts for me on their shows. I appeared as a guest on variety shows, even as a host on some of them. People in the street asked for my autograph. But it all ended as abruptly as my mother's affair with the ex-president. Mummy said it was time to return to Paris, we had a big fight, and that was that. *C'est ça*."

In Beirut, we had no problems at Customs and Immigration— apparently, they were not on the alert for Timothy here. As soon as we were settled into the sleazy hotel Ariana Airlines had provided for our one-night stopover, I began making phone calls and at last could tell Timothy that I had a birthday surprise waiting for him. In no time we were in a taxi heading across town to Tele Beirut—I even remembered how to say the address in Arabic. When we arrived, the same program director who had hired me ten years before greeted us and agreed to exchange favors: Timothy and I would watch the reels of my show in exchange for a news crew Leary interview.

In the comforting darkness of the screening room, my head on Timothy's shoulder, we watched a very young glowing girl slightly resembling Brigitte Bardot conduct interviews and perform skits, fully at ease with the cameras. Dozens of expressions flowed over her face, and her enthusiasm spread to the school kids singing songs on the show. Performing a magic act one moment and a funny monologue about pets or plugging products the next, she never faltered. *Who was this me ten years ago?*

"You're great," Timothy whispered again and again. "I'll make you famous. Soon, you'll be known all over the world."

Little did we know how prophetic his words would be.

After the interview, we went in search of friends of Timothy's friends from Switzerland. The afternoon sun was low and hot, melting away in perceptible waves over the lapis Mediterranean. Still burnt orange from the hepatitis, I was reluctant to move at full speed as we wandered past lemonade vendors whose tinkling silver and copper cups strung across their backs made my head ache. Everywhere, ragged and dirty children pulled at our clothes and begged for money. At last, a white Cadillac stopped and we climbed into the back seat. Immediately, the young couple in front passed us a hashish joint. I inhaled deeply, hoping that the dope would bring my energy back up as it sometimes did. It was my 27th birthday and I wanted to celebrate but felt weak and nauseous and stricken by a sensation that I was going to die. I was not really tired; I was dying. Life was draining out of me with each exhale. I made a supreme effort to keep my hand in Timothy's so I could borrow on his strength.

The car had stopped and he was carrying me to the elevator in a white high-rise. On the 14th floor we entered a completely empty apartment with long corridors and huge bedrooms—a wedding present to the young couple from their parents, but no furniture would be forthcoming until the wedding in May. I collapsed on the wall-to-wall carpet of the huge empty living room and tucked my knees under my chin, already very stoned on hashish when Hassan, a tall Lebanese with narrow eyes and a thick mustache, produced green tabs of LSD.

"Take this," Timothy said, handing me a tab, "it's your birthday and whatever happens, this will make you feel better. I've kept my promise to take you to the seaside for your birthday. Beyond the balcony is the Mediterranean glittering under the stars." He grinned.

I swallowed the acid as he watched, flashing on Huxley's death in *A Timeless Moment. Shit*, I thought in a moment of lucidity, *I'm the one who's going to die here*. Like so many other things in my life, what I had imagined was happening, all right, but in a twisted way.

We watched the city and the sea from the balcony for a while, then I asked Timothy to take me back to our sleazy hotel room because I wanted some private time with him before our flight in the morning. On the way back, the acid was peaking and I began feeling excited and alive again. At a pharmacy, I jumped out of the cab and bought a bottle of black hair dye.

At the hotel, we hopped into the bath together and I smeared black paste all over his silver hair. He was laughing, totally amused and without apprehension, all the while kissing and caressing my breasts. We moved from the bathroom to the bed and were making love when I remembered the goo on his head that should have been rinsed out after twenty minutes, however long ago that was. So we frolicked our way back into the bathroom, but the black dye had taken full effect: Timothy had a full head of purple hair. We loved it.

The next morning he looked like the Acid King himself in a silver lamé shirt, purple satin pants, and hair to match. I wore high-heeled platform boots, a pair of light blue Levi's, and a white sweater with a big pink sun on it. On my finger was the gold tantric ring. The change agents were ready to fly.

When our plane took off for Kabul, I was sandwiched between Timothy and Dennis. A long shiver went through my body as Timothy whispered something in my ear. I couldn't make out the strange word and asked him to repeat it.

"*Prestomico*," he whispered, "the word used a few seconds after launch, when a spacecraft reaches the velocity at which it can no longer return to the Earth."

Yet more prophetic words.

33

THE AFGHANI CONNECTION

Kabul, January 19, 1973

Out the window was the blue expanse of a cloudless sky over magnificent snow-laden mountains that could have been the Alps. We were descending into Kabul International Airport. I squeezed Timothy's hand and glanced at Dennis in the aisle seat. He looked distinctly tense.

Glancing back at me, he reconfigured his face. "We'll check into the Intercontinental," he said, "then I'll go out to Rayatollah's house and tell him you're here." To me in my still-orange skin, he added, "A few good nights sleep and you'll be fine."

I was filled with anticipation, imagining the Far East to be much as it was at the time of Marco Polo, with lounging camels and colorful vendors. Outside, the air was crisp and clean, and the light reflecting off of the mountains was the color of pomegranates. Inside the terminal, Dennis made his way toward the window where an Afghani immigration officer was stamping passports while Timothy and I sat down on a bench to catch our breath and share a hug and kiss, relieved to be together and safe at last. The refugees had found their sanctuary.

Suddenly, a short man with a clipped moustache was standing over us. "Are you Timothy Leary?" he asked.

His voice held an unnerving tension that cut into my skin. Then, without waiting for an answer, he snatched both of our passports out of Timothy's hand, thrust a calling card in their place saying *James Senner, Attaché, US Embassy, Kabul*, turned on his heel, and headed briskly out of the terminal.

Timothy jumped up and started yelling. "Hey you! My passport! You stole my passport!" Every cell of my body was struck rigid with terror.

Dennis, frowning and looking helpless, came up to us with a couple of shabby hippies I took to be American. "This is it," he shrugged, "they're taking us back to the United States."

One of the hippies asked Timothy, "What can I do for you?"

"Give me some money, I'm going to need it," Timothy replied.

The young man pulled a billfold from his jeans and with a weak smile gave Timothy twenty dollars.

An Afghani woman in uniform approached and said in English, "I am from immigration and I want to see your passports."

"A man from the American embassy named James Senner was just here," Timothy said, reading the card in his hand. "He took our passports right out of my hand and went off with them." He pointed. "That way, over there."

Without acknowledging what Timothy had said, the Afghani woman replied, "If you have no passports and therefore no visas, we will have to arrest you and incarcerate you until you are deported."

Timothy tried again, assuming an offended, patient tone of voice. "We have passports, but they have been stolen by my own embassy."

Then, he lost it and started yelling. Men in trench coats moved to surround us. I grabbed Timothy's arm as I watched Dennis hurry out of the terminal. At that point, I thought that he at least had been able to get away and hoped he might find some help for us.

A man in a black leather coat emerged from the trench coats. "You have no papers," he said, "and must come with me to the airport police station."

"No, no," I said, reading the name and function off of the card Timothy was holding, "James Senner, Third Secretary at the American Embassy, has our passports. Check with him." I was having trouble breathing.

Assuming a stern expression, the Afghani policeman pretended not to understand. Timothy and I gave each other a look that said, "Let's get on with it."

We followed the man to a stone and mud hut just outside the terminal. I was really afraid now and started crying very hard. Timothy braced me tightly with his arm and said, "Dennis was right. They're going to take me back."

A man in uniform was sitting at a tiny desk in the corner of a square room with a mud floor pretending to read some papers. Only a desk lamp and two small barred windows provided light, like the sheriff's office in American cowboy films, except no amiable cowboys in sight. Timothy looked pale and frightened and I could not stop shaking, but no one seemed to notice or care. I forced myself to approach the man at the desk and ask him what was happening. He signaled that he spoke no English.

Timothy came up beside me and insisted, "We want our passports back. We demand to be returned to Beirut. This is an international scandal."

I backed him up. "Call the British embassy. Get the Consul on the phone immediately. You cannot detain me or you will be in big trouble."

The chief of police had been watching all of this from the doorway as if he had nothing better to do. Barking at the soldiers in Afghani, he leveled his gaze at us and called across the room coldly in good English, "We are now going to take you to prison until we decide what to do with you." Pointing his finger, he continued. "You will go to the men's side, and you to the women's prison. The charge is that you have tried to enter Afghanistan without passports."

My whole body ached from my illness and the impact of his devastating words, but my mind was suddenly crystal clear, racing and calculating. This was a moment for total obsession, and I knew something about obsession. I strode over to the chief of police who was much taller than I and locked onto his eyes a look of intense determination charged with icy hatred. In a very low voice I slowly said, "As you can see, I am very ill. Look at my eyes. If you separate us, I assure you that I will die and you will have to take responsibility for a terrible scandal. I am the daughter of powerful people in Europe, a British national. I am completely innocent and have committed no crime in your land or elsewhere. You will regret what you are doing now. I am telling you not to separate us or I will die and you will regret your stupidity for making me a martyr in whatever crazy deal you have made with the Americans." Having spoken, I let my eyes roll back inside my head and my knees buckle.

Timothy swept to my side and caught me. The Afghani was leaning over me, checking me out. The intensity of my determination had reached him. I had spoken to him in English, but in German he said, "I can see that you are a real troublemaker. Wait here, I'll be back."

Timothy led me to a chair and sat me down, kneeling beside me.

"This is a terrible nightmare," I whispered to him. "The Afghani secret policeman is really a German, probably a Nazi war criminal who wandered off the beaten track." Laughing at my own joke did not prevent my mind from racing away with terrifying questions. "God, what is going to happen to us? Will they torture us? Will they kill us? Does anybody know we're here?"

"Don't worry," Timothy soothed me, "they're making a deal with Nixon. They're going to trade me for as many helicopters and tanks as they can get. They won't hurt us, we're too precious to them." He had seen through the whole situation.

Suddenly, six soldiers erupted into the mud police station, surrounding and pushing us toward the door. Grunting and prodding us with the butts of their machine guns, they boarded us onto a jeep, Timothy and I in the back, men hanging from the side bars. It was now after sunset. Colors everywhere had deepened to mauve and a dark, deep pink that blended with the red earth. I pulled my light shawl over my shoulders, shivering with cold and fear. This was the most exotic place I'd ever been, the farthest east I'd ever traveled, and here I was in a military jeep rumbling off into oblivion.

We drove a few kilometers down a rocky dirt road toward what looked like the center of town. The soldiers hustled us out of the jeep and into another hut where they made us sit on two folding chairs. The room was filled with men and women in colorful scarves sitting on the floor and sprawled against the walls holding chickens and pigs. An unattended sheep wandered around the room, the bell on its neck tinkling erratically. Against the far wall, a man in a red turban was sitting next to a small brass wood-burning stove closely observing two men who were yelling at each other. The violent stream of Afghani sounded like the tower of Babel. I had spoken five languages since I was twelve and added Arabic when I was fifteen, but this was like nothing I had ever heard. The language was so disorienting that I lost all sense of where we were.

"This must be a tribunal of some kind," Timothy said in a low voice, "an Afghani version of night court."

The two men ceased yelling, but the room was still raucous with the sound of cackling chickens and complaining women.

Timothy got up and approached the man in the turban. "If you are a judge, you must recognize the mistake being made here. We are being detained illegally. You have no right to keep us here. We have done nothing wrong. We demand that our passports be returned to us so that we can check into the Hotel Intercontinental."

Except for the cackling of the chickens, a hush came over the room. The man took a long look at both of us. "I am the judge of this district," he announced proudly. Once again, I was surprised that anyone in this remote place had such a command of English. "I am acting by the laws. I know that you have escaped from prison in your own country. Also, you have tried to enter Afghanistan without passports," he continued, shifting his eyes to me to indicate that he meant both of us. "This is not allowed. You will go to the Plaza Hotel and remain under house arrest until we decide what to do with you." He looked at me again and smiled. "Don't worry, you will be able to rest soon."

Timothy tried to protest, but the judge waved him down and issued a quick hard order to the soldiers who then led us out of the hut, prodding us again with their gun butts. The sun had set but everything outside looked like it had been shot through a lilac filter with bright light. For the first time, I noticed the extent of the maze of cobblestoned streets lit by gas lanterns snaking off in several directions. People were standing about but the scene was uncannily quiet, as if everyone were walking about in Abu Kassim's slippers. I felt immediate warmth toward the colorful, soft-clad strangers milling about. In quest of a pair of eyes to witness our situation, I scanned the faces, but everyone was preoccupied with their own little theatre.

Prestomico. We had taken all the acid at lift-off in Beirut and the last of the dose was definitely in effect. I had the excruciating urge to linger over every amplified sight and sound, and simultaneously to crawl out of my uncomfortable skin. When I saw the glowing tangerines stacked in a squat pyramid at a food stall that were roughly the same color as my skin, I took a few halting steps toward them on the uneven cobbles. Coming down from acid always made me thirsty. In a salutary act of kindness, a soldier ducked around me, snatched up a handful of the tangerines, and handed them to me as we turned to remount the jeep. Ecstatic, I peeled the skins and tossed them languidly into the street like Hansel's breadcrumbs.

Far from the usual *haute couture* I had come to associate with the name, the Plaza Hotel was a rundown adobe building of two uneven floors. Even the z from *Plaza* was missing. I felt dizzy and slightly delirious as they pushed us through the creaking entrance to a "reception room" lit by a single bare bulb. Paint was peeling off the walls and a heap of cane chairs had been tumbled in one corner. No one at the desk, no sign of a telephone anywhere. Obviously, this Plaza had not been a hotel for some time.

"This doesn't look so good," I whispered. Timothy just arched his brows and squinted.

A peculiar hush had followed us in from the street and continued to dog us to the second floor where we were locked into a room with three cots and no windows. The only light filtered from the hall through a single opaque pane in the door. I felt a draft and the distinct presence of creeping things. After the door was resoundingly locked, Timothy and I stood for a long moment staring into that lonely shaft of light, then collapsed onto one of the cots. Neither of us spoke for what could have been hours or minutes, there being no way to sense the passage of acid time nor the direction it might be taking.

Suddenly, I had an idea. "Let's take our clothes off and get in bed naked. This way if they want to take us anywhere else, we can refuse to get dressed." (The truth was I was terrified they were going to take us out and shoot us.) I undressed and climbed under a rough grey blanket. Timothy sat next to me and rubbed my temples to dissipate the terrible migraine that had seized me the moment we'd stepped off the plane, then he too undressed and slipped in beside me. Through the frosted glass in the door, we could see the silhouettes of soldiers moving back and forth in the hallway. Besides guarding us, they played cards, shouted at each other, made threats, and cheered.

I must have slept because the next thing I knew I was staring at the ceiling, my eyes glazed over with dreams. I smelled fear, plus I needed to go to the bathroom. I kissed Timothy's face in the semi-darkness and whispered, "I need to get up and go to the bathroom, but I'm afraid. What should I do?"

He stirred and sat up, then lifted me toward him and whispered that we must both get dressed. He got the guards to open the door and used minimal words to explain what we wanted. His voice sounded old and far away. Suppressing sniggers, two soldiers led us down the hallway to a doorless room with a tiny sink and toilet, the white bowl stained and clotted with brown deposits. We froze just inside the doorway, holding our breath in unison, staring at the bowl as the soldiers edged up behind us, waiting and watching in silence. Timothy stepped past me as if he were going to use the toilet first. As I leaned against the doorjamb and folded my arms across my tummy, he pulled a handkerchief from his pocket, wet it under the dripping faucet, then got down on his knees and began scrubbing the filthy edge of the bowl.

34

AEGEAN DREAMS

We passed the next day in a listless funk, unable to keep any conversation going for more than ten minutes or so. Timothy was pensive, keeping to his thoughts. He took a moment now and then to speak comforting words and massage my forehead; my body had turned a still deeper shade of livid orange. Every time I looked at him, I remembered the expression on his face as he knelt to clean the toilet. The switch for our single bare light bulb was outside the door, so we had to ask a guard to turn it on and off. A few times a day, we were brought *chai* and flat bread.

Dennis was allowed to visit us at about six that evening. He looked haggard and edgy, unshaven, with deep circles under his eyes, but his clothes were surprisingly neat and clean. "My poor friends," he began, "Kabul is crawling with English and American press trying to find out what has happened to you two. Rayatollah's neighbor told me he left for the mountains two days ago and nobody knows when he'll be back. I tried to get an audience with the king, but he also is out of town, and other members of the court are vacationing in Kandahar . . . I have an appointment tomorrow at the American Embassy, but I'm afraid if I go there they'll arrest me. Your situation looks pretty bad, Tim, I'm sure you're going to be deported. As you suspected, it must be some deal with the Nixon people."

I glared at him steadily, unable to sort out my impressions. He too had taken refuge in Europe but was walking around outside, while Timothy . . .

But at least he brought us some lunch from the Intercontinental: two club sandwiches bulging with chicken and bacon and all the trimmings, fresh tangerines and oranges. I laid out the sumptuous feast at the end of the rusty cot where the three of us sat in a huddle. Timothy pulled a Marlboro out of one of the several packs Dennis had brought. As soon as I took a huge bite of the club sandwich, I felt light and nauseous.

Noticing my discomfort and grinning mischievously, Dennis said, "I managed to score some hash from a vendor at the market. This will take care of you." He lit up a chunky joint, puffed deeply, and passed it to me. The taste of fine Afghani green was lovely, with a strong sweet nuance I could not quite place. "Opium," Dennis remarked, "Afghani hash often has opium in it."

Immediately, I felt the anesthetic effect seeping into my body and bringing relief. We three sat in silence as the oppressive grey room began to transform—even the single naked bulb glowed more cozily. Sarangi music playing on the transistor radio at the guard's station down the hall filtered under the door like an exotic perfume. For an instant, I could register where I was without feeling impaled on a shaft of searing pain and fear.

Dennis said he had to leave but promised to return with candles and other treats. "I love you," he said to Timothy, "and I'll get you out of here one way or another." Then he put his arms around me and kissed me lightly on the lips. I felt how thin and wiry he was, recalling his years of hatha yoga. It was the closest bodily contact we'd had so far, too close for my comfort, but I let it pass since he was our only lifeline in this forsaken place.

The next morning we were awakened by two men in black suits, black shirts, and black ties identifying themselves as secret police of the King of Afghanistan. I tried to imagine what American films they had been watching. They stood side by side, their backs to the door, and watched us as silently as Poe ravens. Timothy talked to them in a nervous, exasperated voice, but they said nothing. I began to doubt that they understood a word he was saying when one of them broke silence.

"Your views are interesting, professor, but of no importance in this situation. You are a very important person in your country and we don't understand why. We are told, but don't understand. Can you explain who you are and what is so important about you?"

Timothy sighed, whether from relief or exasperation I couldn't tell, and plunged into a monologue that was by now becoming quite familiar to me. "I'm a political refugee. I have been persecuted for my ideas in the United States and was imprisoned for what I think, not anything I did. You must realize that this can happen in America, too. Against my choice, I had to leave my country and become a man without a country. I was hoping that the King of Afghanistan was an honorable man, brave enough to accept Joanna and me as his guests for a while. Unfortunately, I see I may have been wrong about that."

The two agents exchanged looks, then the one who had spoken before shook his head slowly. "I still do not understand your problem, Mr. Leary, but I will tell you that all is not as you suppose here in Afghanistan. The king will not last much longer. We are a free people and we will never accept submission to any outside power. Afghani people are strong and proud. You ask to be free, and we have our own struggle to be free. At this time, professor, you must understand that we can do nothing for you." (The Soviet-Afghanistan war would begin in 1979 and rage on until 1988.)

After they left, I began sobbing uncontrollably until the sobs turned into choking laughter, shaking me like a rag doll. "What a situation," I sniffled. "Not only are we left in this fucking cell to rot, but the whole country's about to go up in flames." Suddenly, revolution didn't look all that romantic. I dropped facedown onto the cot and buried my face in my hands. "I feel like we're starring in *The Great Escape* but haven't been coached on how to bust through this wall and jump onto the BMW motorcycle."

Timothy rubbed his hand up and down my back. "You came to free me, remember? Now, we must free ourselves. We are perfect lovers and whatever happens we are going to be transformed."

I continued to weep nonstop as the tedious hours crawled by. I was terribly hungry but could not digest anything. The *chai* brought in throughout the day was certainly safer to drink than water from the tap down the hall, but left me on edge. At night, I could not sleep for caffeine and obsession and clung to Timothy's body like a drowning woman as he made love to me, rocking me softly and whispering, reassuring me with extravagant words.

Midday of the third day of our internment, a handsome brown-skinned Afghani dressed in elegant slacks, a yellow shirt, and red velvet vest was admitted. Ali, favorite nephew of the king, was in awe of Timothy.

"I went to school in Berkeley in the late Sixties," Ali informed us, "I have read all your books, Dr. Leary. I have also taken a lot of LSD and followed your guidance about how to have a trip that is spiritually directed." His words glowed with respect.

Despite the circumstances, I listened intently. I had not yet read any of Timothy's books and had no idea what kind of guidance Ali was talking about—or was I getting guidance when Timothy whispered to me, which he seemed to do a lot?

Effusive and generous, Ali gave us some high-grade opium to ease the boredom of confinement and proposed to do an interview with Tim on the spot. "I have brought a tape recorder so we can have a good talk which I can take to my uncle. He will hear your words and recognize what kind of man you are, then maybe he will give orders to set you free."

"Great idea, Ali," Timothy said, "let's do it. But you must insist that I am not here alone. Joanna has been involved in this terrible mistake and is completely innocent. No matter where I go from here, even if I have to return to the States, I won't go without her, nor cooperate unless she is included in my every move."

I felt both proud and alarmed by what he was saying but couldn't sort out the nuances. I was so exhausted, it was practically impossible for me to maintain a coherent thought for more than a few seconds.

Throughout the long interview, I lay supine on one of the cots, drifting in and out on an opium sea. Soon, I was really gone, as was my hunger and fear, floating with slow drift of the blue Aegean on a balmy summer day. My body with its hepatitis and raw, frayed nerves dissolved into the crummy straw mattress as if into a cloud. I felt a bliss like that of a child in the womb. Now and then, I caught Timothy's attention and winked at him. Without dropping a stitch in the animated conversation with Ali, he would wink back with sparkling eyes. Eventually, I was aroused from my opiate Aegean by Ali.

"What should I bring for my next visit, Joanna?"

A slow, underwater voice reeled off candles, incense, some Rolling Stones tapes like *Let It Bleed* and *Sticky Fingers*, more hashish and more opium.

Ali smiled and nodded. "Keep the tape recorder and I'll be back with the rest."

I slipped back to the Aegean while Timothy was walking briskly around the small room, taking a bit of exercise or working off the energy generated by the interview, ebullient and irrepressible, his feet not even touching the floor.

That night for the first time since we had entered this nightmare, I slept soundly, dead to the world.

35

WE WALK THE PLANK

January 19, 1973

The next day, neither Dennis nor Ali reappeared, but around midday the door was flung open and we were roused by several soldiers.

"You must get up!" the leader shouted. "You are coming with us to the airport! Now!"

I turned to Timothy and clapped my hands. "Bravo, Ali! The interview must have worked. We are going to be set free. I'll bet they are putting us on a plane back to Beirut."

Timothy was aglow and hugged me ferociously. "You see, it works! I told you that perfect love conquers all."

I was so thrilled to be getting out of there that I took no account of how weak I was from the combination of not eating, being sick, and smoking dope. In four days my jeans now hung on my hips, my hair was greasy and smelling of opium, and my legs as wobbly as Bambi's. Timothy put his arm around my waist and helped me down the stairs and out into the impossibly bright day and street noises so amplified that I had to keep staring down at the red dirt beneath my feet to stop my head from bursting. His wide and breezy stride carried me along as though I was his Siamese twin along for the ride.

In their usual fashion the soldiers prodded us with their gun butts toward the waiting jeep that then sped us to the runway and up to a 727 with PAN AMERICAN painted in bright red along the fuselage.

"This is not a good sign," Timothy grimaced.

At the foot of the stairway stood a seedy Pakistani doctor who wanted me to sign a makeshift document reading, "I, JOANNA HARCOURT-SMITH, HEREBY RELEASE THE AFGHANI GOVERNMENT FROM ALL RESPONSIBILITY FOR MY PHYSICAL CONDITION IN THE EVENT THAT I DIE ON MY TRIP ORIGINATING FROM KABUL INTERNATIONAL AIRPORT."

With the soldiers crowded around us, Timothy read the statement over my shoulder. Before I could say anything, he turned to the doctor and snapped, "Miss Harcourt-Smith will not sign this paper until you give us back our passports." The doctor glanced sharply at one of the guards and the muzzle of a machine gun glanced off my spine. The doctor held out his ballpoint pen and clicked it.

"Signature and date, please."

I signed. Entire patches of my visual field were missing.

The soldiers then gestured that we mount the stairway. Timothy's purple hair was glinting luridly in the bright sun and somewhere on the periphery, people were snapping pictures. Suddenly, the chief of police we had encountered on the first day, the one who had spoken to me in German, appeared at my side as if disgorged from a crack in the ground. He made to take my elbow and assist me up the stairs. I balked and threw all my weight toward Timothy. We both froze on the spot.

"I will not enter this airplane until my passport is returned and I am told where this plane is going," Timothy announced, setting his face into the hardest expression I had ever seen on it.

His eyes steady as steel, the policeman replied, "This plane is going to Beirut and your passports will be given to you as soon as you board."

Timothy and I looked at each other, then at the stairs, pulling closer together, waiting for the strength to do whatever we were going to do next. When we finally made our move, it felt like we were stepping over, or into, an abyss.

36

THE PRODIGAL SON RETURNS

Cairo, January 19, 1973

Fighting gravity all the way, Timothy and I took the long, slow eighteen steps up the stairway of the PAN AM jetliner. At the doorway to the first class cabin, we were greeted by a tall, formidably built man with a thin beard and full tan. His grinning mouth revealed impeccable white teeth. "Burke's the name and dope's the game. BNDD, stick 'em up," he quipped. "I'm here to bring you back to the United States, Dr. Leary."

I couldn't believe my ears and thought wildly that everything might take on a different meaning if only I knew what BNDD stood for. The truth was, BNDD was kidnapping us, what today is known as an *extraordinary rendition*.

"Bureau of Narcotics and Dangerous Drugs," Timothy said in true telepathic form without looking at me.

Burke, still beaming, handed me my passport with a first-class Kabul-Los Angeles ticket tucked into it. He also handed over Timothy's passport, cancelled on every page except the last where it had been stamped *Valid only for return to the United States*. In addition to his first class ticket, he'd been issued a special US ID. Next to the entry for profession it read "Philosopher."

Burke gestured for us to take our seats, but Timothy held back. "There is no extradition treaty between Afghanistan and the United States. This arrest is illegal."

Burke smiled confidently. "You're wrong there, Professor. This is an American plane, you are standing on American soil." The glint of triumph was in his large brown eyes.

It was a full flight and we were the very last to board. People in coach class were leaning into the aisle to gander at the first-class passengers who had caused the delay. I moved to take my seat, too exhausted to stand any longer. Even before we had time to get buckled in, the plane was taking off. Two agents were sitting behind us, both dressed as Burke look-alikes in blue suits, white nylon shirts, impeccably knotted ties. They nodded slowly, parodies of old-time acquaintances. As they stretched out and opened their jackets, I noticed the big .357 Magnums they were packing—definitely not the kind of magnums I was used to when flying first class. Still, even this was a relief from the accommodations of the past four days. Timothy, on the other hand, looked tense and hyper-vigilant, but I was too exhausted to concern myself with what he might be thinking.

As the jet climbed, Timothy said in a stage-loud voice, looking straight ahead, "I am being taken back to be locked up again. I know what it's like, monotonous and ugly. It will be tough, but I can face it. I know how it works in there, you just have to obey the rules and things go smoothly." Turning to me, he continued quietly, "It will be much harder for you on the outside. I wish I could be with you to show you California and introduce you to everyone. It's very sad what's happening to us, but it can't change our fate altogether. We still have the Perfect Love." He put his arm around me. As I cuddled into his shoulder, he whispered, "Let's watch carefully for a way to escape, maybe during one of the stopovers. I'm not going to let them get away with this." I let him know with my eyes that I understood.

At lunchtime the stewardess brought me a vegetarian meal of rice and steamed vegetables. "Just what you need for your hepatitis," she confided with a smile. I was impressed, and spooked, by the efficiency of the BNDD operation. I chatted with her a little and found out that we were due to land in Istanbul before reaching our ultimate destination of Orly Airport in Paris. When she left, I turned excitedly to Timothy.

"Listen, this is great," I whispered, "there's a good chance we can get away at some point. We're going to Paris where we'll have to change planes and I can get us out of this mess. When we get there, I will run for a French immigration official and tell him who you are and that you have been illegally kidnapped by American authorities. The French love intellectuals and will protect you from the Americans," I assured him, jerking my eyes toward the agents behind us. "They will separate us from these sinister guardian angels. Perhaps they will have to put you in jail, but I'll get the best lawyer in Paris—I already know exactly who to call—and we'll fight your extradition to the United States."

"Bravo, *faites un scandal*," Timothy said, his face taking on that uncanny glow of radiant confidence that was so irresistible and endearing. Once again, I felt the thrill of how close we were.

An hour later, the captain's voice announced that due to our late departure from Kabul we would not be able to land at Orly as the airport closes at ten o'clock. Instead, we would go on to Frankfurt where passengers could make alternative flight arrangements. He made the usual apologies for inconvenience and signed off.

This change in plans jolted me out of a fantasy of me cruising around Paris showing Timothy where to get the best croissant and the best *saucisson et fromage*. Surely the BNDD had changed our destination because they knew the French would never collaborate in such a travesty of justice. Besides, the US had a stronger hold on Germany, given that it was still under sanctions for war crimes.

But how could these BNDD have the power to do that? I cursed myself for not suspecting that the BNDD men might overhear me discussing my plan with Timothy. We were in a different world now; I would have to watch every word I said, even the whispered ones. Timothy agreed with my analysis of what had happened.

"I wonder how the other passengers feel about this," I said angrily, snapping my red Cricket at a Gauloise. Puffing furiously, I ripped a few pages out of my diary, tore them into half a dozen strips, and wrote carefully on each one, three in French and three in English, *I am Dr. Timothy Leary. I have been kidnapped illegally by American authorities.*

Please help me when we get to Frankfurt. Alert the press and the police. Do what you can to help me.

Telling the narcs I had to go to the bathroom, I bypassed the first class toilet and slipped through the curtains and walked down the aisle to the back of the plane, dropping the crumpled slips of paper in the laps of some of the passengers, many of whom were complaining bitterly in French about the change in flight plans.

Since there was no guarantee the notes would produce results, I had another plan for Frankfurt. As we prepared to land, I called the stewardess. "I badly need to see a doctor. I am very, very ill and feel so weak I don't know if I'm going to live." I spoke with urgency, wondering if what I was saying was actually true.

When we landed, a wheelchair was waiting for me at the gate but no doctor as I had requested, no one whom I could persuade to collude with us and get us outside help. Herded by a pack of eight agents, we were taken into the empty Pan American first class lounge presumably sealed off especially for us. Immediately, I curled up on a huge black leather sofa, the best thing I'd seen in weeks. I had to get some real rest to keep my mind clear enough to keep working on our escape.

When I awoke just before dawn, I smelled coffee brewing and heard the distant, muffled sound of someone being paged. All around me, narcotic agents with Timothy among them were breathing deep en masse, covered in airline blankets on the thick wall-to-wall carpet. There must have been a change of guard in the middle of the night, given that a new man was standing at the lounge entrance. When he saw me stirring, he winked at me as if we shared some rare secret. Now strong enough to get up, I drifted over to ask him if I could make a phone call. Sure enough, he said, as if it were the easiest thing in the world.

From a booth just outside the lounge, I placed a collect call to my mother in Paris who had been up all night with the French and British papers. I detected a touch of pride in her voice as she commented on how much coverage we were getting. I assured her that Timothy was completely innocent.

Returning to the first class lounge, I went into the bathroom to freshen up. I desperately needed to brush my teeth, but five minutes of rummaging through my bag turned up nothing but the realization that I did not even have ten cents to my name.

After breakfast, Timothy and I boarded PAN AM Flight 102 to London, where we would stay an hour and a half before taking the ten-hour non-stop polar route to Los Angeles. Perhaps we would have a chance in England.

At Heathrow, a flock of British immigration officers escorted our entourage to a transit area. One of the thirty-seven came up to me and said briskly, "Miss Harcourt-Smith, you are home now, come with me."

Defiant, I said, "No, I won't come. Even though I am British, I am going to follow Dr. Leary wherever he goes. I am not leaving his side under any circumstances. Whatever is done to him will have to be done to me, as well."

The officer looked at me, then turned away to confer with the BNDD agents. Suddenly, Timothy and I were being escorted to an escalator. I became excited. Now for the first time since this nightmare had begun, we were going to have some real exposure to the world outside. As we approached the transit lounge, I could see a frantic cluster of newsmen and photographers. *Fabulous*, I thought, *now this insane drama is going to take a different turn.*

The transit lounge had been prepared especially for us. At an oval table a woman from Immigration was pouring our tea from a huge pot into a nice china service, and there were biscuits and scones as only the English can make them. The press were chomping at the bit behind a rope, rigorously enforced by airport security. There was not a moment to waste. Timothy led me to the rope and we faced the clamoring crowd.

"I am here in Britain to demand political, intellectual, and spiritual asylum," he said, assuming an elegant and magisterial command. "Joanna and I believe the British have a great tradition of fair play. I am being returned to the US from a country that has no extradition with the United States. My capture is an illegal act and I demand asylum here, or at the very least to be sent back to Switzerland, Austria, Algeria or Afghanistan, countries in which I have been allowed to live freely. Until this moment, Joanna and I have not had one single chance to tell anyone the truth about what is being done to us. Your government has a responsibility to act in a way that is free and independent of American affairs. In my case, the American government has clearly violated all rules of procedure, and disregarded international laws. Don't cooperate with them."

When he finished, the head immigration officer standing nearby in his stunning blue and gold uniform told him flatly that any such request was impossible as he was on a blacklist of unwanted and undesirable persons, citing that Dr. Leary had smoked marijuana three years before while visiting John Lennon and Yoko Ono.

"Well, don't think this is the end of me yet," Timothy replied, half to the officer and half to the press, "this is doing nobody any good and before it's over a lot of heads will roll. Some people in high places in the States are already quaking in their shoes now that I'm on the way back."

To Burke lurking at my shoulder, I said, "He's right, it's not over, it's just beginning. It would be funny if you were to lose us after all this trouble, wouldn't it?" With a mixture of menace and mischief, I couldn't help adding, "I hope you get screwed for this."

Burke responded with a cavalier laugh, at which point the press erupted in full fury, most of their questions directed to me, wanting to know what my father Cecyl Harcourt-Smith and grandfather Arpad Plesch would think of my escapade.

"I don't care what anybody thinks," I retorted, "I am with Timothy. Where he goes, I go; what he does, I do."

My former ideas about what I might do to save the moment were spinning with no center of focus. It might be that I could save myself by withdrawing from the drama, but that was all. Later that day, our pictures would be on the front pages of all the London papers, with headlines like that of the January 18, 1973 *Daily Express*, "JOANNA FLIES OUT WITH 'LSD' LEARY" next to "NIXON RACES FOR PEACE."

When we were finally ushered onto the non-stop flight to Los Angeles, we were again given the two front seats in first class, with the Feds right behind us. I had no idea what would happen now. I had no US visa, having burned my green card in Vienna. But somehow I wasn't worried: being fully committed to staying with Timothy was all that mattered. Everything else would follow.

As we leveled out at 30,000 feet, Timothy was miles away out the window, absorbed in his own thoughts. I put my hand in his and said nothing. After a few minutes, I decided to see if I knew anyone in first class. Sure enough, I spotted Putzi's uncle, *Günther* Sachs von Opel, a German playboy I knew quite well from Paris. For years he had been the star of the winter scene at the bar of the Palace Hotel in St. Moritz, renowned for the flair of his seductions and was once married to my idol Brigitte Bardot.

Günther greeted me with a warm hug, exuding his marvelous air of ease. He was 36, tall and strong, with an aquiline nose and thick lips accentuating his German good looks, wearing a dark red silk scarf, a light blue shirt under a blue blazer, and grey flannel pants. I told him about our frightening adventure, then introduced him to Timothy. Charged by the combined attention of these two elegant men, I suddenly felt enormously energetic. The atmosphere in the cabin took on a manic edge as the stewardess began plying us with the usual complimentary first class champagne.

Along with our BNDD guardian angels, we moved to the empty upper lounge. I arranged cushions so that Gunther, Timothy, and I could sprawl out on the floor like pashas, then ordered more champagne and half a dozen Reuben sandwiches. We ate voraciously in a huddle as the pitch of excitement rose a few degrees higher. It was beginning to feel like many other trips I had taken in first class, a party with no limits in sight. Even the narcs were getting in on it, downing champagne and looking unabashedly thrilled to be along for the ride. Although I knew I must still be very sick, my old sense of power was making another appearance. I hadn't felt its full force since Timothy and I had left Switzerland. Drinking champagne non-stop, I relied on my uncanny skill to concentrate on the moment.

To Timothy, Günther was another example of the "hedonic elite" he was always talking about, and Günther approved of Timothy's natural ease and elegance. We told him about our stay at Chalet von Opel at Christmas, then Timothy explained his present situation at length. I was struck by how casual he sounded about going back to prison. He was much more concerned about abandoning me than his own fate, particularly regarding my serious need for medical care. His concern warmed me through and through. He entrusted me to Günther, who solemnly accepted the responsibility.

"As soon as the plane has landed, I will take Joanna straight to the Beverly Hills Hotel and get the care of the best doctor in Los Angeles," Günther promised.

Timothy thanked him and the party rolled on.

37

THE QUEEN OF DIAMONDS

Out the PAN AM window, Timothy pointed out the coast of California through a pair of binoculars we borrowed from the increasingly amiable narcs. I'd never been to California, but the name held enormous mystique, like the hymn sung at Woodstock, *If you're going to San Francisco, be sure to wear some flowers in your hair* . . .

"This is my world," Timothy smiled, "and now it's yours to play with." Opening his address book, he continued, "You are the Queen of Diamonds and these are your subjects. All of my contacts are in here. A lot of people will be waiting to see you. Many of them do not understand what I've been saying and have strong opinions about me. You can handle that, though. Call Art Kunkin first thing. He owns the *LA Free Press*. Tell him to organize a press conference for you. Then, call Allen Ginsberg . . . " He thumbed through the book, marking names he wanted me to call. "They're all good friends of mine and they'll help you."

In Europe, Timothy had never made even the vaguest mention of these people, and now our lives would depend upon them. For 49 days,

I had been no further than ten feet from this man and could not fully register that we were about to be brutally separated.

"What do you want me to do exactly?" I asked with a lump in my throat.

"Tell everyone that you are my wife and explain to them exactly what has happened to us. Get my lawyer to file an affidavit demanding that I be returned to Afghanistan." He looked into my eyes. "I'll meet you back in Kabul in three days."

Well, that was concise enough, simple and reasonable. At the moment, it sounded like a good plan. Three days. He wrote a note: "THIS IS TO INTRODUCE JOANNA HARCOURT-SMITH. SHE IS MY VOICE, MY LOVE, MY LIFE. SHE IS DESIGNATED TO ACT IN MY BEHALF. PLEASE ASSIST HER IN ANY WAY YOU CAN TO HELP ME GET FREE." He signed it, "Timothy Leary AMERIKA 1973."

As the plane rolled up to the gate at LAX, Timothy stood up and put on his parka, knowing it could be a little cold in California at this time of year. He suddenly looked very sad as he stuffed *Newsweek* in one pocket and *Time* in the other, explaining, "It's going to take a long time for me to be processed and I want to have plenty to read." Then he took me gently into his arms and said goodbye with tears in his eyes suddenly only grey, the blue having vanished. Oddly, I was not crying. In fact, I felt excessively calm, smashed from all the champagne.

"From now on until I get out of prison again, there is very little I can do for you," he reminded me. "I regret it, but don't worry, I'll be out soon. Come and see me as soon as you can. I'm pretty sure they'll house me at Orange County Jail. I love you and always will."

And so we walked off the airplane and up the gangway. Another narc greeted us halfway, identifying himself as Agent Snyder. He read Timothy his Miranda rights, handcuffed him, then took him through a door as immigration officers approached me and made me follow them into an office. I walked in a daze, each step as uncertain as the next. My old sense of running on autopilot was so intense that I felt as if I were leading myself on a leash. After keeping me waiting for forty-five minutes, the immigration people handed me a green card, told me curtly that I was now on my own, and showed me the door.

It was dead silent in the bathroom as I mechanically powdered my nose, put on blush, dried my eyes, and pulled the comb through greasy opium hair. In the mirror, I stared at the pink sunburst on my sweater and straightened the long string of wooden Tibetan prayer beads Timothy had given me in Gstaad. I retrieved the long lambskin coat I'd dropped next to the sink and glancing at my Rolex, turned to find Günther and the waiting limo.

The opaque sliding doors of the transit area parted and I walked into a writhing horde of reporters twenty feet deep. Flashbulbs snapped, microphone booms dangled, and cameras whirred. From a dozen directions, people screamed my name, assaulting and cajoling me with questions. Television lights flashed over me like comets caught in a freeze-frame. I braced myself and said, "I am Joanna Leary, wife of Timothy Leary. He is my life and my love. I have chosen to speak and act on his behalf."

Bardo Express

PART III

Mind at Large

Reflecting on my experience, I find myself agreeing with the eminent Cambridge philosopher, Dr. C.D. Broad, "that we should do well to consider much more seriously than we have hitherto been inclined to do the type of theory which [French philosopher Henri-Louis] Bergson put forward in connection with memory and sense perception. The suggestion is that the function of the brain and nervous system and sense organs is in the main eliminative and not productive. Each person is at each moment capable of remembering all that has ever happened to him and of perceiving everything that is happening everywhere in the universe. The function of the brain and nervous system is to protect us from being overwhelmed and confused by this mass of largely useless and irrelevant knowledge, by shutting out most of what we should otherwise perceive or remember at any moment, and leaving only that very small and special selection which is likely to be practically useful." According to such a theory, each one of us is potentially Mind at Large. But in so far as we are animals, our business is at all costs to survive. To make biological survival possible, Mind at Large has to be funneled through

the reducing valve of the brain and nervous system. What comes out at the other end is a measly trickle of the kind of consciousness which will help us to stay alive on the surface of this particular planet.
  Aldous Huxley, *The Doors of Perception*, 1954

38

THE IRON DOOR

January 20, 1973

I awoke in a pink and yellow suite at the Beverly Hills Hotel. Outside were palm trees and strong sun. After seeing a doctor the night before, I'd watched myself screaming "Timothy Leary is innocent and no matter what I have to do, I will prove it" on national news. On NBC, Tom Brokaw reported that Timothy's bail was $5 million, the highest ever set for an American citizen, and called me a disheveled acid freak. Welcome to America.

From room service, I ordered orange juice, an English muffin, and black cherry preserves, then had a fit when they said they didn't have black cherry.

At eleven, Art Kunkin, publisher of the *LA Free Press*, picked me up to drive me to the Orange County Jail. Art was short and stocky with a long greying beard, a blue shirt frayed at the wrists, and shabby corduroy pants. He was very nice and sweetly deferential toward me, but I really couldn't understand why he didn't dress better.

From the cross-town freeway, Southern California struck me as little more than ugly billboards and a thousand off ramps. At last, we exited and stopped in front of a low white building where press people were swarming like insects, shouting and snapping pictures.

"I have nothing to say," I responded, flashing my most charming smile. "First, I will talk to my love."

A guard in an ugly beige uniform with a bulge of fat above his belt stopped me. "You need to be processed."

"Processed, what is that?"

"We need your ID, you have to be fingerprinted. What is your relationship to the prisoner?"

"I'm his wife," I said with aplomb.

"This way, then. Step through the metal detector. Thirty minutes," said the fat man.

In a small room with a chair and a black telephone, another beige guard with a gun stood beside me as Timothy appeared on the other side of a window in an orange jumpsuit, smiling gleefully, and smoking a cigarette. Belying the smile, his eyes were red and bloodshot from being interrogated all night. Picking up the receiver on his side, he pointed toward my telephone, his lips moving. At last, I filled in the horrible picture and picked up my receiver.

"How am I going to live with the fact that we now come into the same room through different doors and must speak and look but never touch?" I cried.

"Calm down, my beauty, it's all a mistake. I'll be free soon."

Getting hold of myself, I turned to the business at hand. "Your friend Art Kunkin has organized a press conference at the *LA Free Press* office this afternoon. What should I say?"

Timothy beamed. "Make a scandal! Tell them, 'You can't imprison love!' Tell them I am free, even in prison." He seemed to be having a good time, as if the cold visiting room with its down-and-out people and coffee vending machines and slamming steel doors was really a concert hall in the Palace Hotel and we were listening to a string quartet.

"Go to San Luis Obispo and get a house," he said over the telephone. "A woman named Betsy will contact you, she will have money for you and help you. I'm being transferred to the California Men's Colony, the prison I escaped from, only this time they're going to put me on the maximum-security side in solitary confinement. There will be a trial, I'll be acquitted and freed. Just wait for me at the house and I'll come soon."

Our half hour was up. He hung up, blowing kisses through the glass window. I rushed to press my lips against the cold glass, then he was gone, swallowed by the iron door.

39

ANGEL OF MERCY

A few days later, Betsy showed up at the Beverly Hills Hotel in a black Mercedes. She had dark skin, black woolly hair, sparkling black eyes, and an ephemeris under her arm. After introducing ourselves, she grinned.

"Timothy says you're a Capricorn with a very interesting chart—many planets in your 12th house, the house of karma."

"I don't believe in astrology," I retorted dismissively.

She looked startled. Timothy Leary's woman does not believe in astrology? "Then, you know the Tarot?" When I didn't respond, she added, "I also give great massages. Lie down, I'll show you."

She was right; the massage was a godsend for my hepatitis-wracked body fresh from an Afghani jail. Her hands emitted that same loving feeling I had been recognizing ever since the first morning at Timothy's house on Lake Zug.

"Will you be my secretary?" I asked, not knowing what else to call what I needed from her.

"Yes," she replied, "thanks to friends of Timothy, I'll be your wheels and look after you." She pulled a huge wad of $100 bills out of her pocket.

So we went house hunting, rolling down Highway 101 smoking fat joints Betsy had rolled at breakfast. The California coast north of Los Angeles reminded me of the Mediterranean, only more dramatic and abrupt. *This* was the Southern California I had expected—seagulls, sandpipers, white beaches.

"Who gave you the money?" I asked finally.

"The Brothers."

"What is the Brothers?"

"The Brotherhood of Eternal Love, friends of Tim's who smuggle hashish from Afghanistan back into the US. Before Tim was arrested in '69, he and Rosemary lived on their ranch in Palm Springs. He's their spiritual leader, their guru."

"I hate them!" I lashed out angrily. "They are the reason we were arrested in Kabul. I read about the Brotherhood in *Rolling Stone*. They are making all the money, but Timothy is the one taking the blame."

Betsy let my comment ride. Just north of San Luis Obispo, we found a nice house on the beach in Cayucos not far from Morro Bay. Compared with European beach houses, the American version was a little piggy's house built of straw that the wolf's breath could blow away without trying. The walls did not seem thick enough to protect or ground me, but I comforted myself with the fact that Timothy would be only a few miles away. His escape trial was set for the middle of February, less than a month away.

40

THE SORCERER'S APPRENTICE

One morning Dennis' conspiratorial voice called from the Los Angeles County Jail to say that he'd been arrested at LAX when he'd flown back from Kabul. "Come and visit me. I'll tell you what's going on, it's very interesting."

Strangely, I was eager to see him. Now less a shady sorcerer's apprentice, on this side of the ocean he felt like an ally in that he was the only one who had known me in Europe, the only link between my life, the free Tim Leary I had fallen in love with, and the grinning prisoner now at the California Men's Colony. I wanted to ask him a hundred questions about Timothy's drug-dealing friends and the poets and gurus who wanted to organize benefits and political rallies. I wanted him to help me understand where I was and what was happening to me.

As Betsy set out for Los Angeles, we were stopped 25 miles out of San Luis Obispo and an irate officer made Betsy walk the line, obviously not understanding that being stoned was not the same thing as being drunk. I had a bad taste in my mouth for American police in general, but especially now that they were becoming my frequent escort. Betsy and I were both on their subversive list due to connections to Counterculture movers and shakers.

Dennis looked like an agile monkey in a big cage all by himself. He was housed on the 12th floor of the downtown Los Angeles County Jail—old, musty, built in 1925 and justly brought down later by the 1994 Northridge Earthquake. When I leaned toward him and put my hands on the bars, he did likewise and whispered, "I'm working for the Feds."

"How can that be?" I forced a smile. "I thought we were on the other side."

"Working for the new Drug Enforcement Agency—the old BNDD is merging with it—is the only way Tim is going to get out of jail." He was adamant.

"First, don't you have to get out of prison?" I asked mockingly, catching a foul whiff of urine and sweat that almost made me gag.

Casting a furtive glance toward the guard making his rounds, he whispered, "The Feds just put me in here for a few days so no one would think I'm working for them. An agent named E. Donald Strange is my contact." He grinned. "He masterminded Tim's capture and return to the States. After you left Kabul, I went to the American Embassy and the DEA offered me a deal: work for them and they'd pay my way back to the US instead of letting me rot in Kabul. You know I didn't have a cent and wanted more than anything to be with you and Tim, to help get him through this tricky situation." He snorted. "Besides, I hate dope dealers. They're all using Tim to make money—carrying his picture in their wallets so when they get busted the Feds think Tim is masterminding their operation. Tim is the naïve PR man for every petty dope peddler in this country—all the nobodies making money because he broadcast the message, 'Turn on, tune in, drop out.' You know: kill the messenger. But none of them will lift a finger to pay his lawyer or get him out of prison. I don't mind busting a few, if it will help you and Timothy."

His slightly mad look made me realize the sorcerer's apprentice was still very much alive. I didn't trust him, but he was all I had. Here I was, new on the scene, destined to be the Mata Hari of Timothy's freedom—Mata Hari the infamous French spy-agent-provocateur who mystified both French and German intelligence during World War One—and I knew next to nothing about who was who and what was what on the American political scene, much less what had already gone down in the Counterculture. I was in desperate need of information. Dennis may have been the Feds' informant but he was also mine, and the only one who knew who I was and how much Timothy loved me when we had been together on the same side of the wall. I counted on him serving me above and beyond any of the other game pieces on his board because I knew he was in awe or in love with me.

"Gurus like Rammed Ass and Ginsberg," he ranted, "want Tim to stay in prison so he can become the martyr of the hippie cause. The more *political* hippies appear to be, the more credible they become to the ones the Feds are really after, like the Weathermen and Black Panthers. Timothy serves as a wedge between the Counterculture and the Nixon regime."

I listened closely, realizing *les règles du jeu* were in play in the US, as well.

"The day you were returned to California was the day of Nixon's second inauguration, get it?" Dennis glanced around furtively. "That same day, Meyer Lansky, the big Mafioso hiding in Cuba, was kidnapped and returned to Miami. Nixon needed a powerful front page for his law-and-order platform." He snorted again. "Who are we kidding? We're all puppets trapped between Nixon in Washington and Reagan in California. Let's get Tim out of prison and head back to Asia where people are gentle and hate Americans for all their games."

I had a headache and had to think. What would Mata Hari do? Those Nixon people would be at my feet in no time if that was what was needed to spring my Beloved.

At the Beverly Hills Hotel, Betsy and I took refuge in the Polo Lounge. I said nothing to her about Dennis' situation, given her relationship with the Brotherhood. As I sipped a few tall vodka and tonics, the bubbles nicely tickling the roof of my mouth, I thought, *I can free Tim from the politicians* and *the hippies*. I didn't know how many doubles a double agent could have, but at least Dennis would be secretly working for the Feds *and* for me.

41

CASE CLOSED

February 19, 1973

The escape trial in San Luis Obispo on February 19, 1973 came and went, the upshot being five consecutive years for escaping the California Men's Colony on September 12, 1970. Timothy had been advised by his attorney Bruce Margolis to be as far out as possible during his testimony and to plead temporary insanity, which broke my heart: he certainly didn't need more negative publicity. But he'd looked handsome in the blue suit and yellow tie I'd asked John D'Amecourt in DC (still technically my husband) to send—the very blue suit John had worn at our wedding. In one of the pockets was a note saying, *Good luck.*

On the witness stand, Timothy had told the jury that he felt like an explorer from the future who, while visiting the 20th century, had been captured and put into a cooking pot and stewed over a fire while a bunch of natives stood around waiting for him to be well-done so they could eat him. I wasn't allowed in the courtroom during his testimony but watched the soundless scene through a small window. When it was finally my turn, I lied and said that one of the narcs had offered me hashish on the plane coming to the States. My lie proved useless and I was ashamed of it.

Dennis called every day of the trial. He was out of jail and living in Southern California with Robin and their child Orion. "Tell Tim that I'm working hard at being a great informant so the Feds will trust me. The narcs need a lot more money from Congress so the DEA can become bigger and more powerful. Strange—the guy who engineered your capture in Afghanistan— testified to Congress that although the State of California might not be able to prove that Timothy Leary was an international dope peddler, he still has to be stopped and imprisoned and the key thrown away because he's an ideological trafficker corrupting the life and future of a whole generation of American and European youth." He chuckled. "And yet, strange enough, I like Don Strange. You'll like him, too. He's a funny little man, short and powerful, with a slow, soft Louisiana accent. His father's a state supreme court judge in New Orleans . . . Got to go, Peachy. Lots of stupid, greedy dope dealers to bust. Tell Tim I love him."

I was astounded. I had always thought of "the government" as a big, grey, faceless block of drab people going to work in ugly places lit with incandescent lights, the walls plastered with railway and public utilities posters. Now Dennis was telling me that government agents were manipulating people for budgetary reasons, just like the elite Michel Hauchard world I came from: Don Strange had moved Timothy and me back to California on the world chessboard so he and his friends could get more money and power from Congress.

I didn't know about being a "great informant," but Dennis was right: winning at this game was first and foremost about finding out who the players were on both sides. With Dennis on the government side and me on the hippie side, we would show everyone that there were no sides and no secrets worth keeping. Then, when everything was out in the open, we'd open the prison doors and let my beautiful, innocent prisoner out.

As I left the San Luis Obispo courtroom, the additional sentence and 108 charges already pending seemed pretty desperate to me. For courage, I invoked Mata Hari, Mrs. Andrei Sakharov, and Jeanne d'Arc. Inhabiting my mind with heroic women would help me plot what Timothy called escape routes, Mummy having drummed into me the belief that I could open any door, whether the Queen of England's or a peasant's.

42

TRIPPING IN PRISON

March 1973

Just before Timothy was moved to Folsom State Prison twenty miles northeast of Sacramento, Ram Dass and Ginsberg threw a benefit in Los Angeles to raise money for his escape trial lawyer Bruce Margolin. Not once did they ask me to come up on stage and give Timothy's fans a report on his condition, even though I'd just seen him drugged up on the antipsychotic Thorazine (chlorpromazine), slurring his words, his eyes bloodshot, saying that guards had come into his cell in the middle of the night to wake him and confiscate his pens, pencils, and paper and all the rest of his meager possessions, such as my letters and the few books he was allowed to read. *To hell with the poets and gurus,* I thought. A young couple had agreed to take me the 150 miles to San Luis Obispo in time for 8 a.m. visiting hours, so I told them I was ready to go when they were. When we left at about four in the morning, Allen was chanting with Ram Dass beside him in a full lotus.

In the backseat of the couple's Ford Pinto, with their sleeping baby's head on my lap, I took out a tiny tab of Orange Sunshine I had been saving for a rainy day, thinking how delightful it would be to greet Tim while peaking on acid. After twenty minutes, I began to feel the familiar tingling in my spine, the tightening of my neck and jaw muscles. When the young woman in the front seat turned to ask how I was feeling, her face shone like a star as minute increments of expression moved across her face second by second like weather as feelings and thoughts occurred to her. How *real* feelings and thoughts were, literally changing the shape of people's faces! Silver filaments of light ran among the child, the couple, and myself, linking us in a pulsating *love* like an electric current, the four of us in our little mechanical luminous egg traveling through the velvety darkness of Highway 101. I felt warm and safe with these strangers, united by the kind intent we held in common, on our way toward a man we all loved in different ways. How simple it all was.

Out the window, an everyday California dawn was on its way, spectacular in its lilac and pink understatement. Tears sprang to my eyes as a huge exaggerated sun rose, spilling gold everywhere. Almost to San Luis Obispo, we stopped for breakfast at a truck stop. With a large, silly grin on my face, I was absorbed in watching the baby hungrily eat her pancakes. Even the graveyard waitress' ill humor was wasted on me. Like John D'Amecourt what seemed a lifetime ago, I stared at my hands ribboned with veins as great and productive as the Amazon River as they held the heavy white mug of coffee, almost hearing the currents surging beneath my skin to and from my heart, irrigating every cell, every tiny DNA molecule in my sacred body.

I looked up and fixed my big pupils on my traveling companions. "Why are we outlaws for choosing to alter our perception with chemicals?"

The young woman answered in a soft voice, "Our society has gone insane. The real narcotic is the 9-to-5 trance most people live in. The government is afraid that our generation will wake up to harmony, that we'll reconnect with true tribal wisdom and practice loving participation and no longer need to sanction their patriarchal blame game of policing and protecting us from our instincts." Her partner nodded and they both smiled sweetly at me.

They dropped me at the prison gate just before eight. I sailed through the checkpoints, the metal detector not picking up that I was high on LSD, nor detecting the two tiny pieces of blotter acid hidden in the depths of my belly button. Timothy intuitively knew I was high and was elated. Putting his arm around me, he whispered, "I know where you are," then darting his tongue into my ear, "and I know who you are, too."

When we settled at a table in the corner of the visiting room, I smoothly transferred the blotter acid from my belly button to my mouth, then leaned over and delicately deposited it on his open lips with a kiss. Within half an hour, he joined me in the psychedelic world. The old mischievous Leary look returned to his eyes and shimmering sensuality to his body. We stared into each other's eyes joyfully, both of us recognizing that ultimately, confinement is limited to the body only. Our spirits danced together once again. I put my head on his shoulder and closed my eyes. We remained in deep tantric dialogue for three hours, thanks to the swift and sensuous language of the spine.

43

ARE YOU GOING TO SAN FRANCISCO?

During our two-month stay in Cayucos—before tearing down the set and moving into San Francisco—Betsy and I realized it was impossible for us to go anywhere without being followed by unmarked cars packed with government agents in seersucker suits. Strange crackling noises and interruptions told us that the telephone was tapped, so when I felt like it, I would pick up one of Timothy's books, perhaps *The Politics of Ecstasy* or *High Priest*, and read into the telephone, figuring the narcs might as well learn something worthwhile while on the job.

    San Francisco was the beautiful city in America to be in, city of the happening Counterculture. Market Street, hilly and spilling down to the ocean, reminded me of Tangiers on a winter day. North Beach felt a little like Paris with its pastel houses crammed together and pushing their spires up into the sky, the outdoor cafés and lingering aroma of espresso, the delicious delicatessens and specialty shops. People were out and about, walking their dogs and talking with one another on sunny streets, and on weekends neighbors brought out lawn chairs, drank white wine, and laughed late into the night. Every day was magic theatre in San Francisco.

My studio—a room with a fireplace and a bathroom paid for by the Brotherhood or other invisible benefactors—was on a small steep *cul de sac* near Coit Tower. I had no money but plenty of hashish, marijuana, and LSD. Not having money for food suited me fine because I liked to keep very thin—thin being as powerful as having money. I had one embroidered Afghani dress, the perfect outfit for the imprisoned acid king's official paramour holding court and smoking endless joints with Om-chanting hippies hanging on my every word. At last, I was as important as I wanted to see myself, and every day a glowing letter awaited me in the mailbox.

I called and made an appointment with Timothy's attorney Melvin Belli, who had tried many famous cases, from Errol Flynn to Jack Ruby and Sirhan Sirhan. His office was on the edge of Chinatown and appropriately decorated in red velvet, black lacquer, and black leather. Belli himself had white hair and a large body—a bon vivant and womanizer—and had recently married a woman about my age. I told him that Timothy and I wanted to have a baby, but that he had been moved to Folsom Prison, D Block, where murderers and other sordid criminals were serving life sentences.

"I like the idea," he said, no doubt thinking of the publicity, "let me think for a moment." He took a long drag on his outlawed Cuban cigar, squinting at me through the smoke. "I'll assign a lawyer to work on Dr. Leary's appeals, but in the meantime I'll write a brief to petition that his sperm be released in a vial. That way, you can have artificial insemination." He looked very pleased with himself.

Sitting in the deep black leather armchair in my only dress, I wasn't thinking so much of publicity as of becoming one with Timothy even while he was in solitary confinement: a cosmic thought for a cosmic couple. Wanting another child had little to do with the fact that I had already given up two. Maybe for Timothy it did—maybe he wanted to make it all better for me by giving me another baby. But for me it had more to do with how ever since Mummy's Spanish chauffeur raped me as a child, I felt compelled to get special attention from men through sex, seduction being the end game. Dinner, driving me around (I had never learned to drive a car), calling me, and giving me money were not enough to stay safe. The only way was to manipulate and bind them to you, and the surest way to bind a man to you was to have his child. I wanted Timothy's baby because I wanted him for life, and this time it would be different—or so I told myself.

Childhood trauma had made everything *unreal*. I could make love for hours because I wasn't there. I could hold a scintillating conversation and secretly believe the person wasn't talking to me because there was no me. I played and exchanged hundreds of roles like skirts or pairs of shoes: Sarah Bernhardt, Joan of Arc, Brigitte Bardot, Scarlett O'Hara. Plus seeing myself through the lens of role upon role meant seeing others the same way: the Imprisoned Philosopher, the Sorcerer's Apprentice, etc. If someone didn't play a role I could see, he or she wasn't memorable. Being poor wasn't real, either; it was simply the role I was playing in San Francisco during the fall of 1973.

Over that year and a half before the Watergate hearings, two anxious women obsessed over the telephone between Spain and San Francisco about one man, talking, puffing deeply on cigarettes, one on American cigarettes in Europe, the other on French cigarettes in California. Quite the international family portrait.

"Be clever with these newspaper people," Mummy advised in her Garbo voice. "They are vicious and you must come out looking good. You represent Timothy and must say what he would say. When you visit him, listen well, then repeat to yourself what he says so you will remember. You must not be a little whore with these famous men you meet at radical cocktail parties, like Abbie Hoffman and Jerry Rubin. It will turn out badly for you." She laughed. "You have found a good, powerful man. Don't make him look bad, and if you do, my little nymphomaniac Desdemona, don't ever tell him the truth. Think about what I've taught you. Never tell the truth about those things. Lie, lie, lie. It's much better that they don't know."

"But, Mummy, I . . ."

"Oh stop it, I know you as if I had made you." More laughter. *"Bon!* I must get off the phone, *Bonanza* is about to come on and then I go to play bridge at the club." *Click.*

Some days, she even believed I was still a virgin, perhaps because it made her feel younger. But on most days she thought of me as *une dévoreuse d'homme*, a man-eater. True, it never even occurred to me to say no to any man who wanted me. Free love was part of the Sixties *raison d'être*, and yet the truth was that I had been this way long before joining the Counterculture.

44

THE FOLSOM PRISON BLUES

It was now early summer and quite hot. Every Sunday, Betsy drove me to Folsom Prison in the black Mercedes. On the way, we would stop and have frothy A&W root beers, drinking them in the car in silence, me smoking cigarettes and Betsy a joint.

Folsom Prison looked like a turn-of-the-century European fortress built of grey stone blocks, the picture of maximum security. At one o'clock, in my threadbare Afghani dress, I would stand in line with wives wearing their best, sexiest dresses. I longed to feel united with these multicolored women, but didn't; we'd met at a common crossroad but were from different worlds. The female guards knew it, too, and therefore were particularly harsh with me—not just strip-searching me but making jokes at my expense whenever possible, like how afraid they were of getting high on LSD from touching my clothes. But at last I would walk down the alley between buildings toward the visiting facility, my heart pounding, tears standing in my eyes. Having paid the price of shameful entry, I was on my way to the only person in the world who loved me.

Even in his regulation prison blue denims, Timothy looked elegant, and of course there was his usual smile. His eyes looked clear, so I assumed they weren't drugging him. We were allowed to hug once at the beginning of the visit and once at the end. After clutching at each other as long as we dared, we would sit at one of the round tables. We couldn't hold hands, but our knees touched under the table and our eyes over the table. He lit my Gitane, then his Camel. I loved the way his eyes lingered all over me.

"How is it, my love?" I asked, shaking slightly. I gazed into the blue-grey eyes of the man who was supposed to protect me and keep me safe, who in turn was being held in the most unsafe place in America.

"They have me in a cell next to Charlie Manson. When I arrived, Charlie sent me some coffee and cigarettes. He likes it in solitary, says that's all he's ever known except for a few years outside. We have long talks. He knows there is no right or wrong, just different ways of using the capital of energy that makes us who we are. He feels he's God, with the divine right to destroy lives." Timothy shook his head. "I don't approve at all. As you know, I think conditions have come together to make us what we are so we can exercise kindness and compassion in order to arrive at permanent ecstasy with one another."

I nodded and touched his hand lightly. "Every time I come to see you, my beloved, I carry you outside with me. I talk to everyone about you and how unjust it is that you are in such a horrible place. I went to see Ferlinghetti at City Lights the other day. He and Allen Ginsberg want to come with me to see you next Sunday."

He nodded, then said gently, "Let's have lunch," leading me by the hand to the vending machines.

Belli's writ to petition Timothy's sperm was denied; no part of Timothy Leary was going to be allowed to leave solitary confinement. As one of the most dangerous men in America, his DNA and genetic makeup were no exception.

45

GINSBERG REDEFINES PRISON IN SANSKRIT

Dennis came to see me once in a while at the little studio on Alta Street. His hair was thick and long, and he wore brightly colored viscose shirts with huge pointy collars. He was having a blast working with the narcs, and his latest ambition was to qualify as a CIA agent. He loved conspiracy and undercover work but was afraid he wouldn't be a valid candidate because of his record. To Pink Floyd's "Money," he launched into an inspired monologue on revisionist revolution.

"The way to change the government is to infiltrate it, work inside the System, and continue to take LSD so as to retain a strong overview of the game. Tim's only way out of prison is to cooperate and tell the Feds everything he knows about the Weathermen and the Brotherhood of Eternal Love."

I was incredulous. "You're crazy. You know he's on the side of the Revolution."

"There is no revolution, Peachy. Everybody is busy making money one way or another, don't you see? Dealers want lots of money so they can become politicians, bankers or stockbrokers. No one on *either* side wants things to change. Hippies want to have what other people have—cars, washing machines, freezers, health insurance—they just don't want to work for them. And no one but you, Tim, and me understands the politics of ecstasy."

I leaned over to change the tape. It was time to air out the room, and the conversation, with the Eagles. "Dennis, you're becoming as cynical and boring as a narc. Go away and be with your new friends. I'll do my revolution without you. All I have to do is get Timothy out of prison."

Undaunted, Dennis continued. "I talk to Don Strange about Timothy, how he's a Harvard professor, a straight guy like him. After all, Tim's father was Eisenhower's dentist. What Leary really is, I tell him, is a serious psychologist, the man who designed IQ tests, the man who went into Massachusetts prisons and helped convicts leave behind what landed them in jail, the writer of a very respected textbook called *Interpersonal Diagnosis of Personality*, the man who invented group therapy. He's not a dope dealer, I say, but a serious researcher corrupted by the very tools he used to research the mechanics of the human mind." Dennis laughed. "That's what I say to Strange."

"But Dennis, you're forgetting he's also the man who advocated LSD on *The Johnny Carson Show* and in *Playboy*—the man who escaped from prison with the help of bomb-throwing revolutionaries, the man who said, 'Aim for life, shoot to live.' Believe me, Dennis, the Reagan and Nixon administrations are not ready to forget, much less forgive." I raised my eyebrows and looked at him as the Eagles sang—

> *'Relax,' said the night man,*
> *'We are programmed to receive,*
> *You can check out any time you like,*
> *But you can never leave.'*

"Well then, Peachy, go along with your revolution and I'll go along with mine, and eventually you'll see I'm right. Only the government can free TL. We'll meet somewhere down the road when you begin to understand what this is all about." Dennis had all the certainty of a religious convert.

Handing him a Coors from the fridge, I poured myself a double shot of Jack Daniels.

"We're different, Dennis. You don't really know me." I looked at my glass. "At least my friend Jack never betrays me." I meant it as a joke, but it didn't sound like one.

Dennis walked to the door, waving his beer at me. "Be careful of Allen Ginsberg. He hates women."

The following Sunday, I heard obnoxious backfiring on the street, along with the rattle of a broken muffler. Out the window, I watched Allen emerge from a typical beat-up two-toned hippie VW bus idling in a cloud of smoke.

At my door, the rabbinical-looking poet was briefer than brief. "Let's go, we don't want to be late."

Ferlinghetti drove—another tall, Etonian silver-haired man like my father and Timothy. During the drive, the two poets talked to one another about Timothy, comparing him to Ezra Pound and Wilhelm Reich, both of whom had been persecuted, tortured, and broken by the government that boasted having no political prisoners. I sat in back, having no idea what to say to two Beat poets who obviously had nothing to say to me. The truth was I was jealous of Timothy's friends—Ginsberg, Kesey, Ram Dass, all of them. They had no sympathy for me—a superficial European debutante looking for love in all the wrong places—and viewed me as an intruder, a usurper of the rightful place of the real wife, now on the run. Rosemary was the real acid queen. The only thing I had to hold onto was that Timothy loved me like nobody had ever loved me. Despite my sexual escapades, I felt I was being loyal to someone and sticking to something important for the first time in my life. But Ginsberg knew none of this, nor would he have cared had he known.

After passing Vallejo, Ferlinghetti pulled into a hamburger joint at the edge of a field of iceberg lettuce and we each ordered a juicy cheeseburger with dill pickles and greasy fries. At a bright orange picnic table, the two Beats continued talking while I watched pink bloody juice run down into Ginsberg's salt-and-pepper beard.

At Folsom, the guards made us wait an unusually long time before letting us into the visiting room. Timothy wasn't at the door to greet us.

Instead, they led us to a glass cage and told us to sit in front of it. Fear crept over the edges of my mind. Other prisoners and their girlfriends and wives were sitting around us unwrapping sandwiches, peeling oranges, their scene warm and friendly while we stared at an empty glass cage.

At last, Timothy was led into the cage, his hands and feet shackled in heavy, noisy chains. He sat down with difficulty. It was then that I noticed with horror that his head had been barbarically shaved and lines drawn on his skull still caked with blood. His face had not been shaved for days.

"*Namasté*," Allen said, putting his hands together and inclining his head.

"*Om shanti*," Timothy responded with a wan smile and similar but chained gestures.

"What has happened, Timothy?" I cried.

He shrugged. "This morning two guards came into my cell and shaved my head, and when it was time for the visit, they shackled me without any explanation."

Ginsberg asked if Timothy had a copy of *The Tibetan Book of the Dead*. When he said he didn't, Allen recited verse in Sanskrit for some time, which seemed ridiculous to me—reciting Sanskrit poetry at a time like this?

Our hour gone, Ferlinghetti promised to send books from City Lights and Timothy asked Ginsberg to help take care of me. As we were leaving, I said to the two Beat poets, "It's so hard to leave Timothy in that monstrous cage."

Ginsberg responded with what I thought was either disdain or delusion. "He is not in prison."

Was this a Buddhist joke, a Zen koan? Only much later would I realize what Allen meant. The prison system challenged those in the revolutionary underground who had had their eyes opened by LSD and Eastern spirituality, and the Beat poet chose to respond to the inhumanity Timothy was undergoing by revealing that it was a spiritual, not a political, issue.

Later in the underground press, Ginsberg would call me a CIA sex provocateur and say that I had arranged Timothy's capture in Afghanistan and flown back to the US with him to gain access to his friends. At the time, I hated him for his lies, but later realized that Allen had fallen prey to the divide-and-conquer game the Feds wanted him to fall prey to, as many of us did.

46

THE THREE FATES OF WATERGATE

Summer 1974

Timothy agreed to an interview for a six o'clock broadcast by a Sacramento news team and they passed the footage to me. When I saw it, I was annoyed with how *happy* Timothy sounded. With such a happy camper, how could I possibly rally support to free him?

Nor were his Belli lawyers in their three-piece gabardine suits, glittering gold pinky rings, and Rolls Royces particularly helpful. Oh, they loved to chat with me about the complexities of the case, but beneath it all they didn't have much hope for Timothy's appeals, despite my pulling the stops on seduction. Appeals were set aside and rejected right and left. Timothy was in the vise grip of *les règles du jeu* and invisible personalities pulling strings and, as they say in American gangster movies, putting the squeeze on him. In fact, I wondered if Dick Nixon, in the highest office in the land, wasn't having his strings cut by a similar squeeze.

Like millions of Americans during the summer of '74, I was addicted to watching Nixon's power base disintegrate day by day on live TV. I would awake at 6:30 in the morning, turn on the television, and sit up in bed drinking my muddy French roast coffee while the Watergate players keeping my man in prison lost more and more ground. The big question that summer was, Did the President know about the break-in at the Democratic National Committee headquarters at the Watergate office complex in Washington, DC on June 17, 1972? The answer was obvious, but proof was another matter. So far, the burglars were known and that they were paid out of a slush fund of the 1972 Committee to Re-elect the President, for which Timothy's old Duchess County nemesis G. Gordon Liddy, the first cop to ever bust him, had been counsel at the time. Nixon's first denial had been a televised speech to the American people on April 30, 1973, the second just four months later on August 15. Finally in April 1974, he'd announced that he was about to release the infamous tapes, and now the fat lady was about to sing.

At the end of the summer, Dennis called while I was following the latest episode like a soap opera addict. "Watch carefully, Joanna, this is it. You see that man who was just whispering in Sam Dash's ear? That's the man who's going to bring Nixon down. His name is Officer Butterfield, a nobody, but a nobody that Nixon appointed to tape everything said in the Oval Office."

"You mean the question, 'Did the President know?' will be answered?" I was overjoyed.

"Ha! Not only did the President know, but the President knows it's on tape."

Thus began the dance of special prosecutors and subpoenas for the Oval Office tapes. History was being rewritten weekly. Vice President Agnew was out of office, and Gerald Ford was next in line for an unelected presidency. Timothy was still the most famous prisoner in America, but not for long; powerful Republicans like Haldeman, Erlichman, and John Dean were getting ready to do time.

"There are two kinds of time," Timothy explained to me during Watergate, "hard time and easy time. If you're smart, you'll do easy time—a few hours of meditation, an hour of yoga in the morning and at night. This is the third time I've read *Gravity's Rainbow* by Pynchon. There's books and the prison grapevine, which by the way is very smart *and* very funny."

On Watergate nights, I would drink alone in front of the television, hating Archie Bunker for being the archetype of the mentality keeping my dream man in prison. Between sitcoms, I would swallow a lovely little blue Valium 10, then late at night phone my mother in Spain and talk incoherently, as I had done since I was sixteen years old. Finally, I would pass out on the floor or in my bed in front of an indifferent, laughing Johnny Carson. Freeing Timothy Leary may have been a heroic task for an intelligent, well-traveled woman like myself, but it was also boring and lonely.

47

STARSEED

Once Timothy's 1973 book *StarSeed: Transmitted from Folsom Prison*, came out, ideas got wilder and wilder, in part due to his idea that the purpose of comets is to streak through the universe and seed planets with star dust, which, given a large enough timeframe, become us. Thus we are all extraterrestrial beings, and our purpose is to leave planet Earth and search the universe for our origins. If the Imprisoned Philosopher said it, it must be true, and I for one couldn't wait to get off the planet with my love in the most perfect little space ship we could find. Obviously, Timothy was thinking that space was a far better home than Earth.

After mornings in bed with Watergate, I would shower away my hangover, then talk on the phone with people about how we could free Tim. The range of escape ideas gave new meaning to far out: stage an all-out war on Folsom with grenades, tanks, and machine guns; change clothes and places with him; a massive dose of acid to de-materialize him, like Captain Kirk beaming up from a Klingon ship. Budding New Agers thought that since Timothy had spoken at length about how we create our own reality, he must like being in solitary in the bowels of Folsom.

Now that I was getting streetwise, if the idea sounded *Starseed* enough—like the soft-spoken hippie in Kansas who said he could build a flying saucer in his backyard—I'd hang up and walk briskly to a pay phone down Alto Street, listening the whole way to Bob Marley and Fleetwood Mac playing the soundtrack for the movie that was my life, puffing furiously at a Gitane, wondering *Do I look as good as Ali McGraw in* The Getaway? as I passed thrift stores, psychedelic posters glowing under black lights in shop windows, and blissed-out hippies sharing spliffs on Grant Street.

"Here's how we'll do it," I would whisper into the pay phone receiver all the way to Kansas. "I'll be naked in the saucer, wearing long white satin gloves and a machine gun. Huge speakers will blast 'Nights in White Satin.' We'll descend into the Folsom yard when Timothy is scheduled to be outside, snatch him up, and take off. The guards will be paralyzed with fear. You will pilot the spaceship while Timothy and I make love.—I'll talk to Timothy and call you back, just start designing it."

Then I'd hang up, fish in my bag for another cigarette, and walk to the Starseed office above the Little Fox Theater on Pacific Street that film director Francis Ford Coppola was paying for so it could double as the Free Tim! headquarters. It was in that office that the faithful cosmic secretary Betsy typeset the entire prison StarSeed Series, including *NeuroLogic* and *Terra II: A Way Out*. Strangely, Timothy insisted I'd co-authored all three books because of the information he'd received as transmissions through me. While it thrilled me to think I was Timothy's female cosmic transmission tower, it was also somehow disturbing, much like the feelings Arpad Plesch had inspired in me as a child.

In between touring with rock bands and ingesting large amounts of cocaine to give me courage to plead the Imprisoned Philosopher's cause on stage, I gave lectures on space migration, then would spend hours on Telegraph Avenue in Berkeley selling Timothy's books to passersby to raise gas money for my trips to Folsom, or pay the electric bill. I had never been poor before, so it was kind of fun playing Impoverished Revolutionary and Wife of Imprisoned Dissident in this latest installment of *magic theatre* that Timothy and I had been drawn into.

48

THE HUNDRED DOLLAR MAN

At the Starseed office, Betsy held up a small piece of paper. "A man named Franklin called, here's his number."

Sipping the cappuccino I'd picked up at Enrico's, I called Franklin and we made a date to meet at the Top of the Mark in the Mark Hopkins Hotel at seven o'clock. I liked him immediately because he knew where to meet and what to say, a welcome change from hippies. On the way home, I stopped at a vintage clothes store and bought a pink and teal silk crêpe dress, calf length with a tight waist, and a pair of purple suede pumps with a rounded toe and thick heel, all for twelve dollars.

From the Top of the Mark on a clear night, you can see all of San Francisco, from the pyramid tower to the Embarcadero, the ocean undulating in the distance. The *maitre d'* showed me to a table. I ordered a vodka and tonic, then pulled out my compact; a little powder and pink lipstick and I was ready for Franklin, the mystery man.

From behind me a fire red hibiscus appeared. I put it behind my ear and looked up. He had deep blue eyes, a broad forehead and short beard. He didn't smile.

I didn't find out much about him that night other than that he was charming, attractive, and secretive. Even his name was a secret, "Franklin" being a nickname he'd picked up because of the hundred dollar bills he carried around. He wanted to know everything about my life, yet had no desire to share his. When he drove me home in his Ford Mustang, I asked when we would get together again. "I'll call you," he said with a smile.

The following week he came over without calling. This time his gift was not a red hibiscus but a large amber marble of opium. We heated it up on the tip of a needle and crumbled the soft earth-like substance into a pipe. Everything about opium intoxicates: the smell, the taste, the high—like floating in the womb again, gently bobbing about in warm life-sustaining fluids.

It being early fall, I was curled up in front of the fireplace, mesmerized by patterns in the dancing flames. His voice reached me from far away.

"I'm an LSD chemist. I synthesize and manufacture Clear Light."

"Wow," I purred, "the Chemist of Clear Light. Franklin, this opium is the best, so enticing—" I stopped short of adding, *like you*. Well-being permeated my body and I longed to be touched and caressed.

He took several transparent little vials out of his pocket, each filled with hundreds of tiny transparent cellophane squares. "I'll give you a few hundred tabs of Clear Light so you have as much as you want for yourself and your friends. Don't ever sell it, though. Go forward and you're all right, but look back and you'll turn into a pillar of salt." Seeing my puzzled face, he translated. "You're being followed and watched, so be careful."

My limbs were so heavy, I couldn't even raise myself up to say goodbye. "Thank you," I managed in a weary voice.

After he left, I lay by the fire until it was nothing but small glowing embers. I was attracted to the awesome power he had given himself by manufacturing LSD, but he was not Timothy the media figure, the writer, the Harvard professor, the passionate philosopher of the future. As a woman, I felt that I could only be something by being attached to a powerful man; otherwise, I was nothing. Avidly, I read everything Timothy wrote so I would be totally knowledgeable about my lover's thoughts and deeds. I was the devotee of a great man, just what my mother said I should be, except that that man was now behind bars and could provide neither sex nor money nor any form of protection. Something was wrong, but I believed there was no other way, no other choice than the course of events unraveling in our *magic theatre*.

49

COPS AND ROBBERS

Dennis called often from Laguna Beach, urging me to convince Timothy to turn state and federal evidence, the Feds having assured him that Timothy could do himself a lot of good by doing so.

"Otherwise, it's lots of fun running and gunning. You know what narcs' biggest regret is? That they can't go and enjoy a good old massage parlor so they drink Boone Farm wine and talk about getting anonymous blow jobs. All in all, though, it's fun being legit, and it pays well. With my record of dope dealing arrests and jumping bail to join Tim in Algeria, it blows my mind that I'm not in jail."

"But what about the people you're busting?" Franklin flashed through my mind.

"I don't care. It's a war between cops and robbers, and I've been taken prisoner. Considering that I got caught, I'm in pretty good shape for a prisoner of war." He sounded positively smug.

"What do you mean, prisoner of war?" *What a load of crap*, I was thinking.

"In the war between dope dealers and narcs for control of drug profits, not to keep kids safe. And it's just beginning. It'll become an all-out war in the next ten to twenty years, like in the Twenties and Thirties when there was all-out war between the Mafia and the newly created FBI. The new DEA couldn't have hoped for a better media poster child than Tim to remind the public what a life-saving agency it is—you know, how he's killed more young people than the Vietnam War, thousands jumping out of windows on LSD, thinking they can fly, or thinking they're oranges or bananas and peeling their own skin off. Meanwhile, the DEA pumps illegal drugs into the streets, and more dealers, too, just to keep their jobs."

Missing the implications of his last comment, I gasped. "Peeling their skin off?"

"Peachy, that's just government rhetoric, like lampshades made from Jews. Everyone has to earn entry to those huge state and federal funds allocated for law and order agencies. Remember when Nixon ran on his law and order ticket? And today he's barely staying out of prison himself!" Dennis laughed. "Weird shit. Wait until you understand what's really going down in politics. You'll shiver with fear and scream with rage. It's all a big dirty piggybacking game. But don't worry. Tim can outsmart them, if only he agrees to infiltrate their ranks."

50

MUMMY AT FOLSOM

Christmas 1974

A year after I thought I was escaping to freedom with Timothy, my mother decided to visit the man in Folsom Prison. At the San Francisco Airport, she looked worn out and well dressed, her hug brief, her kiss a peck on the cheek. She looked Betsy up and down with contempt, no doubt thinking, *Badly dressed, acne pocks, frizzy hair, in desperate need of a makeover.* Her first words to me after a year and 10,000 kilometers of separation were, "My God, Joanna, you've put on weight. Have you been eating those horrible McDonald's?" *Better than your Polish dumplings in butter and bread sauce!* I screamed inwardly, it being too soon for a fight.

At Folsom, *Christian Science Monitor* and *Rolling Stone* writers trailed after Mummy in her black and white suit, white satin blouse, sheer stockings, high heel pumps, two strands of pearls, and a huge gold and ruby Cartier ring. Mussolini may have been one of her lovers, but the trip to Folsom was one of the great events in her life. This time, I wasn't stripsearched. In fact, we floated through the electronic doors because she treated the prison guards as if they were the Polish servants her father beat regularly in the courtyard of their estate. Once Timothy was brought in I watched jealously as she did the same thing she had done with each of my lovers since I was fourteen, proving to me that twenty-seven was still too young to get the kind of action and attention I craved. The two of them sat there as if I did not exist, though from time to time Timothy threw me a wink.

"You look just like Joanna's father," she purred, "handsome, very handsome."

"You are very elegant and beautiful yourself," Timothy responded, catching up the hand with the ruby ring and kissing it. "As soon as I get out of here, we will come and see you in Spain."

"Yes, yes, I will await you impatiently, please get out soon." She blushed and batted the few mascara eyelashes she had left. I fixed my eyes on her stiff coiffured hair and told myself that Timothy would not really want to make love to a woman who never brushed or combed her hair. I trusted no one, certainly not my mother. In France, when a mother and daughter are in love with the same man, it is considered a good sign for the longevity and power of the patriarchy.

Suddenly, Timothy kneeled in front of her in his regulation prison denims and asked for my hand. Fiddling with the two tiers of pearls around her neck, she said, "Yes, yes, you may marry her, but hold her on a tight leash so she does not get out of hand the way she has with me. But I know you of all the men she has been with—such a pity—will know how to handle her psychosis."

I was barely flattered. How could he marry me? His wife Rosemary was on the run and divorce was not possible until she surfaced and dealt with her legal problems. Like Scarlett O'Hara, I pushed it out of my mind.

In the spring, Mummy tagged along on my *Starseed* lecture tour during which I showed Folsom footage of Timothy to college students and spoke about space migration. One night, I held court at a professor's home, lecturing after hours about the benefits of LSD, then distributed Franklin's Clear Light. At Western Washington University in Bellingham, Washington, I gave a passionate Free Tim! speech and a young man with a full head of red hair timidly handed me an early copy of his manuscript, *Another Roadside Attraction*. Instinctively, I added Tom Robbins to my list of future eligible men.

In Eugene, Mummy and I visited Ken Kesey and his family. Kesey was jovial and kind and loved to drink as much as I did. We spent three long nights getting drunk together, fantasizing about everyone turning on to LSD so they could witness their own beauty and the perfection of the universe. While we talked and smoked and drank, Mummy smoked and watched television with the Kesey children and Ken's wife Faye made blueberry preserves and canned tomatoes from their vegetable garden. Watching Faye take lids out of boiling water and screw them onto mason jars filled with fragrant fruit, I envied her simple gestures, and how early every morning, no matter when she'd gone to bed, she made cornbread or muffins for the children to eat before going off to school. I tried to imagine being connected with the simple continuity of life, but I was as far from being like her as Timothy's space colony orbiting Earth, and clueless as to how to get there. I had been fashioned by Mummy, an empty shell who had passed onto me her bottomless need for personal power by categorizing everyone as useful or useless objects. And the Kesey children painfully reminded me of the two small children I had abandoned to the care of their fathers for the sake of an imprisoned man twice my age.

I was in a solitary confinement of my own making as far from the freedom I coveted as the man in the moon.

51

TRIPPING WITH FRANKLIN'S CLEAR LIGHT

Mummy returned to Europe and Timothy was moved from Folsom Prison to Vacaville Medical Facility halfway between Sacramento and San Francisco. Due to the temporary insanity defense that Margolis talked him into, a battery of psychologists and psychiatrists now had access to his LSD-saturated brain. But at least I saw him more often. We'd hold hands and kiss each other's cheek outside at a picnic table under the California sun, and when he'd return to solitary confinement, I'd return to my steady diet of hippie freaks, cognac, strong marijuana, and soothing Valium.

    Then Franklin titillated my humdrum stoned life by asking me to take an acid trip with him. He picked me up one night and we stopped at Tower Records on the way out of town to buy all the tapes on my list, from Mozart's "Don Giovanni" to the Stones' "Exiles on Main Street." Franklin laughed all the way back to the car. "Do you really think we can listen to that much music in twelve hours?"

We crossed the Golden Gate Bridge in silence. I wanted to make love with this man in his thirties with greying hair cut short, his fingers long, his palms wide. I imagined him caressing me, soothing my body while we soared together on Clear Light. It had been a while since I had tasted the pleasure and power of good sex. I'd rolled around with Tony Russo of Pentagon Papers fame under his cluttered desk in Santa Monica, but neither of us had much longing for the other. Then there was underground revolutionary Abbie Hoffman one night in my narrow studio bed, a liaison due more to logistics than true desire in that he was on the run and needed a place to stay. Perhaps for both, I was a touchstone to Timothy Leary.

Franklin and I drove along coastal 101 for about two and a half hours, listening to music and talking. Outside, a slow rain began to dot the windshield.

"Since Timothy has been in prison, I haven't taken acid with a man I really like . . . ," I said hesitantly. I could just barely see his face illumined by the instrument lights.

"I want you to taste this acid and tell me if it is as good as I feel it is. I've spent the last ten days in the mountains distilling the ingredients for thousands of Clear Light tabs." He looked over at me. "LSD is just a miniscule amplifier that turns up the volume and power of experience."

"Why do you do this, Franklin?" I asked. "Why take the risk of being an outlaw LSD chemist? Is it for the money?"

"We're all messengers and mirrors for one another. Everything is a mirror of what we are—the ocean out there, this rain falling on the windshield." He chuckled. "It's all done with mirrors, you might say. LSD turns up the intensity of the message or, if you like, renders the image so bright, so lucid, that you can no longer ignore it. Sometimes, the images and messages are hard to bear, and other times they are so extremely beautiful that you just want to cry at the tenderness and perfection around you."

I knew exactly what he meant. Not even Timothy had described it this way.

"When I am tripping," I began hesitantly, "I keep returning to a hard-to-bear place where I feel so confused and alone that nothing makes sense. LSD opens up such horrible contradictions that I don't understand the why of anything. Is it because I am too young?"

He put his hand on mine. "There is a flow, a weave, a wave to everything. Perhaps this time on *my* acid, you will understand."

We drove on through the coastal rain in silence until we descended into a cove. Near the edge of the water was a large wooden beach house with a porch light shining our welcome. We carried our bags of groceries into the house and I gasped. A queen-sized bed covered with a huge American flag was in the middle of the large living room, a bright fire crackled in the fireplace, overstuffed velvet pillows were scattered over the floor. In the kitchen we unpacked our provisions: grapes, peaches, English muffins, coffee, half and half, and squares of dark Swiss chocolate.

"We'll be comfortable here," Franklin smiled, giving me a light hug. "No one will disturb us for the next twelve hours. Make yourself comfortable while I bring in our music and bags."

I stretched out in front of the fire, took my platforms off, and wiggled my toes. At last, Franklin joined me in a generous white cotton caftan. Silently, we toasted our champagne.

"The time is now," he said, producing a small vial filled with white powder. "This is the magic powder for you, the crystalline extract from which I make thousands of hits. Put out your hand and receive."

I was terrified. What if this time I could not come back? What if I went insane? Inside my mind, I heard Mummy's cigarette voice: "WHAT'S THE DIFFERENCE? YOU ARE ALREADY MAD, IT WON'T MAKE YOU ANYTHING YOU ARE NOT ALREADY." I put out my shaky hand and Franklin tapped a thin ribbon of shining powder along the lifeline of my palm. Quickly, I licked it. In turn, Franklin tapped powder into the black lid of the vial and poured it onto his tongue.

I got up and put on Iron Butterfly's "In a Ga Da Da Vida." Except for the amber light cast by the fire, the room was dark. Shadows danced on the white walls. Outside, waves pounded the beach. In the distance, I could hear a fog bell sounding sad and deep. I closed my eyes and dozed off, the noise of a log shifting in the fireplace finally startling me awake. Franklin was sitting in the middle of the American flag in a full lotus, watching me with amusement. Great warmth emanated from him.

"How are you?" His voice traveled the distance of centuries to me.

I tried to respond, but Mummy's voice boomed, "DON'T TRUST, DON'T CARE, EVERYONE IS OUT TO GET YOU. DESTROY AND BETRAY." And yet Franklin looked so peaceful, so kind.

The fog bell had become the sound of a funeral procession.

"I am . . . I am . . . I am . . . alone . . ." *Was that my voice?* I tasted tears. *Were they mine, or the ocean's?*

Over the distance, Franklin's gentle voice said, "No, you're not alone. Everything and everyone that ever was is with you. Look at the fire." I followed his gaze into the flames. "Trust the fire." He got up and walked to the French doors, opened them, and gestured toward the dark beach. "Trust the sand under your feet. Feel the truth in the wind. TRUST."

Following his voice, I walked out the French doors and onto the beach. My fear awoke and I stopped. I wanted to turn back. My heart was pounding in my throat like a Moroccan drum. The Outside was too big, the stars, the ocean, the wind. I couldn't manipulate or control them. Panic shot through my solar plexus.

Then, Franklin's warm breath was against my cheek. "Everything is in Everything."

I tried to turn away from myself but found myself enveloped in Franklin's embrace—not a sexual embrace, more like floating in a huge bowl of warm vanilla pudding, surrounded but not held or constrained.

"You are enough, you don't have to do anything."

Who said that Not Mummy. I pulled away, ran inside, and threw myself on the bed. Curled in the fetal position, I covered my face with my hands. "I can't accept anything!" I screamed. "I have to fight to the end! This is a battle to the death, survival of the fittest, the bravest, the most beautiful . . ." My voice trailed off as Cat Stevens sang:

> *Morning has broken like the first morning*
> *Blackbird has spoken like the first bird*
> *Praise for the singing, praise for the morning*
> *Praise for them springing fresh from the Word . . .*

Franklin stood looking kindly down at me. Through his eyes I saw a young woman thrashing around on a huge American flag, struggling to be born to herself.

52

A MEAN SCENE

Dennis' warning about Ginsberg came back to haunt me: in the underground press Allen had said I was a CIA sex provocateur, telling anyone who would listen that I had arranged Timothy's capture in Afghanistan and that working for the CIA was why I had been flown back to the US with Timothy. I plowed through the rumors, staging a Free Tim! benefit at the Chinese Theatre where we would advertise on radio and local TV about showing every bit of film footage ever shot of Jimi Hendrix starting at midnight after the regular films. Dennis came up from Laguna Beach to help me organize it. We drank and smoked and talked late into the night, after which he slept in his sleeping bag on the floor in front of my fireplace. Of course, he had his own take on things.

"Tim is using you, he doesn't really love you. He cares only about himself and getting out of prison, and will use anything or anyone who'll help him out of that hellhole. I know you sleep with people who promise to help you, but you're wasting your time giving your body to people who just want to be with Timothy Leary's girlfriend." He looked into my eyes. "I love you, Peachy. I've loved you since the first night you came to Lucerne. He's using you, I tell you. Just tell him to cooperate with the Feds and he'll get out."

Infuriated, I grabbed the tequila and chugged straight from the bottle. Wiping my mouth with the back of my hand, I tore into him, shouting at the top of my lungs, my voice filled with cold hatred. "I don't want you to talk like that! What do you know? He's not using me. We love each other and I am going to get him out of prison and we will have a baby. You'll see. Neither Timothy nor I need your pitiful tips!"

In two strides, Dennis was toe to toe with me. Small but strong, he grabbed me by my shoulders. "Open your eyes, Peachy! You're 28 years old and smarter than you think. You know these things as well as I."

Struggling to break free, I dropped the tequila bottle and kicked it against the door. Its transparent fireworks sprayed the wall.

Still gripping me, Dennis tried to get me to look at him. "Peachy, you don't really know Timothy. His first wife killed herself with carbon monoxide and he didn't find her until morning because he'd blacked out from overdosing on martinis. Don't you see how he uses women, one after the other? Marianne, Delsey, Nina, Rosemary, and now you. Rosemary's in a psychiatric clinic in Switzerland fighting for her sanity. Is that what you want? I love you, don't you understand? I'm young, intelligent. Let's go back to Europe together."

When he let me go, I picked up his pale blue sleeping bag, ran to the door, and threw it out onto the wet street.

He grabbed me again. "I want you and Tim to hear that he will stay in prison forever unless he shows the Feds he's not a dangerous man. They have no plans to let him out. Do you hear me?"

I had no fight left. My eyes and heart heavy, I looked past Dennis out the window at Coit Tower on Telegraph Hill. Dawn was hovering over the city. Across the alley in a small garden, tall sunflowers were getting ready to lift their heavy heads and follow the sun across the sky.

I said listlessly, "Tonight is the Hendrix benefit. I have a radio interview at ten and must get some sleep, Dennis, so I can say the things that will attract a lot of people to the benefit."

He dropped his arms and went outside to retrieve his sleeping bag. Despite our scene, his eyes still twinkled when he came back in, while I gave him my most hateful glance. Pulling a brown wallet from his back pocket, he gently removed two carefully folded pieces of white paper and unwrapped them on the glass coffee table. Brown powder in one, white powder in the other. "China brown heroin, and pure pharmaceutical German cocaine," he crooned.

Exhausted, we sat on my bed rolling joints of tobacco and hash and snorting lines of cocaine and heroin, a warm, sexual current running back and forth between us. We held hands, a little dismayed by the power of our feelings. Dennis sounded surprisingly shy when, after a long silence, he said, "I love you and want to help you out of this mess."

Outwardly silent, I inwardly argued with myself. Mummy had often called me Lady Chatterley for my attraction to the lower classes.

But the benefit went well. From midnight until seven in the morning we adored Hendrix and I gave words of hope to the faithful hippies anxious for news of their fallen guru. And the take was good: $2,500. Everyone thought the money would go to the Timothy Leary Defense Fund. Well, I was the defense fund. I would be able to pay my rent for a couple of months and buy a few delicious treats like Guatemalan coffee and French cheese and mustard. Then I would continue to go each week to the horrible visiting room at the Vacaville Medical Facility near Vallejo to keep Timothy going.

After we cleaned up, Dennis and I walked back to my studio in the falling rain and he got into his car and headed back to Laguna Beach and his assistant narc job. *Still a sorcerer's apprentice*, I thought humorlessly before falling into bed, exhausted but encouraged by the pile of five dollar bills scattered on the carpet next to the ashtray overflowing with dead Gauloise.

I didn't awake until three the next morning. The full moon was flooding my bed and sobs were shaking my frail body. I was in love with the most far-out man in the world and felt deeply, irretrievably lonely with no one to call. I wanted to be held by someone who would tell me what life was for and what a person had to do to become happy. What I had learned on acid with Franklin was fading. How was I ever going to be able to fill the bottomless emptiness that devoured my every experience?

I lit a Gauloise with one hand and grabbed the bottle of cognac with the other. Brown fragrant firewater burned my throat. Today was visiting day, which meant getting up at seven. Betsy would drive me to the prison and Timothy would make me feel good. Meanwhile, the words *He's using you* ran around and around my brain like a broken record, playing even as I kneeled over the toilet bowl dry-heaving like a horrible prayer at a horrible altar.

53

UP AGAINST THE WALL

Betsy was on time. At a quarter to eight, I heard the bubbly sound of the old black Mercedes muffler. I threw on a pair of black pants, a Mexican pink t-shirt, and a black scarf around my neck, catching a glimpse of myself in the bathroom mirror—black scarf and green face, definitely not a good color combination.

The visiting room buzzed with small children. Pimply-faced men in starched denim uniforms stared with lust and pain at their wives and girlfriends. Mothers and sisters were there, all with dark circles under their eyes and savagely bitten fingernails. I did not want to be a part of this scene anymore. I wanted excitement, glamour, closeness, and above all, protection.

As usual, Timothy practically skipped into the large visiting room with his grin in place. We hugged, chose a round table, and sat down.

"I've been waiting for you all week," he said exuberantly, squeezing my hands between his. "Joanna, your letters are so funny and tender, I get them every day after breakfast." He squeezed my hands harder. "I promise you this imprisonment won't last much longer."

I jerked my hands away. "How can you say that, Timothy? It's been *two years*. Every day Belli's lawyers say there is absolutely *no hope* for your release. All of your appeals are exhausted and people are writing letters to the parole board begging them not to let you out." I looked deep into his eyes. "People are afraid of you, and—this is hopeless."

I began sobbing. His optimism about his captivity was a maddening double bind. On the one side was the man needing to get out and swearing it would be over soon based on nothing, and on the other there I was out on the street, discovering more and more just how tightly locked those iron doors were. But the truth was that I was furious with him, furious that each visit he whispered loving words but like my father was not there for me, was unreachable while I was out there somewhere dangling on an elastic cord, ready to be pulled back when he wanted me. My first husband Nico had left for Greek military service shortly after our marriage; my second husband John spent his time playing backgammon or poker. I was tired of words and promises.

Between sobs, I choked out, "You are not getting out of here unless you know something I don't. Besides, Dennis says you are using me." Mascara tears fell like acid rain.

Timothy shook his head. "You shouldn't talk to Dennis, he's a vain and stupid Gemini. You must know by now how much I distrust Geminis." He began a discourse on astrology, as if it were the most important thing in the world to understand at that moment, Timothy's Libra birth sign being the most evolved and Capricorns good at social responsibility.

I sighed. "Dennis knows how to get you out, but you won't listen to anyone!" I ripped the wrapper off a Reese's Peanut Butter Cups and stuffed one in my mouth. "Here, you write legal briefs for convicts who look up to you and they tell their girlfriends they're hanging out with a guru. But me, out there—" Peanut butter stuck to the roof of my mouth and chocolate to my fingers as I began to cry anew.

He stared at me as if finally comprehending my condition. "All right, I'll try it. Why not?" His voice was cheerful, and his blue-grey eyes had taken on an odd mixture of tenderness and cold determination. "Send a telegram to the FBI and tell them I'm ready to cooperate. What was the name of that FBI agent who wants to talk to me?"

Already, the fearless and beautiful Mata Hari was invading my soul. "Frenchy," I said. "I'll do it as soon as I get back to San Francisco. We'll show the government you are an innocent man and a brilliant scientist of the mind. Of course, they're dying to meet you, like everyone else. Now we'll be together soon. I'll hold you in my arms for months and make you feel like the happiest man in the world." I positively shone.

The canned voice of the warden announced the end of visiting time. Convicts and families shuffled slowly toward the electric door between two worlds.

On the way back with Betsy, I said nothing about what Timothy had decided. I had to be careful. Betsy would disapprove of federal cooperation. But I was pleased, given that I was on no side at all, or perhaps I should say on one side only: the release of Timothy Leary, no matter the price. The end of winning what you want justifies the means.

That night on Alta Street, I composed the telegram that would change everything: *Timothy and Joanna Leary ready to cooperate with FBI, DEA, and any other interested agencies. Signed, Timothy Leary from Vacaville Prison.*

54

WALKING THE LINE

Dennis was thrilled when he heard and asked if he could come and stay with me for a while so he could oversee Timothy's and my great government caper.

Before he arrived, Franklin, whom I now saw quite often, asked if I knew where to get ergotamine tartrate, the primary chemical for manufacturing LSD. We were walking along the boardwalk on Embarcadero. Ships were passing slowly at my feet and a fat seagull was evaluating a piece of a tourist's fallen hot dog. My answer came swift and strong.

"I can get a chemist to come from Switzerland with it. How many pounds do you want?"

"How much a pound?"

"Ten thousand dollars," I responded straight into his attractive blue eyes.

"Seven pounds, then. I need seven pounds to make the next batch of Clear Light."

It was not true that I had a source for ergotamine tartrate, but a diabolical plan was germinating in my mind. To be a true Mata Hari,

I was going to get what I wanted from both narcs and dealers: money *and* freedom. Neither was complete without the other.

When Dennis arrived, he looked good with his Southern California tan and good haircut. He'd been excited about the government caper, but when I told him about the Franklin caper he was ecstatic.

He called his DEA connection, E. Donald Strange, to tell him that Timothy and I were ready to talk. *Talk about what?* I wondered somewhat fearfully. Oh well, Timothy would take care of that end. Then we waited and waited. Nothing from Strange.

By then, I had a crush on a young lesbian with long dark hair and unshaved legs. She and I made long, languorous love, enjoying each other's curves and soft skin while Dennis lay on the floor in his sleeping bag. How delicate a woman's mouth felt under my lips compared to the greedier, harder lips of a man. Making love at least gave me the illusion of the kind of intimacy I yearned for within, and Timothy would be goaded on to pursue his release by the erotic stories I would whisper in his ear during our next visit.

Finally, Don Strange called Dennis: an appointment in two weeks at DEA headquarters in LA. Dennis would bring me in so they could question me about Timothy's desire to cooperate.

The next day I had lunch with Franklin at Enrico's and told him what he wanted to hear. "I can deliver the ergotamine next Wednesday. I'll rent a room at the Embarcadero Holiday Inn. Come at seven but don't show up without the money, Franklin: $70,000 cash—for the Swiss chemist, of course."

I saw greed—either his or mine—in Franklin's beautiful eyes. I wanted him to want me, but instead he wanted to make more acid to make more money, just as my family loved money more than people. Well, I would show this bedeviled meditator. He would regret not turning his attention to who I was rather than to what my role as Timothy Leary's paramour could get him.

I returned to Dennis triumphant.

55

ROOM 660

As usual, Dennis had an inexhaustible stash of heroin and cocaine. I did not question its origins, I simply snorted and smoked it all, having developed a voracious appetite for the high the combination produced, a feeling of well-being and invulnerability—and of course the wrenching nausea that accompanied heroin oblivion. I felt I could do anything as long as I had enough of these drugs.

Dennis had built up two years' credibility with the DEA and had a DEA plan that never failed to relieve Franklin of his money without getting caught: First, rent two adjoining hotel rooms and an extra room on a different floor. Ask the buyer to meet you with the money in one of the adjoining rooms, then explain that money and dope in the same room mean two worlds of trouble, not just one, in case the police are tipped off and looking for evidence. Once you have the money in hand, count it to make sure it's all there, then give the buyer a key to the room on whatever floor and tell him to go and pick up the dope. As soon as he leaves to get his stuff, step into the adjoining room and lock the door behind you in case the buyer has a lookout in the lobby—you don't want to be seen fleeing with the money, so lay low in the adjoining room until after the buyer discovers there's nothing in the room upstairs and comes knocking wildly at the door of the room where he left you and the money. Finally, he leaves, at which point you leave.

I bought a metallic Halliburton briefcase like the one James Bond carried in *Goldfinger* and filled it with the most precious things I had accumulated since arriving in California with Timothy: the gold tantric ring he gave me in St. Moritz when we first made love; his address book with a veritable top one hundred of the famous and less-than-famous who had experimented with acid through the years; two of Timothy's original unpublished manuscripts; and my mother's gold and pearl wing earrings made by Cartier in Paris before the War. Next, I spent hours calligraphing a letter to Franklin on beautiful parchment, telling him that if I could fool him, a worse person than I could probably get to him and have him busted. I asked his forgiveness and told him I knew he had made huge amounts of money, and that most likely this caper was a signal that he must stop being a chemist and enjoy life and good fortune from now on.

With the last of my money, I bought a turquoise and black silk wraparound dress that contoured my body perfectly and could be opened in a second by pulling on the black bow at the waist.

Dennis asked uneasily, "Are you really going to spend our last one hundred and twenty dollars on this dress?" We were standing in a dressing room cubicle on I. Magnin's second floor. "He's only going to be with you five minutes."

Impatiently, I explained. "The dress is just another way for me to tell Franklin I love him and that I find him extremely attractive. I want him to know that so when he does not get what he paid for, he will still know how beautiful he is to me." It all seemed highly logical.

But Dennis didn't trust my logic. He jerked the brown curtain toward the wall and pulled me toward him, whispering in my ear, "I can't stand it anymore." His breath was hot and the bristles on his cheek irritated my skin.

I pushed him away. "Don't spoil it with your stupid jealousy, Dennis. This money is going to set Timothy and me free."

Betsy, my faithful secretary for two years, intensely disliked Dennis and stormed out of my life. It was just as well: I was sure she was still reporting to the Brotherhood and they probably knew who Dennis worked for. Deborah, a smart and beautiful Japanese-American, replaced her and became a member of the gang that would soon own a lot of cash. After we got the money, I would rent a suite at the Hyatt Hotel down by the wharf and experience some of the luxuries I had done without during my two years of poverty. Seventy thousand dollars was enough money for many nights in good hotels. After all, I'd been born in the best hotel in the world.

On the day of the caper, we posted Deborah in the Holiday Inn lobby. In my silk wrap-around, I went upstairs to one of the adjoining rooms, the only one I had rented in my name, and waited for Franklin to call from downstairs while Dennis waited in the other room with his ear to the wall. At seven o'clock exactly, the buzzer rang.

"I'm in the lobby, can I come up?"

"Yes, of course, I'm waiting for you." My breathing was erratic but in the mirror my face looked calm. This would be the best part I had ever played.

A faint knock. I opened the door. Franklin looked elegant in his tailored beige cashmere coat and dark brown Gucci loafers. He smiled and hugged me. "Good to see you, I'm excited about our transaction," he said softly.

I sat on one of the beds. "Sit next to me and I will pour us some champagne."

Franklin opened the Dom Pérignon in the silver ice bucket and I poured two glasses. For a moment, we sipped in silence, looking into each other's eyes. I knew he was searching for the truth in my eyes, granting himself another minute in which to check things out before presenting me with the cash. As I looked back at him, I only allowed myself to think of how much I loved him, giving him the silent message that he could still ask me to run away with him instead of just transacting a sordid exchange of goods.

He put down his glass and moved toward his black leather briefcase—the moment I had been waiting for. My hands were trembling; I needed to control my emotions or I would blow the whole deal. He took a small brown folder out of his case.

"Here's the money, seventy thousand dollars in one hundred dollar bills for seven pounds of ergotamine tartrate. We are going to turn on the world." He pulled a thick wad of hundred dollar bills from the folder—clean, crisp, and new. Greed glowed like gold between us, the money on the glass table next to the telephone a magnet devouring all of our energy. From that moment on, there was no room for love, either mischievous or friendly. Now it was only market value changing hands as fast as possible. I counted every note, recalling the precise gestures of every bank cashier I had ever seen.

"It's right," I said with a smile, thinking, *Now I just have to get him out of here.* "The ergotamine tartrate is in the Halliburton in Room 660 on the sixth floor. Here is the key to the Halliburton, and here is the key to the room. It's been wonderful doing business with you, Franklin." I beamed.

He took the keys and walked to the door, turning to say, "Next week, let's go out to dinner and celebrate."

I closed the door gently behind him, leaped for the money, ran to the communicating door and stepped into the adjoining room, locking away forever where I had put the screw to Franklin.

Dennis threw himself into my arms. "We did it, Peachy, we did it!"

"Shhhh, somebody might hear us." My whole body was shaking violently.

Dennis calculated Franklin's every move. "He's on the sixth floor. In a few minutes, he'll discover that the key you gave him doesn't open the briefcase. He'll panic, run down to the room next door. No one will answer because you and the money are safely locked in the next room with me." He looked at me and grinned even more. "Sit down, I have a little treat for you."

On the bedside table were four thick lines of white powder on a small mirror. I rolled one of my new one hundred dollar bills into a narrow cylinder and sniffed the powder up into my nose and my brain, then up the other nostril. I lay down on the king-size bed while a warm wave of wellbeing cruised through my body. In the distance I heard muffled sounds of someone knocking and knocking at a door. A few minutes or hours later, I was in the deep, detached sensory world of heroin. Over a great chasm, I could hear Dennis' muffled voice.

"Okay, the coast is clear. Deborah says Franklin drove away with the Halliburton about half an hour ago. C'mon, Peachy, let's leave this place." In a heroin dream, I put my fortune into my deep tapestry purse, slipped on my pink pumps and left, clutching a fresh bottle of champagne for the road.

Dennis and I spent the evening drinking champagne at Deborah's crummy little studio in the Mission, knowing that no one would find us there. At three o'clock in the morning, I decided to go and wake up Bill Choulos, one of Timothy's Belli lawyers, and offer him all of the money to free Tim. Deborah drove me out to Bill's mansion in Sausalito and I rang and rang the doorbell until his sleepy voice asked who was there. After he let me in, I threw the seventy thousand on the heavy antique kitchen table.

"How much will it cost to free Tim Leary? I have plenty of money now." My voice was surprisingly clear, probably due to the coke Dennis had plied me with after the initial heroin hit.

Besides being an attorney, Bill was also partners with the infamous Mitchell brothers who produced successful porn movies like *Behind the Green Door*. He was wearing a crimson velvet robe and black velvet slippers. We had made love several times during the past few months at his *pied-à-terre* in San Francisco, sometimes even with his official girlfriend whom he had properly initiated into chronic infidelity.

I picked a big juicy cherry from the silver bowl now surrounded by hundred dollar bills. Bill looked at the money, dismay registering on his pleasant *bon vivant* face. "Joanna, I hate to disappoint you, but in this political climate all the money in the world won't get Timothy Leary out of prison. Ronald Reagan will run for President and win before that happens."

I was shocked. Ever since childhood, I had seen over and over how money could buy anything and anyone. What was it about my present lover that made him such a threat to people in power? *Well,* I thought, *I'll find out next week when I infiltrate the Drug Enforcement Agency and the FBI.*

56

MAKING LOVE WITH MR. D

After the Franklin caper, I could no longer resist making love with Dennis: ripping off the soft-spoken outlaw the night before had bonded us in a very sexy way. Together, we had been powerful, determined, fearless, and now we had enough one hundred dollar bills to cover a king-size bed. Appropriately enough, Mummy had flown first class from Paris to San Francisco, so we three took several rooms at the Hyatt Embarcadero, the kind of hotel where the maid turns down the bed at night, lights the bedside lamp, and puts a mint on your pillow.

In the middle of the afternoon, Dennis knocked at my door and I knew what was going to happen by the shivers running up my spine. I was both afraid and excited. My love for Timothy protected me, so there was no way I was going to fall in love. Dennis may have been clever and loyal, but he was ordinary looking, short, and worst of all, the son of an Italian hairdresser from Culver City.

"Hey Peachy, your mother and the others have gone to Enrico's for a coffee." Desire made his voice sound deeper than usual.

Leaving my cigarette in the ashtray, I passed a hand through my hair and put my arms around him. "Let's do something dangerous and *risqué*," I dared.

His body was small but agile with years of doing yoga naked in the Southern California sun. I could feel his ribs but also how much he wanted me. No, I would not fall in love with him as I often did with the men I slept with. This would be for the sheer pleasure of sex and to congratulate ourselves for getting the seventy thousand. We kissed.

"Your mouth tastes peachy, your hair smells like summer peaches, I've wanted you so long," he murmured into my hair.

On the bed, he kissed my face all over, entering my mouth with his tongue, unbuttoning my creamy silk shirt and kissing my tiny breasts, his tight curly hair tickling my skin in a delicious way.

"Tim shouldn't leave you alone like this, you deserve to be made love to, to be adored," Dennis breathed, pressing against me.

"Wait," I protested, "I'm going to pay you for this beautiful act." I jumped up from the bed, grabbed my purse, and took out five thousand dollars. "This is for you to make love to me with more passion than you have ever made love in your life."

Dennis flew across the room and grabbed me with enormous strength. When we landed on the bed, he pushed up my skirt and entered me very suddenly, an intense, hungry look in his eyes. To my surprise, my body shuddered immediately with a deep, long orgasm as I continued to gaze into his wide-open eyes. He stayed inside me and held me in his arms for a long, long time.

The afternoon sun was setting over the bay. Seagulls called to each other in deep, throaty sounds. In Dennis' arms, I thought about all the men I'd had sex with since arriving in San Francisco, all in the name of the Revolution and free love but actually motivated by drugs and longings for conquest and power. No wonder that afterwards I always felt lonely and lost in a strange land.

The Wednesday after the caper, I went up to Vacaville in a rented Rolls Royce, drinking Jack Daniels out of a carafe of Baccarat crystal. I reasoned that there was no reason not to use the money for comfort since it could not free Tim through the legal system, anyway.

Timothy admired my courage in pulling off the scam. "I'm happy you now have the money to live the way you deserve. By the way, yesterday I got a letter from Franklin saying, 'Joanna is beautiful, let her fly free like the wind.' The only other thing he said was, why didn't you ask him for the money?"

I laughed and raised my eyebrows. "Because he would never have given it to me. You have to make people do what they want to do, just as you have to make them do what they don't want to do." I laughed again much harder, putting my hands on my hips and skipping from one foot to the other.

He sighed, no doubt exasperated by my child's logic. "Please send some money to my daughter Susan," Timothy said, kissing my cheek, "also buy me three books I'd like, Kesey's *One Flew Over the Cuckoo's Nest*, John McPhee's The *Binding Curve of Energy*, and Julian Jayne's *The Origin of Consciousness in the Breakdown of the Bicameral Mind*—oh yes, and a carton of Camels."

"Okay," I said, "but next week I won't be able to visit. I'll be in LA talking with the Feds. Is there anything special you want me to tell them?" I lit a Gauloise with the gold lighter I'd purchased at Tiffany's, then held it up. "Do you like my new toy? It's completely electronic."

Timothy watched me. "Tell the Feds I want to get out of prison so I can be with you."

After the Hyatt, Dennis and I rented a beautiful house on Mount Tamalpais northwest of San Francisco with a huge bedroom and skylight almost as large as the ceiling itself, a sunken living room, and a large cedar deck with a hot tub under redwood trees. The first floor had a Japanese bath exquisitely tiled in red and white and aquamarine. Through the windows, the lights of San Francisco shimmered in the distance.

We made love in the Japanese bath, our legs wrapped around each other's hips, pearls of sweat on our foreheads, our hands foraging over each other's bodies. I was not in love with Dennis, I told myself, but our bodies fit together in an exquisite way, and it was nice to have a man in the house after living alone for two years. We would lie together in the big bed under the skylight, listening to the rain fall gently above our heads.

Then I decided to play my most seductive piece of bravado on him: a *ménage à trois*. Offering another woman to the man I was with was one of my favorite courtesan tricks. "Let's offer ourselves to the most beautiful, expensive call girl we can buy in all of San Francisco," I said impishly.

So we drove to an escort service in San Francisco and hired a young call girl named Mary with milky white skin, brown eyes, and generous breasts who looked to be no more than nineteen to be with us for a couple of hours, then returned to the house on Tamalpais. She took off her short skirt and t-shirt and was sitting on the aquamarine tiles next to the tub.

"Do you want me to undress completely or just like this? Usually, my clients are old and ugly. You two are so beautiful, I want to make love with you."

Dennis gazed at her breasts cupped in black lace. I undid her bra and kissed her lips, the two of us falling into the warm, fragrant water with a splash and a laugh.

From outside under the redwoods, I heard Dennis call, "Come and look at the stars and I'll tell you the name of each one." *Why was he holding back?* I wondered if he was jealous.

But eventually the three of us made love together. Then the madam called, wondering where Mary was. Our time was all used up, she said curtly, as if she were talking about a parking meter. We laughed and told her that Mary was staying with us.

But the truth was that no amount of sex could satisfy the deep, aching emptiness and loneliness that had been with me since I was a child smelling starched sheets on the narrow boarding school cot, longing for my mother's smell of blond tobacco, expensive French perfume, and Polish skin.

57

IN THE MOUTH OF THE BEAST

Dennis and I stayed at the Beverly Wilshire Hotel in Los Angeles the night before the rendezvous at DEA headquarters. I was very excited about meeting government people with the power to influence Timothy's fate and sat on the bed contemplating the clothes I had bought on Rodeo Drive. What does one wear to meet with one's lover's jailors? A little black suit from Anne Klein, or bell-bottomed jeans and a blue blazer? Once I decided, we watched *Star Trek* while eating lobster and prime rib brought up by a stiff room service waiter.

In the morning, a limousine drove us into South Central LA to DEA headquarters as I snorted cocaine and heroin in the backseat—the infamous speedball combo—feeling a perverse pleasure at the idea of entering the anti-drug sanctuary under the influence of dangerous substances.

A short man in a polyester suit walked down the hall to greet us. "E. Donald Strange, Special Agent assigned to the Leary case," he said with a grin I couldn't categorize. "So you're the famous paramour."

Paramour. What did he mean by that? Was he insulting me, making it clear that he knew Timothy and I were not really married? I sensed that this little man was out to get me. I looked at Dennis, who was decidedly nervous. *Of course he is out to get me, everybody in this place is out to get me. This is the mouth of the beast.*

Strange led us into a large conference room with drapes over windows that might as well not have been there. I sat with Dennis at one end of a large mahogany table facing eight men in seersucker suits. This—not the Franklin caper—would be the performance of my life: Mata Hari facing the French firing squad.

Tony "Frenchy" Le French, a middle-aged man with a moustache, had the opening line. "Can you assure us that Timothy Leary is willing to cooperate with the FBI as well as the DEA?"

"Timothy will do everything to cooperate," I answer with a devastatingly charming smile, "but you will have to talk to him in person so he can tell you that himself."

"We want to find Bernadine Dohrn, the woman heading up the armed revolutionary group called the Weathermen. Since they helped Dr. Leary escape three years ago, he must know where some of their safe houses are located."

"You must ask Timothy about that."

Jerry Utz from the California Attorney General's office turned his swivel chair toward me. "We want to know if you would be willing to help us catch some of the crooked lawyers in this state."

Like Belli? I wondered, though not daring to ask what such a feat would entail. With speedball cool, I replied, "I will do anything to help free Tim Leary from his unjust imprisonment."

Dennis kicked me under the table, then dragged his fingers through his brown curly hair before saying, "What Joanna means is that Tim is now repentant about taking drugs and deserves to be released because he will no longer advocate the use of LSD. In fact, while he was in Austria with Joanna, he made an anti-heroin movie for the Chancellor himself."

This was fun. I liked the attention of all these men. Given a little time, I felt that I could seduce them into letting Timothy go free. My speedball analysis of how the cops-and-robbers game worked ran something like this: Where there are secrets, there are prisons, and prisons require that there be people committing so-called crimes to fill them. Fear is the cement binding prisons together. Keep the prisoners afraid of the guards, the warden, and each other, and keep the people on the outside afraid of the people on the inside. If you didn't buy into the fear, it would all collapse like Humpty Dumpty.

From the distance of my drug-induced consciousness, I heard someone talking to me. I looked around, surprised to see that I was still in DEA headquarters sitting around a heavy mahogany table with law enforcement agents from every federal agency in America wanting me to help them arrest dope dealers, radical lawyers, and pinko-commie, dope-smoking hippies. Was this what Ginsberg meant when he said Timothy wasn't in prison? I flashed on the recurrent dreams I used to have of Nazis wanting to kill me because my mother was Jewish—dreams more real than real. Was I trapped in a waking dream?

Strange was talking. "Next week, we'll go and see Dr. Leary, then have him telephone his attorney in Orange County and ask him to sell you some cocaine. Do you see how it will work, Joanna? Are you ready to begin working with us?"

I heard myself say, "Oh yes, I'm very excited, I can't wait to begin." The voice was Mata Hari (half-seductive) and Helena Bonner Sakharov (half-dignified and hurt). Sipping the insipid coffee that had been brought in, I added, "I'll be expecting you to visit Dr. Leary in prison some time in the next few days."

"We'll be taking him out of prison to talk to him at length," Utz clarified.

Oblivious to what Timothy would go through, all I could think of was that he would get to sleep on a real bed instead of the concrete slab and thin mattress he had become accustomed to in prison.

After the meeting, Dennis and I collapsed in the limousine, had a quick shot of Jack Daniels followed by a Coors chaser.

"Mill Valley," I directed the chauffeur, feeling Dennis' hand between my thighs.

58

THE RIGHT SIDE OF THE LAW

When we got back to the house under the redwoods, everything was gone: Timothy's letters, stereo, furniture, jewelry, tapes, clothes, even my expensive new Chanel makeup—gone. Someone had backed a truck up to the front door and emptied the entire place. Dennis figured it had to be Robin, his blond surfer girlfriend, mother of his child Orion. Since Dennis and I had become lovers, she had been living with Charley, my personal pusher.

I smiled at Dennis. Now that I was an ally of the police, why not call on my new friends? Either the Los Angeles DEA or Mill Valley police, it made no difference. I picked up the telephone and dialed 911. Within minutes, several police cars had shown up and we'd relayed our suspicions.

"I'll place a tap on your phone in case there's a ransom call," Detective Mahoney said.

I was impressed. "That's it! My things have been kidnapped and soon we will hear from the people keeping them hostage."

Detective Mahoney and several cops stayed all night. I served vegetable soup in blond wooden bowls with French bread from the freezer that I'd warmed up. No matter the circumstances, my mother had taught me to be a good hostess.

At eleven o'clock, the telephone rang. Robin's snippy voice sounded in my ear. "You give us $25,000 in cash and you'll get your things back. Call the police and you will never see Tim's precious prison letters again.[6] I deserve some of the Franklin money and I am going to get it, like it or not, bitch. I'll call back in an hour to tell you where the drop should take place." *Click.*

I smiled at the police lieutenant standing next to me. It felt rather good to be on this side of the law after my long haul as a fugitive convict's wife.

"Who is this 'Franklin' she mentioned during the phone conversation?" Detective Mahoney asked. He was sharp.

I cut in before Dennis could open his mouth. "He is my uncle, the renowned Swiss chemist Franklin Hoffman who died a few months ago, leaving me a small inheritance. In her criminal megalomania, Robin is trying to extort some of my poor uncle's money." Real tears flooded my eyes.

The phone rang again. "Motel 6 near the Golden Gate Bridge at noon tomorrow, and bring the twenty-five thousand in cash." *Click.*

It was three o'clock in the morning and the house was crawling with police. There was no way to sleep with all of these zealous men around to protect me. I made strong coffee and offered Swiss black chocolate.

The bust was sensational. Dennis was sure that Robin would foolishly follow the modus operandi of the Franklin caper. At twelve o'clock exactly, Robin was waiting for me in the parking lot of Motel 6 wearing skin-tight jeans and a white halter-top, her long blond hair shining like precious metal. The prospect of $25,000 and screwing Dennis and me was making her smile from ear to ear—but not for long.

"Give me the money and I'll tell you where your belongings are," she said.

I pulled a brown envelope from my canvas bag and handed it to her. She opened it, looked inside, and laughed. "You didn't think I was going to let you get away with Dennis *and* all of Franklin's money, did you?

---

6 Timothy wrote me passionate letters every day, and how and why those 300 or so letters were eventually all stolen from me in 1978, I still don't know.

Now I have the dealer, an unlimited supply of cocaine, and some of that good hard cash." She fished inside the pocket of her jeans and pulled out a motel room key. "Charley is waiting to give you your things."

"Thanks," I said, grabbing the key. As I walked to the door, I turned around to watch the cops grab Robin, one snatching the envelope with the money out of her hand, another handcuffing her.

I knocked at 515. A stern Charley opened the door.

"No silly business," he said, "I have a gun." Sure enough, he was pointing a grey steel piece in my face.

"I gave her the money, we're all clear, so stop pointing that thing at me."

The shabby motel room reminded me of a prison cell: grey walls, a high narrow window with a small patch of blue sky in it. My things were strewn all over the room like a rummage sale.

"She has the money," I repeated, "otherwise she wouldn't have given me the key."

My voice sounded all right, but I was very nervous. It was the first time anyone had ever pointed a gun straight between my eyes, and Charley's silence was unnerving.

"This is going a bit too far, Charley. Drop the gun on the bed and let's talk."

There was something wrong with Charley's eyes. Cocaine, that was it—he was crazed on cocaine, which meant that at this very moment my life might not be worth a snort.

"Charley," I said softly, "it's me. We were friends, remember? I bought so much good dope from you. Let's have a line together and then you can go and join Robin and the money." I knew the police were at the door but would not interfere until Charley dropped the gun.

"I'm going to put the gun down," Charley finally said, "but if you've tricked me, you'll pay."

Then everything moved very fast. The second Charley put the gun down, police crashed through the door, jumped Charley and wrestled him to the floor while he screamed obscenities at me.

After recovering my things, I decided to leave the house in the redwoods. From now on, I would live in hotels with Dennis, until Timothy was out of prison.

Bardo Express

PART IV

The Flash Point

Men die, but the plutocracy is immortal; and it is necessary that fresh generations should be trained to its service . . .
   - Upton Sinclair, The Goose Step, *1924*

Good Being is knowing who in fact we are; and in order to know who in fact we are, we must first know, moment by moment, who we think we are and what this bad habit of thought compels us to feel and do. A moment of clear and complete knowledge of what we think we are, but in fact are not, puts a stop, for the moment, to the Manichean charade. If we renew, until they become a continuity, these moments of the knowledge of what we are not, we may find ourselves, all of a sudden, knowing who in fact we are.
   - Aldous Huxley, Island, *1962*

59

CHARLIE THRUSH

About the time Dennis mysteriously disappeared one morning, saying he was going on a secret mission for the DEA and would be back soon, my second husband John d'Amecourt invited me to Las Vegas where he was waiting out the required six weeks in order to obtain our divorce. Tacky Las Vegas—how different Monte Carlo-style was with its women dressed in beautiful designer clothes accompanying powerful men to the baccarat table, famous Hollywood producers and Greek tycoons spending hours throwing money away just to prove to themselves and others that they were even more powerful than they looked.

    The master bedroom of the Sands Hotel suite John had reserved for me, with its large, round bed and mirrors on the ceiling, struck me as sad in the present context of sealing a divorce and relinquishing my rights to Alexis, now three and living with his paternal grandmother in Washington. Alexis hadn't come with his father, despite my not having seen him in two years. To buffer the pain of my failure as a mother, I suspended myself in a Quaalude cocoon and took a lot of lonely naps on the luxurious bed. Staring at the papers John's lawyer had delivered, I consumed an entire half-gallon of ice cream then made myself throw up. I spent hours downstairs smoking and watching old ladies with blue hair and winged eyeglasses play the slot machines like sci-fi automatons, agonizing over signing Alexis away.

Then I read in *Newsweek* magazine that Timothy had been transferred to a secret location due to having become a government informant code named *Charlie Thrush*. I was outraged that the government had leaked this information and put Timothy's life in danger, and all before the collaboration had even begun! I spent hours panicking, trying to reach Don Strange at DEA headquarters to find out where Timothy had been transferred, overwhelmed by the vast out-of-control chasm my life had become. Finally, Strange and his Southern drawl called me back. "Don, why did your guys leak the information to *Newsweek*? And why didn't anyone tell me he was being moved?" I sipped Jack Daniels to swallow my outrage.

Strange always had an answer. "As for the leak, it didn't come from DEA. It must have been those FBI guys, they never can keep a secret."

The possibility that government agencies were in competition with one another was a new idea to me, as was the idea that working with the Feds meant Timothy and I were working for Richard Nixon.

"Anyway, relax," Strange went on, "Tim has some important things to tell you. He's being detained in a country club prison in Sandstone, Minnesota. We've informed the warden that you'll be visiting him there. You'll love the place, it's much better than any prison he's been in yet."

Shifting the receiver to my other ear, I took off the clip earring that was hurting. *I should really have my ears pierced*, I thought distractedly, asking Strange, "Will I be able to find French cigarettes in Sandstone? Is there a decent hotel?"

Strange chuckled. "You'll find everything you need. It's a charming resort town. Fly into St. Paul. Call me as soon as you've had a chance to talk with Tim, he has important things to talk to you about."

To Strange, I said, "How does it feel that Nixon broke the law with Gordon Liddy and the other Watergate conspirators, and will be impeached?" It was very exciting to say this to a government agent.

"Never," Strange retorted, "he's a good president and no commies are going to impeach him."

I rang the Las Vegas airport and booked a first class ticket for Minneapolis-St. Paul for ten o'clock that night, mentally thanking

Franklin yet again for his dope-dealing money. Leaving a note for John, I signed the papers, fooling myself that I would get my children back when Timothy was out of prison and he and I were married and everyone approved of us and admired us for being upstanding people who had gone through a terrible ordeal. Now, I had to keep fighting to get my man out of the mess he was in. I took a taxi to the airport, happy to leave behind the glassy-eyed gamblers. Las Vegas truly was night and day from Monte Carlo.

60

THE COUNTRY CLUB PRISON

Champagne flowed easily during the three-and-a-half hour flight, and I took frequent trips to the bathroom to snort the coke I had managed to score from one of the croupiers at the Sands and stash in the gold pillbox I'd bought at Tiffany's. I even masturbated in front of the mirror to make my loneliness abate.

No buses or trains went to Sandstone, so I hired a taxi for the two-hour, one hundred dollar trip, chain-smoking all the way as I listened to what the driver had to say about Sandstone Federal Prison.

"Sandstone sprang up about seven years ago around the new white-collar prison. Most of Sandstone works there, eight hundred or so—not counting the twelve hundred inmates, of course." He grinned in the rearview mirror. "You visiting a prisoner? Not going there to teach French, are you? I don't think anyone would be interested."

We laughed as he sped around an eighteen-wheeler with *Courtesy and good driving are my aim. How am I doing?* on the back. A flash of cold fear shot through me.

"So it's minimum security, like the one the Watergate conspirators were sent to?"

"Sure," said the cabbie, "minimum security unless you make a wrong move. I know because my brother is in there for bank robbery. Too bad the kid took such a bad turn. I used to think he was smarter than me."

We arrived after midnight. There was not one hotel in Sandstone. *Charming resort town,* Don Strange had said. But the cabbie said the woman who owned the only diner in town had a couple of rooms she rented out. When I knocked, she answered and I finally went to bed above a greasy diner in rural Minnesota, crying myself to sleep, thinking of the vanished days of bright sunshine, affectionate dogs, swimming pools and glamorous parties. All I had now was my love for a man as difficult to catch as the wind Franklin said I should trust. Pete Seeger was right—

> *Where have all the flowers gone?*
> *Girls have picked them every one*
> *When will they ever learn?*
> *When will they ever learn?*

I could call Dennis. He would rent a car and we would find a nice hotel nearby. With this new plan in mind, I wiped my eyes with the back of my hand, took my usual high dose of Valium, and plunged into heavy sleep.

The next morning, the warden was waiting to have me processed. He let me know that Timothy was now classified as an informant and so once again was being held in solitary, this time for his protection. "I don't want any trouble," he warned. "I run a tight ship so no one gets hurt." His eyes drifted down my body to my black halter-top, tight jeans, pink plastic belt with silver stars on it, and turquoise high-heeled platform shoes. "Tomorrow, you might want to wear something more conservative. Most of these men are hungry for what prison life deprives them of. You don't want to be the center of attention in the visiting room, do you?"

The warden's own hunger penetrated my skin like a poisoned dart, and he had all the power.

"No, sir," I said, doubling my French little girl accent. "It's so hot and humid out, I am not used to the Midwest summer. This is my first time in Minnesota."

As usual, Timothy bounced into the visiting room, his signature Adidas slightly battered, his shoelaces broken and knotted. He smiled, but his blue-grey eyes looked greyer than usual, more lifeless, his lips dry and cracked. A guard hovered nearby.

"What are we doing among these people," he sighed, "a couple of gazelles amongst a pack of rhinoceros? How good of you to come right away. Are you comfortable? Did you find a good place to stay?" He took my hand and caressed it gently.

"No, it's awful, a sleazy room above a greasy diner." I began to sob as he held my hand tighter. "Don Strange lied to me. This doesn't look like a country club prison, and you're booked under that hateful name, Charlie Thrush. Even the guard calls you Charlie." I looked at him through mascara tears. "Strange betrayed us. I hate these government people."

Timothy pulled a crumpled Kleenex out of his pocket and put it in my hand. "It won't be long now until I'm out and we can have a little baby girl as beautiful and intelligent as you," he said.

"Don't say the same thing you always say! It hurts me." I wiped my eyes, blew my nose, and lit a cigarette, drawing deeply on it, inhaling blue smoke deep into my body and my grief. I looked into his sad eyes. "Are you all right? Are you safe?"

"Well, no one bothers me in solitary confinement. I'm re-reading Robert Anton Wilson's *Illuminatus!* trilogy." He paused, probably thinking over how much he should say. "Last night I couldn't sleep because someone kept walking up and down under my small high window singing that Moody Blues song,

> *"Timothy Leary's dead*
> *No no no no he's outside looking in . . ."*

I must have recoiled, for he added quickly, "But don't worry, they can't get to me. I'm the most watched and guarded inmate in the prison system."

I was paralyzed with fear. "They are going to kill you, Timothy, I know it. This is the end. I am sure the government made up this whole deal about you cooperating with them so they could get you killed."

Had the Feds put him here to get him killed, or to make sure he sang? Even I realized that white-collar criminals at Sandstone probably believed what the media said about Timothy being a mass murderer of youth. He'd committed the cardinal sin of preaching the joys of hedonism in a country founded by Puritans, and advocated self-inquiry and questioning authority by any means, including the use of mind-altering drugs. His message was one of a new internal revolution.

Timothy shook his head. "Don't worry, I'll be out soon. It's all very hopeful now. On Sunday, as soon as Jerry Brown dropped the state charges and granted sole possession of my body to the Feds, they airlifted me from Vacaville to some bank building in Los Angeles. They were all there in a huge conference room, Joanna—FBI agents flown in from Chicago, at least five DEA guys, including that Don Strange you've been talking to; two California state attorneys, and all kinds of other guys packing .357 Magnums. *Magic theatre*. Just keep in mind that these primates are all part of the Bardo we're moving through. Remember in Switzerland when we talked about magic theatre not just being a metaphor but a way of experiencing the world when the neural pathways have been opened up by psychedelics?"

He paused and leaned forward. "They all want something from us, my love." I must have looked bewildered because he smiled and whispered, "They want you to do a little espionage for them. It'll be very exciting, and you will be such an elegant spy." His warm breath was on my cheek. "By the way, the DEA guys all agree that you are very beautiful. Even those poor primates can see your radiance. I love you, my beautiful wife."

I put on my best air of bravado. "I will do anything, Timothy, anything to get you out of this horror, anything so we can be together again." The tears began again.

He put his arm around my naked shoulders when I shivered. It was suddenly lunchtime and families were unwrapping sandwiches, drinking root beer, and speaking in loud voices to children running around. Everything seemed normal except for all the light-blue denim shirts and dark-blue denim pants.

Timothy put his cigarette out. "I'm coming before the California Parole Board next month. If you work with the Feds, they'll testify on my behalf. Once I'm officially paroled out of the California prison system into federal custody, I'm sure I'll get out on bail, pending my appeal in Texas. But with two consecutive convictions, a state one in California and a federal one in Texas, it's much harder for me to get out. First, I have to be paroled out of the California prison system." He searched my eyes.

I did not miss the new adamance in his voice; the usual implacable optimism he had shown since leaving Kabul was gone. The change touched me deeply and I resolved to do what I must to get him out.

61

PRESIDENTS COME AND GO

August 8, 1974

The woman who owned the diner drove me to a nearby town that boasted a halfway decent Holiday Inn. After registering, I called Dennis at his father's house in Culver City. He sounded so good. I was lonely and needed someone real to love me.

"Dennis, jump on the next plane. I miss you and have to talk to you. We have to go to Washington. I'll talk to Nixon and he'll understand."

"No, Peachy, turn on your television. Nixon's giving his resignation speech tonight so he won't be impeached. They're letting him get away by nobly taking all of the responsibility and none of the guilt. Starting tomorrow, Jerry Ford will be President and Nixon will walk. Anyway, I'll catch an afternoon plane and arrive late tonight. I love you, can't wait to see you."

I lay on the queen-sized bed listening to commentators discuss Nixon's fate as I thought about Timothy's. Nixon had ordered the break-in at Democratic headquarters, cheated the American people, and yet wouldn't go to prison. Presidents came and went, but Timothy was doing time for next to no crime. Now the Feds wanted to send me undercover to set up people for busts because they couldn't very well let

Timothy out to do it. From prison, he would telephone old friends, lawyers, and political activists he'd known during the Sixties and tell them that he was sending me to them, that I had something important to talk to them about. Then I would buy dope from them or whatever the Feds wanted, and the axe would be returned to Timothy's hand for the final blow: he would testify against those who had once called him friend.

I crammed myself under the flowery bedspread, doing what I always did when I felt afraid: I ran my hands down my chest and felt each rib to assure myself that I was thin enough and therefore powerful enough to endure this latest test. Thin meant I could slip through anything I needed to slip through. At five foot three, I weighed ninety-seven pounds, which gave me deep satisfaction.

Dennis arrived at three in the morning with a rented car, a fresh supply of cocaine, some Thai stick marijuana, a gram of Mexican heroin, and a passionate desire to make love to me.

62

IS THERE ANYBODY OUT THERE?

Minneapolis, 1974

I dressed very straight: a black skirt and black satin shirt, a black suede belt with a gold heart-shaped buckle, sheer stockings, and black high-heeled pumps—just right for Washington, DC. Dennis, on the other hand, was wearing one of his ugly fake silk shirts and a pair of faded bell-bottom jeans. For a moment I wondered how he would look in a three-piece suit. *No, not his style.* At the Minneapolis-St. Paul airport I bought a first-class ticket for myself and economy for Dennis.

"We must save money, so you must travel economy," I said to him. "You're not mad, are you?"

"No, Peachy, I'm just happy to be with you. Besides, I reserved a suite at the Watergate Hotel, so we'll be close soon enough." Dennis was docile. What a relief.

While boarding, there was some commotion around a pink-complexioned man with a double chin and a grey fedora. It was Hubert Humphrey on his way from his home state to Washington, DC to perform his Senate duties, and I was sitting three rows behind him.

After takeoff, the flight attendant asked, "Champagne?"

"Yes, please," I said, draining the glass before she moved on, "I'll take a little more." She refilled my glass with the gold bubbly liquid I loved. Again, I emptied the glass in two deep draughts, thinking, *I'm ready for Hubert Humphrey, I hope he's ready for me.* I stood and walked forward to his row.

"Senator, I am Timothy Leary's wife. I don't know if you know that he is incarcerated in Sandstone and is about to be murdered for being a snitch. I'm sure you would not want that to happen in your . . ."

"Wait a minute, slow down. Sit next to me, here." He motioned to the empty seat beside him and stepped into the aisle while I slid in, smiling kindly. "You are Joanna Leary, I've read about you."

"Yes," I said, warming to his smile, "I'm at the end of my rope. The Feds in California asked us to collaborate with them. We agreed, and now they've betrayed us by publishing in *Newsweek* that Timothy is a snitch. They don't really want us to work with them, they just want him dead." By now, I was sobbing.

He pulled a large white handkerchief out of his breast pocket and handed it to me. "Calm down, child, I'm going to help you. What do you want?"

"I don't know," I snuffled. "I have been following Timothy from prison to prison for two and a half years and getting nowhere. He is still on the inside and I am alone on the outside. With Nixon out of the picture, perhaps Betty Ford might help?"

He nodded. "After the Republican Convention, I knew things would get harder and harder for hippies, yippies, and all of the young people lost in our great nation, without a clue as to how to grow up. Let me ask you, do you still take drugs, or have you stopped since Dr. Leary was put in jail?"

The muffled voice of the captain gave our cruising altitude and estimated time of arrival at Dulles, giving me time to assume my most childlike air.

"Mr. Humphrey, I have never taken any drugs, other than a little puff on a joint that I didn't inhale. This is what I like," I said, pointing to the amber cognac now before me. I could still lie with the aplomb Mummy had taught me. Remember: never tell them the truth.

The Senator lifted his cup of coffee to his lips, smiling, "It's a bit early for me . . ." He sipped thoughtfully. "As soon as we get to Washington, I'll make a few phone calls."

"At least get him out of Minnesota, Senator, and back to California—maybe Terminal Island in Long Beach, I hear it's relatively nice for a federal prison." Thanking him, I returned to my seat.

Dennis was poking his head through the thick drapes separating first class from the tourist cabin. "What happened, what happened?" he whispered, grinning.

63

THE WATERGATE HOTEL

Once in Washington, we moved into a Watergate Hotel suite overlooking the Potomac on the other side of the Beltway.

"I'll bet Hubert Humphrey doesn't do anything," Dennis said cynically. As if to dramatize his pessimism, he had set up his Moog synthesizer in the living room and was making weird Pink Floyd-like sounds.

I flipped through TV channels, nibbling on a Big Mac the bellboy had fetched for me, drinking Dom Pérignon in a tall crystal glass. "No, something is going to happen, I know it. Things are going to change now. I will talk with the wife of the new President of the United States and she will make him understand that the youth of this country love Timothy Leary and want him free." I grimaced at Dennis. "Stop making that awful noise, Dennis." He paid no attention, so I opened the thick white bathrobe provided by the hotel. "I'm still brown from the California sun, Dennis, don't you think? How I miss the ocean . . ."

He stopped pushing buttons on his synthesizer and leaned over to pull on my left ear lobe. "You have the longest ear lobes of anyone I've ever slept with."

I pushed him away.

"Come on, Peachy, don't be so sensitive, I was just joking."

The phone rang. "Hello?" I said.

An echoing man's voice at the other end of the line said, "Joanna Leary?"

"Yes?"

"Can you be at the Triangle Building at nine o'clock tomorrow morning for a meeting with Attorney General William Saxbe?"

"Who is this?" I asked, buying time to hide how astonished I was.

"FBI Agent Marc Rigby. The appointment has been arranged for you by Senator Humphrey."

"The Triangle Building, is that . . . ?"

"It's the office building at the Hall of Justice on Constitution Avenue. Will you be there?"

"Of course," I said, catching my breath, "I look forward to speaking with the Attorney General."

"Bye bye." *Click*.

I threw the receiver on the bed and started jumping up and down on the thick wall-to-wall carpet. "That's it, Dennis! I'm going to convince them that it's a big mistake to keep him in prison!"

Dennis was not smiling.

"What's the matter?" I asked, looking down at him on the bed.

He looked up at me, biting his thumbnail with that nasty look on his face. "Just because you're going to see the Attorney General doesn't mean Tim is out of the woods."

I still had $55,000 in cash from the Franklin caper and was close to accomplishing my mission, and yet Dennis' eyes were as hard as they had been the day he bit my cheek until there were teeth marks and blood. His attitude seemed ominous, even threatening. I took it to mean he was jealous.

"Don't spoil everything with your jealousy, Dennis. There is room for you in my relationship with Timothy. We will still be lovers when he gets out, just not my *only* lover." I pushed my hair back with my hand. "You are not even my only lover now. If somebody really appealed to me, I would fuck them. We're young, remember? This is not about being faithful, it's about pleasure and fun."

He looked me up and down with disdain, then turned and walked over to the small fridge in the bar, took out a miniature Cuervo Gold, and tippled it down in one gulp. Smacking his lips, he said, "I want you to be only with me."

"Who do you think you are?" I yelled. "I'm free, I do what I want, I'm not ready to belong to anyone. Even Timothy accepts that." I was furious.

Next, he pulled out a miniature Smirnoff. "Why are you with me, then? Just so I can help you get what you want? Score drugs for you, follow you around like a poodle?"

I sat down on the sofa. "Come here, Dennis," I said gently, patting the sofa beside me. "Stop this, you know what's going on. We are both trying to make the government see that our generation is not out to get them, that we only want to live in a world where pleasure and beauty have more of a place than violence and cruelty. We want them to understand that we have a perfect right to put whatever we want into our bodies, to alter our consciousness as we please. We are going to make the Feds understand that they have no right to police the inside of our minds. We are the translators, Dennis, the interpreters. We are here to get the message across that Timothy is not a criminal, he is a philosopher like Alan Watts, Ken Kesey, Jerry Garcia, and the others."

Dennis was shaking his head, having already tossed off the Smirnoff's. "I don't care anymore, I only want you to be with me." He dropped his blue velvet pants, naked underneath.

Horror and despair overtook me. "No, Dennis, put your trousers back on. I don't want to be exclusive. What do you want, a picket-fence wife, a Wonder Bread mama? I can't do it. I like fame, excitement, and drama too much for that." I stretched my arms up and out. "Make me a vodka and tonic, will you? All of this bickering makes me tired. After a nice drink, I'll go to bed and get my beauty sleep for tomorrow at the Triangle Building."

64

FOUR AND TWENTY BLACKBIRDS

I was so nervous in the morning that I could only nibble my croissant from room service. My hair wouldn't fall the right way on my shoulders, but my tight black miniskirt, shiny black tights, black creased velvet top, and knee-high platform black suede boots looked perfect.

"Order the car, Dennis, or we'll be late. Press the bellboy button— Hurry, I don't want to get caught in morning traffic."

We drove in silence through a crisp DC morning, the inside of the Hertz rent-a-car hazy with smoke from my nervous chain smoking. Dennis waited outside as I entered the Triangle Building at exactly 8:50 feeling frail, sandwiched between the vaulted ceiling and marble floor of the large entryway.

I stepped through the metal detector with immunity, having left my cocaine and marijuana stash in the car.

"Third floor, elevator on the left, the Attorney General is expecting you." The guard nodded me on my way.

In the elevator was a man in a grey suit, his pants two inches too short, sent to watch me in case I held a bomb between my teeth or legs.

A middle-aged woman greeted me as the elevator doors slid open. "This way, Mrs. Leary." Still no smile. She walked slowly in front of me until we reached a large mahogany door. Cracking it open, she announced, "Mrs. Leary."

A dozen men in dark suits rose from their chairs as I entered, the man at the big desk indicating a chair. I sat down, crossed my legs, and carefully lit a cigarette. The atmosphere was somber and tense.

"You asked to see me," said the man behind the desk who was obviously Attorney General Saxbe, pushing a crystal ashtray toward me. "These gentlemen," he gestured toward the others, "will sit in on our meeting. They are Justice Department lawyers and FBI agents."

No names, no introductions. *Does the AG need so many people to protect himself?* I wondered. He must be as afraid of me as I am of him. At that moment I remembered a trick that always made me feel safe. I looked around the room and imagined each man stark naked. I began to plead my case.

"Timothy Leary is not a drug trafficker, and yet he was sentenced to ten years in prison for possession of $1/100^{th}$ of a gram of marijuana. He is a scholar, a philosopher, like Socrates."

"What about his escape from prison?" Saxbe asked sharply. "What about his going over the wall in San Luis Obispo, and then being brought back from Afghanistan three years later? Is that the deed of a philosopher or a convicted felon?" The zigzag vein on his right temple throbbed beneath his pale skin.

I swallowed hard. "He had no hope of ever getting out of prison. His wife Rosemary was being unfaithful . . . He panicked, sir, a mistake . . ."

"If I was your father, I would spank you hard."

Saxbe's harsh words hit me like a slap on the face and knocked the words out of me. I began to shiver, suddenly feeling very tiny and wanting to run. In a small voice, I made one final try. "At least you could move him back to California. I know that Senator Humphrey does not want him in his state."

65

QUEEN MARY, SAVE US

Someone must have heard my small voice because Timothy was transferred to Terminal Island Federal Prison in Long Beach, the very place I had mentioned to Senator Humphrey. Don Strange called me and told me to move onto the *Queen Mary*, a Cunard luxury ocean liner turned into a hotel just a short taxi ride from Terminal Island. Visiting was permitted daily from twelve to four, so I didn't have to get up early or miss happy hour on the ship. I loved my stateroom with its royal blue bedspread and mahogany cabinets, porthole instead of window, even the noise of oil pumps on the other side of the bay.

Timothy again looked as at ease as he always did when in California. Holding my hands in his, he said that my career as an informant was about to begin. "We're going to have to prove to the Feds that I've become harmless. The more good will and convincing ardor you show in setting up the people I name, the closer I'll be to release." At Special Agent Strange's instigation, he'd already called his attorney George Chula in Orange County to tell him that I was going to call on him for a favor. I was to make him sell me an ounce of cocaine—just enough to take away his license to practice law and make him do some serious time.

We were sitting in the sun on the prison terrace surrounded by high chicken wire with thick barbed wire at the top, light years from the terraces we used to sit on in Switzerland, sipping cappuccinos and eating dark Lindt chocolate. Here, the coffee was lousy and loudspeakers at each end of the visiting area crackled and spat out harsh words on an ongoing basis.

I stared out at the Pacific Ocean as Timothy excitedly talked about conversations he was having with Gordon Liddy in the yard, something about going on a lecture tour together when they got out, debating right and left politics, Timothy advocating the legalization of drugs and Liddy taking the cops' side.

He laughed. "Ironic, isn't it, that he was the first cop to ever bust me at Millbrook in Duchess County in upstate New York." Still smiling wanly at the fickle finger of fate, he added, "Burst into my bedroom with his posse in the middle of the night, looking for drugs."

I nodded and tried to listen, smoking non-stop, frantic about my new role of destroying the lives of people I had no reason to care about. Moral corruption has no limits, no boundaries to hang onto, and his chitchat felt very far away.

"Timothy, what's going to happen when your attorney figures out that I set him up?" I asked, nervously braiding and unbraiding hair around my face.

He put his hand on my knee. "Don't be nervous. It's Chula's fault that I'm in prison. He's an awful lawyer, raised only one objection during my whole trial." Lighting a Camel, he closed his eyes, opened them, and looked at me. "It's so good to be back here in the California sun. As soon as I get out, we'll head for a Caribbean island, St. Thomas or Barbados, somewhere we can be alone together and make lots of babies. I'll hold you in my arms day and night, and you will forget all of these stupid people, Joanna." His tone changed. "At the end of our visit, you'll go with Don and a couple of other narcs to phone Chula and make arrangements to meet with him."

So it was. Waiting for me were the small, round narc Strange with the Louisiana drawl, and Larry Barker, the tall, skinny one with blond hair and a toothpick permanently lodged between his teeth, the jackets of their plain blue suits bulging above the buttocks with the outline of their big .357 Magnums. On the *Queen Mary*, we walked one behind the other along the corridors like Keystone cops. Given that narcs weren't free love hippies—they believed women should be faithful while husbands went to massage parlors—I agonized over the possibility that Dennis might be there. But Room 306 was empty, the maids had come and gone, and there was no second toothbrush, no dirty socks, nothing to make the narcs suspect that I was anything other than the long-suffering young wife of an imprisoned philosopher.

What I didn't know then and would learn only during the hard days of the coming falling action was that Strange and his minions knew all about Dennis the double agent and his assignment to make sure that I stayed stoned and on track for snitching. I was deep in the house of mirrors. The Clear Light days were over, only I was too drunk and drugged to realize just how over they were.

66

VIRGINIA CHURCH AND CHARLIE THRUSH BEGIN TO SING

My brief career as an informant was beginning as *magical theatre* became more and more like a surreal Theatre of the Absurd.

As I savagely puffed on my Gauloise in my *Queen Mary* cabin, Agent Strange sat on the edge of the bed like it was his, then clicked open a briefcase and pulled out a small tape recorder. He attached a wire to the back of the telephone receiver and nodded to me. I dialed George Chula's number. We agreed to meet at six on Monday and I hung up, the two narcs beaming at me like proud parents.

"You did good," Strange said, "we'll be at your suite before six on Monday with Agent Laurie Farmer. She'll outfit you with a bug."

"Bug?"

Strange shrugged. "You're going to go to this dinner with a microphone taped to your body so we can listen in from our van parked outside."

When they left, I ordered a double Bloody Mary from room service, put on Genesis singing "Selling England by the Pound," and sat in the chair by the porthole watching oil pumps hump like huge grasshoppers, concentrating on learning to hate George Chula. I'd only met him once at the Orange County Jail, and unfortunately he had greeted me with a warm smile. He was about forty-five, with silver hair and eyes like a basset hound's. *All lawyers are bastards,* I practiced, *out to rip you off and take everything you have.* No attorney had been able to get Timothy out of prison, so what good were they?

The vodka helped, but the cocaine that Dennis brought back helped even more. I was so quiet, he asked if I was afraid. I looked at him. Did I see a dark, cold streak in his steel-blue eyes, or was it in me? No, I wasn't afraid. I was paranoid. Look at the company I was keeping.

For our few visits before the Chula sting, Timothy and I assiduously avoided what was really on our minds and talked instead of our pending baby girl we would name Chrysalis, both of us knowing that I would have sold my soul to have our little family dream come true. In my mind, I could still see him kneeling to ask my mother for my hand. And yet that was the last I'd heard of marriage—obviously *un geste du chevalier.*

On the day of my rendezvous with Chula, I was "made over" by curly, redheaded Agent Laurie Farmer until I was USDA-approved sexy and wired for sound. Under my aqua velvet pants was a small black transmitter Agent Farmer had taped to the inside of my thigh while running a small wire up my stomach and taping it to my belly button under my silk wrap-around blouse. Bionic Woman was ready to roll.

At the small seafood restaurant in a Costa Mesa shopping center that Chula had chosen, I ordered Clams Casino and began tapping into his guilt about Timothy's conviction and imprisonment in 1969. He had reveled in the limelight of the media circus, and his practice in Orange County had grown and flourished while his high-profile client lost his case.

"I wish there was something I could do," Chula said thoughtfully. "I bring him good dope every time I see him, just to make things easier for him. You know lawyers aren't searched."

Pearls of sweat gathered on my upper lip. I could feel his words zapping under my right breast and racing outside to the unmarked van.

"George," I said, making my French accent heavier and my voice gentler, "I have developed quite a taste for cocaine. Would you happen to have any connections?" A clam slid down my throat.

"No problem, I find cocaine very pleasant myself." George's eyes gleamed as he took a folded piece of white paper out of his breast pocket and slipped it into my black satin bag. "Take this gram home with you."

"Thank you, George, what a wonderful gift. I'll tell Timothy you took good care of me." I flashed him my best smile. Then, pretending to hesitate out of delicacy, I threw him the big hook. "I would love to have an ounce, if it were possible. That way, I wouldn't have to think about it for a while." I smiled.

"No problem, let's meet again next week and I'll have it for you." We agreed to talk in a few days.

From that point on, I lived in perpetual fear—fear that George Chula would find out I was working for the Feds, fear that the Feds would find out I was sleeping with Dennis and high on hard drugs and downers on a regular basis in violation of our implicit contract that I do drugs only when it served the purpose of a sting and never on my own.

And while I was turning myself inside out to get him out, Timothy was happily bunking with Liddy for whom Terminal Island was country club penance for supposedly refusing to cooperate with the Justice Department regarding the Watergate break-in. Thanks to Uncle Sam, they were now literally "on the same side," and when they got out would take their crowd-pleaser vaudevillian act of two old antagonists on the road. When I would rain on their parade by showing up with a long face and a raging rash all over my body, my skin flaking and breaking into angry red welts under my see-through Indian blouse and silk harem pants, Timothy would downshift and console me with our imaginary baby. Then, I would drag home to Dennis who would undress me and soak me in a warm bath filled with oatmeal, smooth Calamine lotion onto my arms and shoulders and breasts, telling me all the while, "Peachy, you mustn't take this cowboys-and-Indians game so seriously. It only *seems* like there are two sides, but there aren't, it's just the one game."

Little did I know how well he knew that.

After the Fourth of July, I was moved to the Disneyland Hotel in Anaheim because Disneyland, appropriately enough, was closer to the Feds' Orange County headquarters. The narcs set up their electronic equipment in the adjoining suite. With three Feds at my elbow, I called Chula who said he'd have cocaine for me in the next couple of days.

I spent the lag time sunbathing topless by the hotel swimming pool, figuring that I was already an informant for the federal government so who would arrest me for being topless? The action was getting so intense that I kept slipping into a quasi-hypnotic trance, no doubt encouraged by the good drugs Dennis had given me before disappearing into the woodwork until I returned to Long Beach.

The day of the Chula sting, the Feds had bugs all over my room. Next door, they were drinking coffee and Boone's Farm wine and gloating over the pleasure they would have in busting this pinko-commie lawyer, leaving me alone to cruise the high ethers of non-reality due to the heroin I'd snorted earlier in the women's bathroom by the pool. They wouldn't let me watch television because it would interfere with the bugs, so I paced and chain-smoked. Light became dark, ocean waves rolled, freeway traffic droned. Finally, George called. Something was wrong, he said, he would be late. A click followed by another click, and the room was silent once more. Three hours later, he arrived, his white shirt opened to his waist, his dark blue silk pants wet to the mid-calf, sand on his Gucci loafers.

"What a night," he said as he came in, "I have a hard time believing what just happened."

"Drink?" I asked, pointing to the bottle of Chivas Regal on my night table.

"Yes," he said, still standing and watching me. My hands shook as I poured.

Then, he grabbed me and held me much too close. "Is something going on, Joanna? Tell me, did you set me up? Is Tim part of this?"

"I don't know what you mean, what is wrong with you?" My head was filling with blood.

"Sit down," he commanded, pushing me down onto one of the straight chairs. Now, he paced as I had, talking all the while. He'd driven down to Costa Mesa to his friend's beach house to get the cocaine. Before going in, he'd decided to take a short walk on the beach when a lifeguard wearing only a beach towel and flip-flops approached, holding a black walky-talky and saying, "Man, you must be important because they're really after you." He'd been picking up undercover police cars talking about George on their band radios for the past hour, following him, crisscrossing all around him on the freeway.

My heart was beating so hard I thought it was going to end up on the table beside us, and my tongue was so dry I could have filed my nails on it. Breathlessly, I asked, "How could they know? Are you sure he was telling the truth?"

He reached into his pants pocket and pulled out a Marlboro pack from which he retrieved a joint and a tiny folded piece of white paper. Sighing, he sat down.

"Let's do some of this," he said. "Of course, I didn't score the ounce. I just sat in my car, wondering what was happening. I just can't believe Timothy or you would . . ." His voice trailed off as he lit the joint and passed it to me.

Exhaling, I said, "George, I have no idea what is going on, but you know how I am followed, how my telephone is tapped, how I am body-searched when I visit Timothy so I never feel free." The suffering on my face was genuine. "One thing I do know, though. You must thank Fate for the 'angel on the beach.'" I meant this.

Abruptly, he stood up. "I'll go now. I wish I knew what was going on. Keep the gram."

The minute he left, the narc posse burst into my room with rubber gloves to collect the meager evidence, a half-smoked joint and a minute amount of cocaine. I sat dazed while they scurried around, my feet propped up on the dresser, so stoned I could not move.

"We got him, anyway," Don Strange was saying, "it's not much, but it's still a felony. We can impound his car for transporting illegal substances, then drag him into court for possession. Damn that nosy hippie on the beach, those pinko-commie faggots are everywhere." Almost as an afterthought, he added, "Are you ready to be debriefed, Joanna?"

His narc voice reached me from afar. I nodded as I poured a double whiskey, hoping I would be as stoned as Lot's wife so I could never look back.

67

THE GUN

By impersonating a *London Sunday Times* reporter, I contrived to meet the dashing and controversial California Governor Jerry Brown and begged him to parole Timothy out of the California prison system, meaning both state convictions, the ten years for possession, and the five for escape. Governor Brown was politically inclined to do this, although I knew that Timothy, Don Strange, and other FBI agents were bending their heads over how I might set Brown up for a cocaine transaction, a scheme that fortunately never transpired. However it went down, once Timothy was out of the state system and transferred into the federal system Terminal Island in Long Beach he still had at least a dime of federal time to do for interstate transport of several grams of marijuana. Basically, the Feds now owned him entirely.

After Chula, we had morning meetings in the US Marshal's headquarters with a smorgasbord of government officials in three-piece suits, after which Timothy was interrogated for hours in a small rural country club jail outside of Sacramento. DA John Milano coordinated the agencies interrogating Timothy, but within a few months would resign as US Attorney to become Timothy's criminal defense lawyer. Art Van Court, US Marshal for Eastern California, and his staff were responsible for Timothy's and my containment as well as safety. Despite his role as our keeper, Timothy and I liked Art, who had been Ronald Reagan's private bodyguard while he was governor of California. The California Feds were interested in compromising liberal lawyers, and Chicago FBI wanted to get their hands on the Weathermen, particularly Bernadine Dohrn and Bill Ayers, who had helped Timothy escape.

My name was now Virginia Church. I was given protective custody status under the Witness Protection Program out of Falls Church, Virginia and moved to an apartment in Sacramento, where I was not allowed to leave the building without escort or make phone calls without permission, supposedly because of threats against my life by angry pinko-commie hippies and dope dealers. What it really did was isolate me from anything familiar.

Timothy had put on weight at Terminal Island, and as I listened to him talk on and on in the white seersucker suit he had requested I buy for him, with his pudgy middle and thinning hair, I couldn't get over how much like a Fed he looked, except, of course, for his trademark blue and white Adidas. When he wasn't spilling his guts, he played handball for hours with federal agents at a safe house near Folsom Lake. I was fascinated by how charmed the agents were by his jokes about being on different sides of the net but playing the same game. Every time he sent me out to bust somebody, the marshals keeping him hidden cheered and assured him that they would testify on his behalf at the upcoming parole board hearing.

Jean Genet, the notorious French homosexual thief turned writer, said that cops and criminals complement each other and are unable to function without each other. Ultimately, both are rejected and cursed by society.

But as talk rapidly moved toward action against the Weathermen, Timothy felt more and more up against the wall. He was no nearer to being released from the 10-year federal sentence and suspected that the Feds would find one reason after another to squeeze him while the promise of freedom became a speck on the horizon. At Vacaville, when he agreed to cooperate, he had said to me, "This had better work fast, or I'll escape again."

So I was not surprised in November 1975, when we were kissing goodbye, to hear him whisper, "Get a G-U-N." To have decided that his only option lay in armed flight and even murder revealed the depth of his desperation, for Timothy was no killer. In my fantasy life, this latest escape plan would turn us into Bonnie and Clyde. Upon my return to the motel, I told Dennis what Timothy had whispered and Dennis said getting a gun would be easy, he knew someone.

The next day Dennis and I drove to San Francisco. I opened the window, the summer air blowing on my face like on one of those poodles with its ears flying back in the wind. Dennis' voice reached me. "You'll have to be nice to the man we're going to see—you know, flirt with him, make him feel good."

I hope he's good looking, was all I thought.

In the City, Dennis finally pulled up in front of a dirty repair garage. Inside, a fat mechanic was bent over a Mustang engine. When Dennis reminded him that we'd come for a gun, he wiped his greasy hands on an old rag and led the way to a dingy desk drawer with a handgun in it. While looking at us, he toyed with the gun as if the mere act of holding it aroused him. Looking straight at me, he commanded huskily, "Come here."

He pulled me onto his lap and slipped his hand under my skirt. Dennis had a strange look of approval on his face, and any kind of approval made me want more approval, whatever it was about. I smiled, fantasizing being in a big bed with Timothy after we killed the marshals and stuck their bodies in the trunk of the car like in the movies.

The greasy man grinned, his hand on my crotch. "It's a hundred dollars plus a little friendliness from you, beautiful."

I wiggled a bit on his lap and finally broke free towards Dennis. "Give him the money and let's go," I said, disgusted and detached at the same time.

Back in the car, I cradled the first gun I'd ever touched. These days almost all the men I associated with carried huge .357 Magnums.

Except for blaming the idea of the gun on me, *Flashbacks* relates beautifully the recognizance journey we took into Oregon to finger the Weathermen safe houses he and Rosemary had been taken to after his escape. Early one morning, our guardian angels US Marshal Art Van

Court and FBI Agent Dan McGowan, an expert on the Weathermen, picked me up. We then collected Timothy at the latest rural jail, Art and Dan in the front seat, Timothy and I in back, the little handgun that Dennis and I had gotten tucked in my boot. As we drove toward the Oregon border, Dan's .357 slipped under the front seat to the backseat floor. I was aghast. *Two guns within reach.* But Timothy picked up Dan's .357, carefully wrapped it in the sports section of the *San Francisco Chronicle* he'd been reading, and returned it to Dan.

I could tell that Timothy was extremely tense about informing on the Weatherman, so when we pit-stopped in the woods just south of the Oregon border, I think I was ready to kill. I had no more will of my own, no life except this endless string of prisons, steel doors clanging in my sleep as well as in real life, and seemingly no other way out of the nightmare Timothy and I had fallen into. There was no me; there was only Timothy's "perfect love." I was ready to kill just so I could rest my mind for a while without feeling responsible for solving the enormous political game surrounding Timothy.

But when we got out of the car to stretch and the two Feds were peeing by a tree, Timothy took me aside and whispered, "I have realized we would have to kill everyone we meet after getting rid of these two." Live by blood, die by blood. His implacable logic and the thought of a subsequent life of carnage woke me from my trance. *Was this real, two lovers clinging miserably to each other in a damp forest?*

In a fog, I heard Dan say, "I'm going to shoot you."

Fear made my whole body tingle. I broke free of Timothy's embrace to face my executioner, but he was only shooting snaps of the famous star-crossed lovers. Inexplicably, the search for safe houses was called off and we turned back toward Sacramento, the gun still in my boot, the barrel digging into my ankle. A couple of days later, I threw it into the American River and told Dennis to never, ever come near me again. Jack Daniels was the only man I wanted around. Since Timothy had been brought back to the US, Dennis was always around, feeding me sex and drugs, and I was sick and tired of his possessiveness like a wasp on honey. At first, I thought my directive had finally worked, and though I missed the sex, I did not miss the man.

68

DENNIS DIES

A couple of months after the recognizance journey, Art Van Court and his top marshal Fred Pierce picked me up before breakfast at the apartment in Sacramento they had secured for me under the Witness Protection Program. Orders from on high said I was no longer Virginia Church but Samantha Weatherfield—surely a psyops reference to the fictional town in the British ITV soap opera *Coronation Street*. Fred loved calling me Sam, making me feel more and more as if I were completely disappearing into a story not of my own making and adding to my growing sense of unreality.

Art and Fred were in the front seat of the black unmarked sedan, I was in the back with no clue about where we were going, except to see Timothy at a safe house. A good 45 minutes later, we arrived at a house near a lake. Around Timothy were John Milano, Assistant DA Jerry Utz, FBI agents, and of course the same cast of DEA characters, E. Donald Strange and cronies. Timothy looked troubled.

Taking me in his arms, he said, "You have to go back to your mother's house in Spain for a while. Dennis wrote our friends the Feds saying that you're his mistress."

The dozen men in dark suits stared at me like disapproving fathers. I imagined them wagging their index fingers as a wave of immeasurable shame wafted over me. Holding onto Timothy's lapels, I sobbed, "I've been so lonely and isolated." Naughty Samantha Weatherfield. Remembering the words of the AG in DC, I wondered if they were going to spank me.

My mind was racing; nothing made sense, however I looked at any of it. Timothy knew all along I was sleeping with Dennis and did not seem to mind. Now, it had become important and wrong. *Why?*

In a mocking tone, Fred Pierce said, "How could we have missed that?" Several of the dark suits grinned as if he'd said something funny.

"Go and pack your things for your flight tomorrow, Sam," Art said.

"I'll phone you every day, my perfect love," Timothy said, hugging me.

I clung to him. What was going on? Why was I going to Marbella? And how could Timothy be two people, one for me and one for the Feds, at the same time?

Unlike California, Marbella was in full winter. Cold rain fell on the Mediterranean in rhythm to my hot tears in the bath. I missed Timothy terribly and could not understand why I had been banished to Europe. Every couple of days, he phoned collect from a pay phone that Marshal Van Court accompanied him to. Sprawled on Mummy's bed, I clung to his voice while her dog Ben sniffed and licked my bare feet. (Mummy said Ben was her husband, which disgusted me.) Every phone call, I begged Timothy to convince the Feds to bring me back, but all he kept saying was that he loved me and we would soon be together.

One night, there was a knock on the French doors opening onto the garden. There stood an emaciated Dennis with large blue circles under his eyes. "I've just come back from a mission for the Feds in Bogota," he said. "I stopped over in Zurich for a few days and saw those people Tim and I were living with when we all met, remember? Come here and let me kiss and hold you. I've been thinking about it for thousands of miles."

He looked forlorn, but I was adamant. "No, I told you never again."

"But Peachy, I want to marry you." Gently, he pushed my hair back from my face with a trembling hand.

I shrugged. "You can't marry me. I want to be with Timothy, he is my love. I've told you that a million times."

Sighing, he pulled out his wallet and unfolded a white piece of paper. "I've got some good Colombian cocaine for you."

Fleetingly, I wondered how he could get through customs with drugs on him but didn't hesitate: the stuff looked good and I hadn't had cocaine or heroin since seeing him almost three months before. Besides, everyone had drugs then, or at least that's what the addict in me said.

After snorting close to a gram of cocaine, I gave in to Dennis' desire. I didn't like myself for doing it, but I did like the power I had over men.

When Mummy came home from her bridge game at the Marbella Club, she was unpleasantly surprised to see the man she had met in San Francisco. The cook had made dinner so the three of us sat down at the dining room table.

Then, like a B-grade repeat of Tim's proposal, Dennis asked my mother for my hand in marriage.

Mummy gasped, then laughed, flicking her Bic at a king-sized Winston and inhaling deeply. In English with a heavy French accent, her raspy Marlene Dietrich voice began cutting him down to size. "Who do you think you are—you, the son of a mediocre hairdresser in some cheap suburb of Los Angeles? Over my dead body. How would *you* keep her in the style to which she has been accustomed?"

I flashed on my small studio apartment on Telegraph Hill, hitch-hiking to Folsom prison in my only dress, and selling photocopies of Tim's prison manuscript on the street in Berkeley. Was this the style to which I was accustomed? I lowered my eyes and stared at my plate of paella.

When Dennis was hurt, his brown eyes turned to dark lightning bolts. "I can support your daughter. I'm going to become a CIA agent."

Liar, I thought, *you're a low level informant.* And yet there was the trip to Bogota, the extended stays in Miami, all the plane tickets he'd shown me. Dennis was coming up in the world but not the world I wanted to be in.

After dinner, I called a taxi and took Dennis to the Hotel La Fonda, where I had hung out with Rolling Stones women and at times Keith Richards and Mick Jagger. Dennis' small suitcase was no doubt packed with his polyester shirts with long pointed collars, and of course he had his little Moog synthesizer metal case. I walked up the stairs with him to the room in the tower.

"If you don't marry me I'm going to kill myself," Dennis blurted out as soon as he closed the door.

His crass emotional blackmail angered me. "Well, if you choose to do that, please don't do it on my doorstep. Have you come all the way to Spain to do this to me? Go and die in Morocco across the Straits of Gibraltar, far away from my life." A cat caterwauled from the street below. Picking up my handbag, I said good night and left.

Downstairs in the bar, I ordered a double cognac. What a terrible headache Dennis had turned out to be. Would I never be rid of him and his sticky, bewitching energy?

A couple of days later, I was invited to a flamenco party on Saudi arms dealer Adnan Khashoggi's boat the *Mohammédia*, the biggest yacht in the Marbella harbor. Dennis had been phoning the house over and over, but I was not going to let him spoil the evening for me. I dressed carefully in long gypsy patchwork skirt, a frilly white blouse, and silver sandals. The *Mohammédia* was packed with the beautiful people basking in drugs served by butlers on silver trays and the talents of the Paco de Lucía dancers and singers of southern Spain. The alcohol and Quaaludes I was doing meant hardly touching the cornucopia of Middle Eastern food on the buffet table. Had the soundtrack been Queen's "Khashoggi's Ship," I might have realized how prophetic it all was:

> *Who said that my party was all over, huh, huh*
> *I'm in pretty good shape*
> *The best years of my life are like a supernova*
> *A huh, huh, perpetual craze . . .*

I awoke at eleven the next morning in the guest room of someone's house with no memory of having left the party. Hung over and perplexed, I grabbed my things and called a taxi.

Mummy was waiting for me on the steps of the villa. "Wash your face and put on something decent," she said, shoving a Valium into my mouth and handing me a glass of Perrier. "Dennis is dead and the *Guardia Civil* want to talk to you. Suicide, they say. They have been here at the house several times looking for you."

I was in a hung over daze as the chauffeur drove me to the police station. A police inspector who had come all the way from Madrid showed me Dennis' passport.

"*Sí*," I answered in my best Spanish, "I know this man. I saw him a few days ago." *Why had someone come all the way from Madrid for a suicide?* I wondered.

"The hotel manager called us when he did not come out of his room," the inspector said flatly. "We suspect suicide. Did he kill himself because of you?"

Terrified by the direction his questions were taking, I flashed on my last scene with Dennis.

The inspector then pointed to what Dennis had said was a Moog synthesizer. "What is this?" he asked suspiciously.

"A musical instrument," I answered dully.

"We'll see about that. I'll have it identified in Madrid."

I could not feel anything other than frozen and afraid. *Had I caused Dennis' death?* Quickly, I chased away this unpleasant thought. I would go and have a Bloody Mary or two at the port bar. Yes, that was a good idea. Everyone would be gossiping about the American's death at the La Fonda Hotel and I would be the center of attention.

Finally, the inspector said I was free to go and could collect Dennis' things at the La Fonda. After bolstering my courage in the port bar, I went to his tower room and found a half bottle of Valium and half bottle of wine on the bedside table—and his diary. On the last page were lines from his birthday brother Bob Dylan's song "Just Like A Woman":

> *When we meet again*
> *Introduced as friends*
> *Please don't let on that you knew me when*
> *I was hungry and it was your world*

Years later, I would wonder about the Feds choosing to house me on the *Queen Mary* and how it fit with that same Dylan song—

> Queen Mary, she's my friend
> Yes, I believe I'll go see her again
> Nobody has to guess
> That Baby can't be blessed
> Till she finally sees that she's like all the rest
> With her fog, her amphetamine and her pearls

I'm not saying that "Just Like A Woman" was written with Dennis and me in mind, but could Dylan lyrics have been used in some terrible Theatre of the Absurd psyop against us? Sadly, back then my ensnared mind was incapable of wrapping itself around the possibility that intelligence agencies don't just manipulate people's lives but their minds, too.

Like an automaton, I went home and called Don Strange. He didn't sound the least surprised by Dennis' death and put me off, saying he couldn't talk now but would call me back. The next day, the *Guardia Civil* called to ask me to identify Dennis' body. Though my memory has blanketed that macabre scene with a dense traumatized fog, I do recall the refrigerated drawer at the Catholic cemetery being rolled out to reveal the lifeless body of a man I knew intimately. I verified the US Navy tattoo on his arm that proved the body was not that of his twin. But it was the *state* of the body that made me throw up on the tiled floor. Autopsy demanded that the body be cut open and summarily sewn back together. The Dennis I knew was now a Frankenstein. On his death certificate, cause of death read *Acute peritonitis and gastritis*—not suicide. I was confused, but refrained from asking.

The following day, Strange called to say Timothy had been transferred to a special unit for high-powered snitches at the San Diego Metropolitan Correctional Center, otherwise known as the Cinnamon Stick, and that I could return now, as if Dennis's death had been the turnkey to return me to Timothy.

It was the end of November 1975 and the bizarre psychological operations Timothy and I had fallen prey to weren't over yet.

69

THE FLOPHOUSE OF MIRRORS

From Marbella to Madrid and London and Los Angeles and finally San Diego, I contemplated Dennis' death. I had spent several sad days with his father who had now returned to California with his son's body. He could not understand why Dennis would have committed suicide in this faraway land. He was angry at me, but primarily directed his grief and confusion at Timothy. Dennis' twin David had fathered two children with Timothy's daughter Susan and had mysteriously become severely schizophrenic. One son locked in a mental institution, now another son dead in the south of Spain—both intimately involved in the fate of Timothy Leary.

After 24 hours of travel, I arrived exhausted in San Diego. Two US Marshals I didn't know met me at the gate. "We're taking you to your hotel and will pick you up tomorrow morning to go and see Timothy at the Cinnamon Stick."

"The Cinnamon Stick?" I was puzzled.

"The new prison recently built downtown on Union Street." Like Tweedledum and Tweedledee, one marshal opened the car door for me, the other stowed my luggage in the trunk.

They pulled up in front of a seedy downtown hotel obviously on the local Skid Row.

"What is this?" I asked. Never had the marshals subjected me to such accommodations. What was going on?

The marshals smirked at each other. "It's just one night. You'll be moved tomorrow."

My room was on the seventh floor close to the fire escape, the view a deserted concrete parking lot. It was 7 pm California time but my body was on jet lag time. I threw myself on the lousy mattress, the springs digging into my skinny body, suddenly worried about my safety. I was tired but wired, and it was too early to go to sleep without some help. *Same solution to a different problem*, I thought: *I'll go downstairs, find a liquor store, and drink myself to sleep.*

Cautiously making my way down the dark, shabby corridor to the elevator, I eventually ended up on the street where there was no lack of liquor stores. Several black men were hovering outside the nearest liquor store, drinking from brown paper bags. I grabbed a six-pack of Coors beer and a pint of whiskey to put me to sleep, plus a bag of ice, and hurried back to the hotel. All the way up on the elevator, a black man stared at me, then got out on my floor, and seemed to be following me down the hallway. The hairs on my arms stood up as a cold sweat broke out on my upper lip.

I stopped at my room and fumbled with my keys, letting out the breath I didn't know I was holding as he passed me and continued to the next room. Inside, I quickly closed the door and chain-locked it. I definitely needed a drink now. After dumping the ice in the bathroom sink and burying the beers in it, I poured a shot of whiskey into a plastic glass, my hand trembling. The brown liquid felt good going down my throat. *I'm safe now*, I thought, walking back into the room.

But then I stopped, frozen by terror as I stared at the thin adjoining door between my room and that of the man who had passed me in the hall. Mechanically, I went to the phone, dialed 9 and the phone number the marshals had given me. Ring after ring echoed in my ear. No answer.

I was lost, immobilized like a deer in the headlights at night. I popped open a beer and drank greedily. The phone rang. *Saved*, I thought. It was Timothy calling from the prison. I spilled out my fears in a quiet voice, afraid of the man beyond the paper-thin door. All Timothy could say was "I'm in prison and can't help you."

Suddenly, the man in the adjoining room started banging on the door between us. "Open the door!" he shouted. "I want to come in!"

Timothy could hear him, too, and frantically told me to hang up and call security, but I couldn't hang up: Timothy was all I had. I was trapped on the phone with a powerless man locked behind steel doors.

"I just want you to save me!" I whispered furiously to Timothy as the black man continued shouting and banging.

"I can't do anything from here, you know that," Timothy said in a pained and frustrated voice. "Call the US marshals. Their job is to protect you." The man was still pounding.

"I tried to call them and they don't answer the phone. If harm comes to me, it will be your fault," I cried. In my despair, I was forcing upon him the impossible. I wanted him to understand that by being in prison he was killing me. The man in the other room was relentless; he was going to break down the door and it was all going to be Timothy's fault.

I hung up and drank more whiskey. At some point during my alcoholic fog, the threatening man stepped away from the door. When I finally came to, the faint light of dawn was trickling though the dirty windows and I was still in my clothes, lying in the fetal position on the bed.

A moment later, strong knocks on the door opening to the hall made me jump up. A voice followed the knocks. "San Diego Police! Open the door."

The clock said six o'clock.

"What do you want?" I yelled.

"Open the door!" the man's voice commanded again.

"Slip your ID under the door," I had the presence of mind to say. He did as I asked. *San Diego Police Department.* It looked legitimate, so I unlocked the door.

Two agitated detectives barged in.

"Did you hear any disturbance last night?" one of them asked. "The man in the room next to yours pushed a prostitute from the fire escape onto the parking lot below. Apparently, he went downstairs late last night, picked her up, and threw her off the fire escape."

His words penetrated my hung over brain like thunder.

"It was supposed to be me, " I said stunned, sitting back down on the bed. "He tried to break down my door last night. I guess he gave up and killed someone else."

As is usual with cops, they asked the same questions over and over. Suddenly, I had a terrifying thought. "Since you have not caught him yet, how do I know he will not try to find me and kill me?"

"Well, we don't know that, do we?" said the other detective. "But we don't think you're in danger. Here's my card. Call us if you see something."

It was broad day when they finally left. Disheveled and afraid, I caught my image in the mirror and looked at myself closely. What did I see? I looked into my own eyes for a fleeting moment—not too long because facing myself was too painful. *You are insane,* I said to my image, *you have become truly insane. No place to go, no one to talk to. Who is the one in solitary confinement now?*

At ten, the US Marshals showed up. When I asked why they had not answered my call the night before, Tweedledee said to me in the rearview mirror, "Probably our coffee break. What happened?"

I couldn't believe they did not know about the murder on my floor, and yet I'd seen how government agencies competed and didn't communicate with each other, the left hand not necessarily knowing what the right hand was up to. While driving to the Royal Inn at the Wharf, I recounted my night of terror.

Tweedledum shrugged and shook his head, his eyes blank. "Not a word."

70

JAMES AND NORA JOYCE

One morning, ex-DA John Milano called to tell me that the Federal Parole Board in Washington, DC had granted Timothy's immediate release. Apparently, Milano had waved the April 16, 1976 *National Review* in their faces and said, "How could you be worried about the man who blasted the Sixties icons in *National Review*?" It was true: Timothy had written an article for William F. Buckley calling the Weathermen a "bewildered, fugitive band of terrorists" and Bob Dylan's songs "snarling, whining, scorning, mocking."

I got out of bed, hung over and exhausted, and threw cold water on my face. We had won. We had succeeded. I was getting what I wanted. The man I lived for was going to be mine. I would be warm and loved at last. He would recognize that I was the one who saved him and reward me in every way for the rest of our lives, despite the inexplicable contradictions surrounding me, such as because of my love for Timothy, my sister had disinherited me and I was denied access to my daughter in Athens—and wasn't I supposed to hate government agents and love the poets and writers who were condemning Timothy and me for snitching?

At thirty, I thought I knew everything, but mainly what I knew was that I had to appear perfect at all times to all people. As an informant for the Feds, I was perfect enough to loosen up the parole board, but to Allen Ginsberg I was a "CIA sex provocateur" and the worst kind of low-life, a snitch. Some even said that I single-handedly brought down the Sixties, but the truth was that the kaleidoscopic revolution of my generation was about to crash and burn because we were coming up against an implacable law and order era that was just getting started. We wanted to do away with corrupt institutions but had no solid plan or power with which to replace them.

Mummy came to San Diego so she could share in the big moment. Together, we found her a nice apartment overlooking the bay with a large guest room and bathroom in which Timothy and I would stay for a while after his release. She got the color television she longed for. As soon as we knew that his parole had been granted, we rented a suite at the La Valencia Hotel in La Jolla just outside of San Diego and stocked it with Veuve Clicquot champagne and a basket of ripe mangoes and golden melons. This would be our freedom-honeymoon suite.

Timothy was released at the Cinnamon Stick on April 21, 1976. I waited at the door of the high-rise prison with John Milano and Mummy, surrounded by newspaper photographers and journalists as excited as we were. At last, Timothy bounced out in his trademark Adidas with a huge grin on his face, picked me up in his arms for all to see, and said, "At last I can be with my beautiful wife. We are going to live together and make many babies."

That night we dined at the excellent restaurant at the La Valencia. Starved for good food after years of institutional meals, Timothy ordered almost everything on the menu, shoving prime rib in his mouth, then lobster, crab, Caesar salad, topping it all off with chocolate mousse, strawberry rhubarb pie, and vanilla ice cream, with cognac and coffee to chase the excessive champagne we'd been drinking. How he ate that night drove home to me his three and a half year ordeal.

But when we returned to our freedom-honeymoon suite, we fought drunk for the first time. For my part, I had no idea how to express my feelings or think of his wasted years. I had suffered terribly and wanted Timothy to say he was sorry and make up for all this pain and fear I felt and probably for all the men who had betrayed me and used me ever since Daddy left before I was born.

Early the next morning, we were still in bed when there was a pounding at the door. Two federal marshals entered, assuring us that without the Witness Protection Program we would end up on a slab. They had orders to take us to a safe house in Salt Lake City, but Timothy was able to change it to Santa Fe. As the marshals left so we could prepare for our flight to Albuquerque in two hours, Timothy groaned, "This is just going to be another prison, I can feel it."

In Santa Fe, we were issued driver licenses in the names Timothy chose: James and Nora Joyce. With our Witness Protection Program government stipend of $700 a month each, we rented an A-frame in the Pecos Wilderness. Timothy made blazing fires, we cooked on a Coleman stove, chilled our drinks in the early spring river, and slept in a double sleeping bag. Bears moved at the edge of the forest while I sunned naked in a clearing near the cabin and Timothy wrote on his manual typewriter.

Now free to be together, we had a hard time connecting; too much water had flowed under our bridge. Truthfully, I did not recognize the man who came out after the better part of three and a half years of solitary confinement. My man without a country had become, like me, an alcoholic. We engaged in horrendous fights. He had an ongoing prescription he'd fill in Santa Fe for meds I never knew the name of; at the *pâtisserie* in the La Fonda Hotel, he groused about Bob Dylan being so negative and yet among his few possessions from prison was a book of Dylan lyrics. When we weren't drinking or fighting, we tried to bring to fruition our many hours of talk about having a baby, but Timothy's years in prison, all the drugs they had him on, and whatever else happened to him there had left him basically impotent. Each month was a disappointment. He was now 57 years old and I was 30.

In childhood, I had learned to be a genius at seeing the worst in every situation, so in the Pecos Wilderness the sound of the river was too loud, the city was too far away, I was cold and felt isolated. Now that I had what I'd desired for so long, the terrible catch was that it did not make me any happier than I was before. I was insatiably jealous of any woman who approached Timothy because of his impotence with me and my conviction that no one could love me.

Mummy was still living in San Diego and wanted to see me. I hated her, and yet she was my most intimate witness. Having no life of her own, she lived vicariously through me and saw herself as the director of my movie. She was my oldest and most intimate enemy. When I told Timothy that I would have to go to San Diego to see what Mummy wanted, he said that if I left, he would leave me. That night, drunk and dramatic, he jumped on the motorcycle *sans* buddy seat he'd bought and headed towards Colorado.

In San Diego, I learned that for once Mummy had not exaggerated her emergency: she had been diagnosed with inoperable lung cancer and was a month or two from death. Disconcerted and fearful at the inconceivable thought of losing my childhood perpetrator with whom I was still pathologically linked—not a day went by without my talking on the phone with her—I called my half-sister Floki, who was vacationing at her house in Sardinia, and asked her to come immediately, then moved into Mummy's apartment overlooking San Diego Bay and near Scripps Mercy Hospital where she was receiving treatment. One of the first things I did was discard her last half-empty carton of Winstons. Floki arrived with her Mexican lover and her secretary; on the advice of friends, she was set on renting a Lear Jet to fly Mummy to Houston so she could get an experimental cure.

71

THIS IS THE END, BEAUTIFUL FRIEND

In the following days, Timothy flew from Albuquerque to be with me as well as appear on the *Today* show. I picked him up at LAX and we immediately went to a bar. While we drank shots of Jack Daniels straight up, he told me he had slept with a woman in Santa Fe. Despite my own many sexual encounters while he was in prison, I was devastated: I was no longer necessary to the man I had tirelessly helped to free from prison. He would not be standing by my side during my mother's illness and death. Besides, he had told me many times how much he hated hospitals, not to mention death since his first wife Marianne died of carbon monoxide poisoning on his 35th birthday.

That night at a friend's house in Los Angeles, we made love with all the passion of our desperate, dying, stained love for each other. For the first time since he'd left prison, it was deep and strong. We were two people making love in a lifeboat after their ship had sunk before their very eyes. We sobbed, knowing that when the lifeboat reached dry land, we would be taking different roads toward separate futures. It was that night that my third child Marlon was conceived. As with my other two children, I immediately sensed it. Timothy gently put his head on my belly and declared he could feel the tiny cells of a new life dividing inside my womb. When morning unzipped the night sky over Los Angeles, I was more confused than ever.

Together, we returned to Mummy's apartment in San Diego. A doctor confirmed that I was pregnant even as Mummy was wasting away and telling me daily that she wanted to die and did not want life support to keep her alive. She looked frail and afraid in the frilly nightgowns my sister had brought from Europe. Back in Mummy's apartment, her small dog Chou-Chou barked incessantly, as nervous and scared as her dying owner.

Mummy's and my relationship had gone through so many stages of love and hatred, the love being more about shared stories of shared years together and our extreme co-dependency. In a real sense, I'd always been in bondage to her. She had been jealous of every attachment I ever formed, so I had never developed lasting friendships and had used men to defy her and escape the hold she had on me. Without Timothy, I would have to learn to survive without anyone to love me and reflect back to me my own image so that I knew I *existed*. When alone, I was nothing; I lived only through the eyes of others and whatever they thought or said about me.

Timothy refused to go to the hospital, saying he'd been in too many institutions during his prison years. We continued drinking, and when night came, fought. One night, we argued over the three-month lecture tour he was going on without me. Pregnant and my mother dying, I begged him not to leave me behind. As Chou-Chou's howls filled the California night with desperation, I blurted out the names of a few of the men I had slept with and played out the humiliating role of the abandoned woman, getting down on my knees as I had done before with so many men, drunk, screaming insults, belittling, telling him to go because I did not need him, spouting things I did not really believe, terrified of showing one ounce of vulnerability. From outside my body, I watched myself with no way of shutting myself up, the burning anger inside spewing out like molten lava. The damage done, I got down on my knees again and begged him not to leave me alone, my voice still sarcastic and defiant because I did not trust anyone to stay and care for me. I hated myself, every drama I initiated adding to my self-hatred and humiliation.

The next morning, I awoke from my blackout and Timothy was gone. He had packed his little Pinto with his meager possessions and left without a word, the drawers empty, the wire hangers dangling. I panicked. Mummy was close to death, Timothy was gone, I was two months pregnant and penniless, angry people wanted me dead, and I was hopelessly addicted to drugs and alcohol, though still in deep denial. Only later did I realize that he didn't want me along so he wouldn't be seen with the Mata Hari now being blamed everywhere for his snitching. In a *Los Angeles Times* interview, he would tell the world that I was the one who had convinced him to cooperate with the authorities, I was the evil one who had set people up out of my perverse obsession with him, thus endangering my life all the more.

It was September 1976. Fall was happening in Europe. *Fall.* An appropriate word.

As Mummy was being airlifted to Houston, she kept screaming to the nurses, "My daughters are moving me so they can better kill me!" Mummy craved safety, Floki wanted her cured, and my attitude was what's the use, since she has told us all her life that she wants to die?

Just three weeks after arriving at the Houston hospital, I sat watching over her while she slept hooked up to machines pumping powerful drugs into her veins. A strange series of events had conspired to bring her, an abused and unloved little girl, from Poland to France and Spain and then end her life in Texas, USA, far from her land of birth. Somehow, her end was connected to the new life growing inside my belly.

The last night of her life, she lay in her Christian Dior sheets and beige cashmere blanket Floki had bought at Neiman Marcus. I sat up all night with her, just the two of us dozing and waking in the blue glow of the television light. The ward was quiet. The private nurse sat in a chair by the door. I curled up at the end of the bed, trying to keep her feet warm, but to no avail: her toes were already icy cold. Toward three in the morning, the time of the dark night of the soul, I climbed into bed and lay next to her, my arms wrapped around her skeleton of a body, caressing her forehead and hair still dark brown despite her age.

She was like the embryo curled in my womb, Timothy's child: precious, important, recognized only by me, abandoned by all others. Not only did I carry the two of them, but also the promise of continuity itself, the promise of fierce survival.

Mummy and I had been exceedingly cruel to each other. Everything I had learned from her about raging, I had turned against her and others, and yet she was the only person I was really close to, the only living proof I had that my self-defeating behavior was not all my fault. I held her in my arms, avidly breathing in her particular scent, that unique smell each of us emanates, that essence that exists only once for each human being and never again. I wished I could bottle her scent so I would never have to live without it. During that September Texas night, in the dark hospital room under the flickering light of the color TV she always wanted on because it was her only window to the world, I knew that I would miss her like I had never missed anyone.

I held her for the next three hours, feeling her life running out through my own body, each of her tentative sighs penetrating me like needles. As she neared death, I realized there were no guarantees that I would survive her long, for I was addicted to the edge of death.

A light went on in the hospital corridor and the morning nurse came in. She was young and very gentle with me. We exchanged glances, knowing my mother would probably die some time today on her shift. I stood and stretched, looking down at my feet on the pale linoleum floor.

"You're pregnant," the nurse said while expertly changing the bottom sheet under my mother.

"Yes," I responded, looking down with a faint smile at my blue t-shirt with an arrow pointing toward my womb and big black letters saying, *BABY*. My eyes filled with tears.

I told the nurse that I would be in the cafeteria and she promised to call me if my mother's condition changed. As I kissed Mummy's face, she opened her eyes for a moment and glanced up at the television, then at me, her expression that of a small, helpless child. At the Hilton cafeteria, I ordered poached eggs with corned beef hash and coffee. My tears fell into the runny yellow yolks, the dry toast sticking in my throat. My mother and I were fused together, like Siamese twins. I had no idea if it was she or I who was experiencing this journey into death.

Mummy died the morning of September 24, 1976, her eyes drifting around the room as if looking over things hidden. I asked her where she was going and she said she was going out to buy a pack of cigarettes. And then it was over. When she simply did not take the next labored breath, I held her feet and watched one precious, solitary tear make its way down the left side of her face.

I left the room and lit up my best friend, Gauloise. Steeped in the interplay of life and death, I wondered if any part of what I was experiencing was real. The tears and sobs wracking my body were all I had to keep grounded. I was lost. Timothy was gone, Mummy was gone, and I had no idea where or how to recognize any authenticity in myself or around me. In a supposedly free country, I felt as though I had collaborated with the *Gestapo*, running, drinking, drugging, wondering every morning if that day would be the day someone would execute me for my betrayal of the Counterculture.

Numbly, I stuffed Mummy's things into a couple of garbage bags, thinking how when someone dies the bags are rarely packed, death being an unpredictable one-way ticket. Nor did Marisya need to worry about wearing the right clothes, as she had done all her life. Dragging my garbage bags, I walked down the hospital corridors sobbing so hard I could scarcely catch my breath. No one stopped to ask what was the matter, death being a normal occurrence on this floor.

I caught a taxi back to the Warwick Hotel where Floki had booked a room for me and a suite for herself and her entourage. I knocked on the door of her suite. Her lover opened the door.

"So it's all over, she's gone," he said.

Behind him, Floki was crying, her face pale, her shoulders bent. I went to her and hugged her. In our common grief, we somehow ended up under a table together, holding hands, crying like lost babies at 37 and 30 years old. Once we'd dried our tears and stood to rejoin the now motherless world, Floki passed a book to me. "Someone dropped this off for you, it's from Timothy Leary."

It was Aldous Huxley's *Island*, a strange and wonderful gift. Immediately, I recalled a lifetime ago when Nicky gave me Laura Huxley's *A Timeless Moment* with the plane ticket I would cash in for my first solo trip to America. Now in *this* timeless moment, I was desperately in need of guidance. I opened *Island* as I might the *I Ching* and turned randomly to this passage:

> *"It's dark because you're trying too hard," said Susila. "Dark because you want it to be light. Remember what you used to tell me when I was a little girl. 'Lightly, child, lightly. You've got to learn to do everything lightly. Think lightly, act lightly, feel lightly. Yes, feel lightly, even though you're feeling deeply. Just lightly let things happen and lightly cope with them.' I was so preposterously serious in those days, such a humorless little prig. Lightly, lightly—it was the best advice ever given me. Well, now I'm going to say the same thing to you, Lakshmi . . . Lightly, my darling, lightly. Even when it comes to dying. Nothing ponderous, or portentous, or emphatic. No rhetoric, no tremolos, no self-conscious persona putting on its celebrated imitation of Christ or Goethe or Little Nell. And, of course, no theology, no metaphysics. Just the fact of dying and the fact of the Clear Light. So throw away all your baggage and go forward. There are quicksands all about you, sucking at your feet, trying to suck you down into fear and self-pity and despair. That's why you must walk so lightly. Lightly, my darling. On tiptoes; and no luggage, not even a sponge bag. Completely unencumbered."*

Lightly. Would I ever learn?

To be continued in Book 2, **Healing: The Journey Home**

EPILOGUE

Are you willing to be sponged out, erased, cancelled,
made nothing?
Are you willing to be made nothing?
dipped into oblivion?

If not, you will never really change.

The phoenix renews her youth
only when she is burnt, burnt alive, burnt down
to hot and flocculent ash.
Then the small stirring of a new small bub in the nest
with strands of down like floating ash
shows that she is renewing her youth like the eagle,
immortal bird.

- D.H. Lawrence, "Phoenix"

It was hard that for so long I needed proof that you had loved me . . .

In June 1995, Timothy came to Santa Fe to give a lecture on Chaos. Something told me it was time for us to meet again; it had been twelve years. I sat in the second row and watched him approach the podium, now 74 years old. He looked so terribly frail, his skinny body swimming inside his Armani suit. For a while, he spoke about computers, his eyes scanning the audience but failing to notice me. I stared intently at him. Finally, his eyes lit up, as did the great Leary grin.

"Joanna," he said, "what a privilege, it's been so long."

I smiled back amidst a rush of mixed feelings.

"This woman was the most loyal and courageous lover a prisoner could ever have," he told the audience. "She stood by me every minute of my imprisonment." Looking at me once again, he gestured, "Stand up, please, so everyone can see how beautiful you are."

I stood, turning slowly toward the three hundred or so applauding people, then turned back toward the stage and gave Timothy the Cleopatra wink. The rest of his talk was devoted to his time in prison—not including, as you might guess, our time as informers.

Later, I read that he had terminal cancer, was living somewhere in Beverly Hills and walking hesitantly with a cane, eating next to nothing, skinny as a blade of grass. In February, I sent him my goodbye fax, finishing my personal business with Timothy Leary. Three months later, on May 31, 1996, the comet Hyakutake stopped to pick him up for his last trip, the one we call death. I remembered how his mother had died at 97 when he was still inside, back when I thought he would live forever if he ever got out of the Establishment's prison.

Squinting up at Hyakutake's long tail like an exclamation point against the dark sky, I pictured Timothy streaking heavenward, the mad sorcerer riding into forever, his DNA packed up, FedEx-ing his undamaged chromosomes, his body giving out but his brain still going at the speed of light. I felt him dying out of me, becoming free of all prisons and games.

> *Then in the shadow of the morning*
> *When all becomes sincere*
> *Then you will see what I tell you*
> *That all the love you once gave him*
> *It all belongs to you . . .*

The Moody Blues, "To Our Children's Children's Children"

During the Nixon-Ford years that Timothy and I shared, the Counterculture was systematically dismantled. From the Black Panthers and American Indian Movement to the diverse unity of good will resonating in *every* country—communist or democratic—consciousness was rising up against war, oppression, and injustice. We-the-people had seen through the Emperor's many costumes.

For a brief time, Timothy and I whirled in the vortex of that dismantlement. Our time together taught me that no life merits the luxury of being merely personal when living in a National Security State that covertly devours its people's rights. Every life is political because only a web of living ideas can create and re-create the democracy that safeguards individual freedom. LSD revealed to me a vision of what freedom could be, but over time I realized that only strong individuals dedicated to running clean can achieve and maintain such visions in the messy struggles of the here and now.

Strangely, Timothy and I tripped and traveled together in Europe and the Middle East for exactly 49 days, the very amount of time that Tibetan Buddhists specify for the Bardo between death and rebirth. And it was true: our acid time together of 49 days was a life between lifetimes, given that acid time is Bardo time.

This is a good place for me to state clearly my position on drugs today. Hard drugs are monstrous tools of destruction: heroin, cocaine, crack, methamphetamine, and their Frankenstein street derivatives. Since marijuana grew in George Washington's backyard, it has become a big genetic business, not to mention the misfortune of inheriting a negative outlaw *set and setting* that often leads to prison. According to Paul Armentano, the senior policy analyst for the NORML Foundation in Washington, DC, one out of eight US drug prisoners is locked up for cannabis possession.[7] So far, Colorado and Washington State have legalized marijuana. May more sane laws than those instituted against the Counterculture in the Sixties follow!

Was Timothy right about change in consciousness being a threat to the Establishment? Certainly illegalizing marijuana, psilocybin, mescaline, and LSD is an effective way for a National Security State to lock away dissidents seeking to chemically alter their consciousness. Sadly, however, many equate "changing consciousness" with temporary escape from pain and confusion over a world seemingly spent before they arrived. LSD is *not* another brand of alcohol, just as Venus is not Liverpool. Instead of a "war on drugs" and punitive, discounting

---

7   Paul Armentano, "Pot Prisoners Cost Americans $1 Billion a Year." *Washington Examiner*, February 10, 2007.

threats, we must open a forum of dialogue between ourselves and with our children. This is my dedication.

Solitary Confinement

> *Before we can understand Manson, we must realize that a prison system is a microcosm of a culture and that the American prison system is run on raw fear and violence.*
> - Timothy Leary, *Neuropolitics*, 1977

The torture known as solitary confinement that has become standard prison procedure was used to break Timothy. Isolation with sensory deprivation, permanent bright lighting, extreme temperatures, and forced insomnia began in America during the Nixon years. Today in an estimated 44 states, supermax facilities confine more than 30,000 people, some in continuous isolation for as long as 25 years. I repeat: *Solitary confinement is torture.* I believe that Timothy agreed to cooperate with the Feds because they threatened him with years of solitary confinement.

He was kept in solitary confinement for "ideological trafficking" among the prison population. Add to that the great crime of being a worldwide ray of hope for youth. For this alone, they wore him down, discredited him, then kept a leash on him for the rest of his life.

But whatever the initial justification or intent, the end result of solitary confinement is to make it so that very few have contact with the prisoner and know what is really happening to him or her. Sometimes when I visited him, his mouth was dry and he could barely speak or move because he was being plied with debilitating and sometimes paralyzing drugs. Once at Vacaville—where SLA leader Donald DeFreeze was programmed to kidnap and program heiress Patty Hearst—they insisted I see Timothy in a straight jacket in a padded cell. There had been a small riot, Timothy said, and the warden had isolated him in this manner so the other inmates wouldn't hurt him. I found this explanation absurd and couldn't imagine why Timothy, a gentle man, had been put in a straight jacket.

Still, Timothy swore he was doing "easy time." Imagining his solitary confinement as a remote cave in the Himalayas, he recited Buddhist sutras to remind himself that Form is Void and Void is Form, i.e. that none of what he saw and felt was necessarily real. He said he kept sane by visualizing being beyond the four concrete walls and out in the world, moving around freely, traveling to exotic levels of consciousness and reality, leaving his body for hours by virtue of having taken at least 500 acid trips. As much as possible, I sent him letters with postage stamps dipped in liquid LSD so that all he had to do was eat the stamp after the letters were censored. He also paid close attention to the prison grapevine that he said was often very savvy and very funny.

But how long can a sensitive man remain in solitary confinement with a 25-watt bulb, a metal chair and table bolted to the floor, waiting months to get a court order for a manual typewriter? How long can he be drugged by guards, yanked out of his cell in the middle of the night, and transferred from one cement cellblock to another? In *Flashbacks*, Timothy compares his condition to that of Solzhenitsyn in the Gulag. Was it just coincidental that *Gulag Archipelago* was published in the West the year Timothy was brought back from Kabul?

WikiLeaks releases about "enemy combatant" detainees and informants at the military prison in Guantánamo Bay make me wonder about Timothy's months and years of solitary confinement— his shaved skull when Ginsberg, Ferlinghetti, and I arrived, the temporary insanity plea giving carte blanche to doctors to "examine" his LSD-saturated brain[8], etc. As Jeffrey Kaye put it in his April 25, 2011 article, "Guantanamo Detainee Files Hint at Psychological Research" (truth-out.org):

> *While the "areas of potential exploitation" often included presumed areas of further intelligence seeking, based upon supposed links of the detainee to the area under consideration, other areas of proposed "exploitation" are vaguer, or seem to imply research into prisoner psychology, or even possible status as an informant or intelligence asset after release.*

Was that also what happened to Eldridge Cleaver? While Timothy was housed at the Cinnamon Stick (San Diego Metropolitan Correctional Center) along with other high-profile informants, Cleaver

---

8 See Colin Ross, *Bluebird: Deliberate Creation of Multiple Personality by Psychiatrists* (2000) for history on the CIA's Project MK-ULTRA and experimentation on prisoners.

turned himself in at the US Embassy in Paris and 24 hours later found himself at the Cinnamon Stick. How does such an intelligent man go from the Black Panthers and Islam to being a born-again Christian and conservative Republican who then flirts with joining Reverend Sun Myung Moon's Moonies before being baptized a Mormon?

After Timothy's release in 1976, he refused to take LSD but drank more than ever. Why was that?

Government informants

I can't condemn Richard Nixon for shutting his mouth because I'm shutting my mouth. I'm not getting paroled until I'm rehabilitated. I'm not getting out behind the lawyers. I've had a chance to analyze, as a psychologist, Nixon's downfall. I've had a chance to see that I'm locked up because of the way I played secrets. I know some people might get hurt. But if I can tell my story and get it all out, karmically, I think I'm free within. And if I'm free within, it will reflect without . . . When I look at Socrates, I see that all they wanted him to do was just say he was sorry. He didn't have to drink the hemlock. Maybe if the offer was poison, I'd take that, I don't know. But it is prison. I'm a rat in a maze, staring at the door, looking for another door and there isn't one. Like it or not, when you're in the prison system, you come out through the system, unless you escape, and that didn't work.

   - Timothy Leary, 1974; quoted in *Acid Dreams: The Complete Social History of LSD: The CIA, The Sixties, and Beyond* by Marty Lee and Bruce Shlain, 1985

I have grown to doubt that our meeting in Switzerland was accidental. Certainly, the high-end gangster Michel Hauchard piqued our interest in each other, but what of Timothy's memory of "creating" me in his cell at the California Men's Colony outside San Luis Obispo before his escape in 1970? In Switzerland, he knew that his days as a free man were numbered, given that the BNDD-DEA knew that the Brotherhood of Eternal Love considered him its godfather and mastermind behind its Kabul-California hashish traffic. Thus he followed Nixon's law and order script with avid interest. Before I showed up at Lake Zug with my great idea for getting him on a boat, his entourage had been expecting his recapture and re-imprisonment at any moment. Not for a minute did anyone believe I could save him from the BNDD-DEA if they wanted him bad enough.

During our Clear Light days of breathlessly tripping and traveling over three continents, Timothy and daily LSD and tantric sex on acid entrained my brain with two assumptions that would hold firm through his three and a half years of re-imprisonment: that he was the unique, powerful protective Alpha male I had been groomed for, and that I was his faithful emissary with a talent for scandals and dramas. Every prisoner needs a tireless ally on the outside, and every prisoner knows that unless you have a lot of money and aren't marked for a fall, lawyers tend to forget locked-up clients very quickly. Next to money, a woman is a con's greatest asset, an insurance policy on the outside—especially an internationally known and connected woman.

Am I saying that Timothy *consciously* entrained my brain and set me up? No, though I cannot imagine anyone better qualified to do just that. At the very least, I am saying that he needed me as much as I needed him, and when he finally bought his freedom, he no longer needed me. For my part, I needed to be destructively, immeasurably wanted by a powerful man who could not go anywhere but to me and through me.

As for the federal agents that Timothy and I fell afoul of, I came to several frightening conclusions during the year and a half I was an informant:

Federal and state agents will subvert each other's efforts if it means procuring more funding from House and Senate appropriations committees for their respective agencies.

They are utterly racist and sexist.

Their big egos thrive on busting people with big names.

They resort to exploitative, threatening language and play games with guns.

I was treated with extreme condescension for my gender, my relationship with Timothy, and for not being American. My crime was guilt by association, for I was in love with the guru of LSD and therefore a person to be used. I became a hostage for love. The Feds had fun christening Charlie Thrush's paramour—Samantha "Sam" Weatherfield, Lucy Brown, Virginia Church—and encouraged me to wear sexy transparent clothing to better lure and bust commie-pinko hippies. They threatened that if I did not offer my charms and youth to the men they wanted to entrap, they would whisk Timothy to maximum security at Leavenworth or Chico where he might have an "accident" for being a snitch. I was passed from one to the other as human bait to assuage their grandiose need to make more cases, bust more pinkos, fill quotas, etc.

While trembling with fear that a lawyer or dope dealer would discover that I was wearing a wire and kill me now or in the future, I clung to the tiny thread of sanity that when the ordeal was over, I would write a book that would describe the blackmail and horrendous sexism and disdain for human life shown by most federal and state agents if they perceived someone to be on "the other side" and therefore expendable. I would tell how US District Attorneys strengthen their cases by turning friends and loved ones against each other until they are refugees from all sides, leaving them broken, humiliated, and exposed—tossed aside like refuse when they have been sufficiently exploited and are not needed anymore.

To this day, I regret my role in George Chula's bust. I managed to botch every other case I was assigned, in the odd moment relaying to the person that it was an entrapment. *Flashbacks* doesn't mention Timothy testifying before the Orange County Grand Jury that Chula had on several occasions brought drugs to him when he came to Orange County Jail to discuss his case, but it happened.

Starseed

Appropriately enough—given that our celebrated love affair had become as unreal as the Starship *Enterprise*—the last place we were together as Joanna and Timothy Leary was at the 1976 Star Trek convention in Oakland. Science and science fiction were closing ranks, and I have pondered what role Timothy and I may have played through the Starseed office in San Francisco and the StarSeed Series he insisted I "co-author" his first year in prison: *Starseed, NeuroLogic,* and *Terra II.* After his release, he would become a futurist lecturer with the StarSeed Series and post-prison books such as *Exo-Psychology: A manual on the use of the human nervous system according to the instructions of the manufacturers*

(1977); *Neuropolitics* (1977); *The Intelligence Agents (Future History)* (1979); etc. Until he was free to lecture, I was sent out as his proxy lecturer on space migration, for which I was being constantly prepared.

When Timothy read *The Curve of Binding Energy: A Journey into the Awesome and Alarming World of Theodore B. Taylor* by John McPhee, he sent me to meet with Taylor in Washington, DC, and then on to Gainesville, Florida to meet with my second cousin Stanislaw Ulam, the mathematician father of the H-Bomb mentioned in the Preface. When astronomer Carl Sagan came to see Timothy in prison, I spent extensive time with him, too. Stan, Taylor, and Sagan were all involved in Project Orion, an interstellar mission study that deeply impacted Timothy.

My cousin Stan was the first scientist to mention *technological singularity*, the future emergence of greater-than-human intelligence that now goes by the names of *singularity* and *transhumanism*. From his release to his death, Timothy played a pivotal role in priming the young for the interstellar missions of which Stan, Taylor, and Sagan dreamed. The evolving headspace went from psychedelics to post-psychedelic *interstellar neurogenetics*, and then in the 1990s from outer space toward cyberspace, singularity, and transhumanism.

As you can see, the multilevel complexity of plots raging around Timothy and the Counterculture bewildered and frightened me. For the longest time, I clung to the failsafe equation of doing whatever I had to so we could be together—an equation that cut like a knife across all moral considerations. Defiant, damaged, and cloistered in a cocoon of drugs, alcohol, and music, I was an outsider even to my own life and didn't know that by burning others, I would burn myself to the bone. Finally, though, like D.H. Lawrence's Phoenix, I would find my way up and out of the ashes.

POSTSCRIPT: UP AND OUT OF THE ASHES

I'm looking for a miracle in my life.
If you could see what it's done to me
To lose the love I knew . . .

The Moody Blues,
"To Our Children's Children's Children"

Shortly before getting sober, I was still getting up from my bed at four in the afternoon, hung over and depressed. Someone seeing me in this pitiless state said to me, "Have you no compassion for God?" The question shot a diamond arrow into my heart. Indeed, I had no compassion for the unique creation I am.

I have been a member of Alcoholics Anonymous for 27 years, clean and sober from the drugs and alcohol that played the centerpiece to Timothy's and my story. Once in recovery, I began to view the treasure hunt of life, *un jeu de piste*, as grace, the intangible law that cannot be bought or sold or owned or faked in any way, the law with a mind of its own hidden behind daily life. Access to grace is often granted those willing to alchemically transmute their suffering. Once amazing grace is with us, we no longer have to fall back on the old methods of error and pain to awaken our awareness.

Meeting Timothy meant beginning to face the fact that the evils implanted in my childhood were preventing me from becoming a responsible, loving adult. With Timothy, I died again and again, killed by the drugs I was taking and my values of stealing, cheating, lying, and double-crossing. Our Perfect Love in our magic theatre may have been an illusion, but at least it left no way out but either death or sobriety.

Timothy's philosophy was that life is a movie set and one should be ready to move on at any time. Devoted to his Buddhist take on detachment that everything passes and changes and no amount of sticky white knuckling will change it, he constantly practiced dying to everything and everyone that might become a habit—perhaps due to Sri Krishna Prem, the guru he had visited in India years before we met, who told him, "Jump from rock to rock with courage and a smile before it sinks."

Once I weaned myself from the crutches of drinking, drugging, and lying, I became the living dead—neither on earth nor in heaven or hell but in a shadowy world of phantoms and unrealities. For a long time, my memories of the stories in *Tripping the Bardo* arose in my mind like shadows on the wall of Plato's cave. At first, there was something grotesque and pathetic about the memories of the girl in her twenties who subjected everyone she met to her dark load of personal history. Then people began arriving in dreams now able to love me as they couldn't in life when I thought I was awake and able to change my story at whim. Slowly, I began to realize that real choice has to be earned by stalking our actions and the hidden stories that unfold through them. True choice is the precious reward of an examined life. Otherwise, we remain driven by our past.

I was living proof that the unloved child makes unloving choices, particularly towards the self, and not loving oneself becomes the recipe for hurting others. The trapped human goes through three phases: fight, flight, and freeze. When I was still drinking, fight and flight were my only strategies—either clawing my way through each day, or running as far as my legs would take me, a vagabond without a country, my children safely tucked beyond my reach. Some men loved me, but what imposter did they claim to love?

Through AA, I understood that I had lost touch with matter—matter in the human world being relationships that *matter*. As I began to recognize feelings and sensuality in the true sense of the words, I slowly advanced from living-dead catatonia to a heightened sense of reality. The world came alive one experience at a time. Reality was still frightening, but no longer the madness and terror of separation. Like a living puzzle, memories began to form pictures that made sense, even when they seemed totally surreal. These were my experiences, and the story of my life was the road I had traced for myself. I came and went from unreality until I realized that being sane is its own reward.

The Buddha, the Dharma, and the Sangha have become places of refuge—the Buddha as a Higher Power, the Dharma as the values I try to practice every day in actions that resonate as integrity in my body, and the Sangha as the community I am a part of, from microbes to elephants and humans. To honor having lived the unfolding, I chose to tell my story not just for myself but for all who are faced with their own brand of odds at every twist and turn in the wheel of fortune between birth and death. A life is at least to be honored for that.

APPENDIX 1

ALCOHOLICS ANONYMOUS STEP 8

Santa Fe, Spring 1990

Dearest Timothy,

    Out of selfishness and ignorance, I committed a lot of mistakes when we were together. I am truly sorry for the pain I might have caused you. I thank you for the loving patience you showed me and the way you welcomed me in, no matter what. I needed approval and you gave me oceans of it.

    I loved you, Timothy. In fact, you are the first person I ever loved, who performed the miraculous operation of opening my heart so that it has never needed to be shut again.

    I feel gratitude and tenderness for you today, so I ask you to forgive me.

    I have been living in Santa Fe for five years. It's a good home for me, and I thank you for introducing me to it.

                    All ways,

                      Joanna

Los Angeles, 7-8-90

Dear Joanna –

My stepson Zach pointed out to me this afternoon that the date was 7-8-90. And that at 34 minutes after 12 noon plus 56 seconds the date was

1234567890

He pointed out that this happened only once in a century.

So, on this amazing day, I take pen in hand to respond to your wonderful letter.

This was an important day in my life—I made a decision which I'll tell you more about soon.

Anyway, it was wonderful to read your tender, wise letter.

You wrote me a loving note a few months [ago] which I intended to answer in kind—but I mislaid it. My usual disorganization.

Yes, our relationship was amazing. Very few people could understand the incredible friendship and loyalty we developed. And I include Maricia [Marisya] in our friendship. How touching that she came and lived in San Diego to be with us. What an amazing person she was. I have often regretted that I was so distracted at the moment of her illness that we did not rescue her from the horrible hospitals and did not make our house on the hill a joyous place for her to recuperate or make her transition surrounded by warm fun and human contact.

Yes, you "committed lots of mistakes" and, yes, those events have caused me many "problems." But looking back at that time of political-social weirdness, who went through more tests, who dealt with the Evil Police-Government Powers with more nobility? I was instructed by the wise words of Havel, the playwright who became president of Czechoslovakia: *Each thinking person who lived through the Communist years was tested in strange ways and made accommodations to the Police Terror. Let us all forgive each other and inquire, compassionately, What are you doing to prevent the police terror from reappearing?*

Through your creative machinations, I was privileged to get to know the agents of the Police Evil—FBI, DEA, Federal Marshals, State Attorney Generals—the bad and the less-bad—all confused humans. And no more evil than virtuous liberals. I do tend to like humans in the individual form and avoid all groups and causes, no matter how virtuous their aims.

There was something comically human about the madness. When I had three marshals whose only job was to play handball with me and type my manuscripts! And Art Van Court?

Who did you hurt, in your wicked betrayals? Poor George Chula is the only one who could claim "real" minor-trivial annoyance—and he understands, and has never complained to me.

One could make a case that you swept through America (using and abusing) my reputation (!) as a Hindu Goddess Whirlwind, testing everyone you met—and leaving one and all better, after the smoke cleared.

This is foolish, late at night talk. But I hope you know that I have never attacked you. I thought that my superficial comments about you in FLASHBACKS were loving and I was a bit hurt when you never thanked me for them. WHAT DOES WOMAN WANT is my favorite novel. Thanks for making that possible.

Anyway, our friendship was amazing and inexplicable.

My life, like yours, has continued to be incredible. I rarely think about you—but when I do it is with pride and respect and affection.

What we went through!!!!!!!!

Please consider yourself "forgiven" which means, I guess, "given" best wishes "for" the future.

You are a rare and special person and you enriched my life beyond measure.

Thanks, all ways.

              Timothy

APPENDIX 2

PRISON TIMETABLE

January 20, 1973 to April 21, 1976

Back from Kabul:
(1) **LA County Jail, LA**
(2) **Orange County Jail, Santa Ana CA**
(3) **California Men's Colony, San Luis Obispo**
    The prison he escaped from. Maximum security.
    SOLITARY CONFINEMENT
(4) **Folsom State Prison**, 20 miles NE of Sacramento CA – March 1973
    SOLITARY CONFINEMENT - Geronimo Pratt on one side, Charlie Manson on the other
(5) **Vacaville Medical Facility (now the California Medical Facility)**, halfway between Sacramento and San Francisco off Interstate 80 – November 1973
    From Vacaville, TL sent the telegram to the FBI agreeing to cooperate. Governor Jerry Brown agreed to drop state charges (5 years for escape, 5-10 years for possession) and pass him over to the Feds for the federal sentence that had been on appeal since 1969. He was then picked up by a helicopter from Vacaville and taken to a meeting in a bank building, then transferred to

(6) **FCI Sandstone Federal Prison, MN** – April 1974
A minimum-security facility catering to white-collar criminals with no love for TL, the most dangerous man in America responsible for killing kids with drugs.
SOLITARY CONFINEMENT.
(7) **FCI Terminal Island, Los Angeles**
(8) **Small jails and prisons in Northern California**
(9) **Metropolitan Correctional Center (The Cinnamon Stick), San Diego**

Made in the USA
Las Vegas, NV
15 February 2023

67568767R00215